HITLER'S GREATEST DEFEAT

HITLER'S GREATEST DEFEAT

The Collapse of Army Group Centre, June 1944

PAUL ADAIR

ARMS AND
ARMOUR

For Rebecca — a charge fulfilled.
This book is dedicated to my children and
grandchildren in the hope that they never have
to face the horrors of war.

Arms and Armour Press
A Cassell Imprint
Villiers House, 41/47 Strand, London WC2N 5JE.

Distributed in the USA by Sterling Publishing Co. Inc.,
387 Park Avenue South, New York, NY 10016-8810.

Distributed in Australia by Capricorn Link (Australia)
Pty. Ltd, 2/13 Carrington Road, Castle Hill, NSW 2154.

British Library Cataloguing-in-Publication Data:
a catalogue record for this book is available from the
British Library

ISBN 1-85409-232-4

Cartography by Cilla Eurich.

Designed and edited by DAG Publications Ltd.
Designed by David Gibbons; edited by Michael Boxall;
Printed and bound in Great Britain by
Hartnolls Limited, Bodmin, Cornwall

CONTENTS

ACKNOWLEDGEMENTS

The material used in writing this book was gathered for the preparation of a training film in the Services Sound and Vision Corporation Campaign Series, and for use at an Art of War Symposium held at the United States Army War College in 1985.

I am very grateful to the Services Sound and Vision Corporation for permission to use transcripts of interviews and archive material. My gratitude is due to the Production Department for their help and encouragement over the years, particularly David Goldsmith, Barry Warden, Ann Carroll, and John Fanner. Major Bobby Shafto eased the military side with customary good humour. I am appreciative of the support of successive Directors of Army Training, above all that of General Sir Michael Gow, GCB, who instituted the Campaign Series of films.

Field Marshal Sir Nigel Bagnall, GCB, CVO, MC, attended several Art of War Symposia and was always ready to help and encourage works on the Eastern Front. For this, I am particularly grateful.

As a basic source for the study of the campaign, SSVC commissioned a translation of General Niepold's book entitled *Mittlere Ostfront Juni '44*. This was published by Brassey as *Battle for White Russia: the Destruction of Army Group Centre, June 1944*. I am very grateful to Mrs Simkin for permission to use the translation prepared by the late Brigadier Richard Simkin.

Generalleutenant a.D. Gerd Niepold, who served as the principal staff officer of 12th Panzer Division during the campaign, first alerted me to the fascinating events that took place in Byelorussia more than fifty years ago. His practical help and encouragement have been of great assistance. I must also record my gratitude to three other senior German officers, who attended the Art of War Symposium at Carlisle, Pennsylvania, namely General a.D. Graf von Kielmansegg and Generalleutenants a.D. Lemm and von Plato. In more than fifteen years' study of the war on the Eastern Front I have been fortunate enough to make many good friends amongst former German officers, who have been long-suffering in answering my continuous flow of questions. I would thank particularly Obersts a.D. Helmut Ritgen and Hermann Rothe, Oberstleutnant a.D. Rolf Stoves, and all my other friends who have helped me over various points of detail.

Amongst those still serving, I must mention Brigadegeneral Harald van Nes for his help over Intelligence matters, and Dr Dieter Ose, whose efforts ensured the success of the Carlisle Symposia, and who has been kind enough to guide me through the complexities of the German Army on the Eastern Front; nothing has ever been too much trouble, and I am very grateful to him for his friendship and encouragement. I am extremely sad that General Didi von Senger und Etterlin did not live to see the appearance of this book.

Dr Rolf Hinze who took part in the campaign, and escaped back to the German lines after an epic journey, has written extensively on the Eastern Front. The eye-witness accounts he has assembled bring to life the harsh conditions of the campaign and its aftermath. I am very grateful to him for permission to quote from his works and for the illustrations he has provided.

I have left my greatest debt to the last. Colonel David Glantz, now retired from the United States Army has been most unselfish in the sharing of his unrivalled knowledge of the Soviet Army. His scholarship and practical help, which has included reading drafts and proofs as well as answering a myriad of questions, have been a permanent encouragement to me. With his normal generosity, he gave me permission to quote from his published works noted in the Bibliography. This book could not have been written without his help.

I wish to record my gratitude to Sidgwick & Jackson for permission to quote from *Hitler's War Directives* the order issued by Hitler establishing the concept of *Feste Plätze*. This is reproduced as Appendix VII. Richard Hanson of Bushwick Books kindly obtained permission for me to quote from Alex Buchner's book *Ostfront*, published by Schiffer Military History.

The illustrations are reproduced by courtesy of the Bundesarchiv, Bonn; Dr Rolf Hinze; and the SSVC. Tony Payne and Chris Marshal of 'Splash' were extremely helpful in preparing the illustrations for publication.

Rod Dymott of Arms & Armour Press and David Gibbons of DAG Publications were very cooperative and eased the path of the appearance of this book. Cilla Eurich drew the maps with much good humour in spite of constant revisions.

Finally, I am especially grateful to my agent, Sheila Watson, for her efforts on my behalf. I have not been an easy patient!

My wife has been most helpful providing an environment conducive to writing and in being generally supportive while I have been suffering birth .

Paul Adair, April 1994

INTRODUCTION

In the South of England during the months of May and June 1944, life was dominated by the assembly of troops for the largest seaborne invasion ever attempted in the history of warfare.

Convoys of trucks and tanks, all bearing a large white identification star, thundered through the towns and villages of the English countryside. It was obvious that the date of the Invasion was imminent and the attention of everyone was focused on the narrow stretch of water separating England from the continent. Ten British and American divisions were destined to land in north-west Europe on the morning of 6 June. Despite the meticulous staff work and planning of the last few months, they were being launched into the unknown, and no one could be absolutely certain that there would not be some unforeseen disaster that would prevent Allied troops from gaining a toe-hold on the beaches. The extent of the prevailing uncertainty can be measured by the fact that General Eisenhower, the Allied Supreme Commander, had gone so far as to prepare a statement to be issued in the event of total failure of the enterprise. No one who heard it will ever forget the feeling of relief when the BBC announced that a successful landing had been carried out.

Throughout that fateful summer the attention of the western Allies focused, naturally enough, on the fighting in Normandy, and the hope that the war could be brought to a rapid conclusion. Little attention was paid to the momentous events that were taking place at the same time on the Eastern Front. To set these in context, it should be borne in mind that while the German Army was deploying 59 divisions in the west (28 of them in Italy), 165 divisions were engaged on the Eastern Front.[1]

The German preparations to repel the invasion were characteristically thorough. To avoid their historical fear of having to fight a major war simultaneously on two fronts, they hoped to prevent the Allies from getting ashore, but if this could not be achieved, to defeat them on the immediate littoral. If this concept were successful, Hitler would have sufficient time to transfer desperately needed divisions, particularly panzer divisions, to counter the enormous superiority which the Soviets were about to unleash upon the German Army in the east.

The first main offensive in the series that Stalin planned for the summer of 1944 was intended to bring about the destruction of Army Group Centre and the liberation of Belorussia, the last area of the Soviet Union still under German occupation. The success of the offensive is the subject of this book. It removed nearly thirty divisions from the German Order of Battle, inflicting greater casualties than were sustained at the Germans' previous greatest defeat at Stalingrad. The main difference between the two was that after Stalingrad Germany still had the manpower and resources to maintain the initiative, whereas the losses in the summer of 1944 combined with the increasing drain of manpower and *matériel* in the west meant that the end for Germany drew inexorably nearer. The gallantry and self-sacrifice of her soldiers, sailors and airmen could not alter the overwhelming odds stacked against them, odds that were inevitable given the manner in which Hitler had conducted the war. The high possibility of defeat had existed from the day that he launched his armies into Russia.

Notes
1. Hastings, Max, Overlord, London, Michael Joseph, 1989, p. 60.

PROLOGUE
'SECOND FRONT NOW!'

On the evening of 22 June 1941, the day on which the German Army attacked Soviet Russia in Operation 'Barbarossa', the Prime Minister, Winston Churchill, broadcast a pledge that the British people would 'give whatever help we can to Russia and the Russian people' in their fight against the Nazi invader. Stalin, who it now appears may have been suffering from some form of mental breakdown, did not respond until he made his historic and moving speech to the Russian nation in which he mentioned 'with gratitude' the offer of aid made by Churchill. This was promulgated a few days later with the signing of an Anglo-Soviet Declaration which outlined mutual military assistance and a pledge not to conclude a separate peace with Germany. There was still no proposal for direct British military intervention.[1]

On 18 July, Stalin made his first proposal that there should be a 'front against Hitler in the west (northern France) and in the north (the Arctic)'. Churchill replied that it was just not possible to consider anything of that scale given the state of Britain's present resources. Stalin countered on 13 September by stating that 'England could without risk land 25-30 divisions at Archangel or transport them across Persia (now Iran) to the southern regions of the Soviet Union for military co-operation with Soviet troops on the territory of the Soviet Union'.[2] Thus was born the concept of Western intervention to take pressure off the sorely embattled Soviet troops, later to be known as the Second Front, which was to cause such bad feeling for the next two years.

Although there could be no question of physical intervention because Britain was herself fighting for survival against overwhelming German superiority, Churchill and Roosevelt agreed at their first meeting in Newfoundland in August 1941 to send much needed military supplies to Russia. This was the beginning of the Lend-Lease scheme which was to play a major role in equipping the Soviet forces, although it was very much played down by postwar Soviet historians. The first aid came from Britain's very meagre war production capacity and was transported by convoy around the North Cape to Murmansk until the losses from German attacks became so great that the convoys had to be discontinued. Eventually the great bulk of aid came from the

United States and entered Russia either through Persia or through the Pacific ports and along the Trans-Siberian railway. This latter route proved capable of carrying as much as the North Atlantic and Persia routes combined.

During the months before the USA entered the war, Stalin maintained his pressure for a Second Front to relieve pressure on his heavily engaged troops now fighting in front of Moscow. Fought in the severest winter for many years, this titanic struggle represented the first major setback suffered by the German Army who were ill-prepared for other than a short summer campaign. It was at this point that Japan attacked American forces at Pearl Harbor, which was followed by Hitler's amazing declaration of war against the USA, which was to seal the fate of Nazi Germany. It is an interesting speculation as to how the war would have developed if Japan had been the main US enemy. Could there have been a successful Second Front based solely on the forces of Britain and her Empire?

Immediately after Pearl Harbor Churchill decided to go to the USA to concert plans with Roosevelt, sending Anthony Eden, his Foreign Minister, to Moscow where Russian troops were about to launch their first large-scale counter-offensive. At the Washington conference, code-named 'Arcadia', the first with the two countries both at war, the two leaders made the momentous decision that Germany was to be defeated before Japan. Among other measures there was a general intention to return to the continent of Europe during 1942, although Churchill felt that 1943 was a more realistic date unless there were some form of internal collapse in Germany. The strategic bombing offensive remained the only feasible way of attempting to relieve pressure on their Soviet ally. Naturally Stalin was disappointed and took every opportunity to express the view that the Soviet forces were fighting the Germans while their Allies stood by idly watching.

In April Roosevelt sent his special envoy, Harry Hopkins, and General Marshall, his Chief of Staff, to London to discuss the possibility of a limited Second Front in 1942 if the situation on the Eastern Front deteriorated to the point of a Russian collapse. The British Chiefs of Staff pointed out that only seven infantry and two armoured divisions could be prepared in time to land in 1942 and that these would not be strong enough to hold a beachhead against the forces that Germany already had available, let alone against reinforcements withdrawn from the east. However it was decided to proceed with the planning of this operation, code-named 'Sledgehammer', in case a suitable opportunity presented itself, or it were necessary to mount it as a 'sacrifice' if

Russia's forces were catastrophically defeated which at that time seemed quite possible. Churchill never thought that the plan had any chance of success and put all his backing behind a second plan, 'Round Up', to attack the continent in 1943 with the 48 divisions that could be assembled by then. But he left the Americans with the impression that he also accepted 'Sledgehammer' and this was to lead to confusion when Molotov, the Russian Foreign Minister, visited London and Washington.

The London talks with Molotov got off to a bad start when he demanded recognition of Russia's 1941 boundaries, including eastern Poland, the Baltic states and Bessarabia. Churchill rejected this out of hand and Molotov then pressed for a Second Front capable of diverting at least 40 German divisions from the German summer offensive which was expected daily. The considerable difficulties were pointed out to him and Churchill added that a landing in North Norway was being considered with the dual aim of drawing off German forces and securing the airfields from which the vital convoys to Murmansk were being harassed. Molotov was unimpressed and continued to press for a cross-Channel attack when he arrived in Washington. Roosevelt at first appeared to support a landing in 1942, but his staff, who were by then more cautious and realized the shortage of suitable landing-craft, ruled out any prospect of such a landing. Molotov was told that no definite reply could be given until agreement had been reached with Britain. On his return to London Churchill told him that Britain would support the landing if there were sufficient landing-craft and it appeared 'sound and sensible'. Molotov saw through this and reported to Stalin: 'Consequently the outcome is that the British Government does not accept an obligation upon itself to establish a Second Front this year, and declares, and that conditionally, that it is preparing some kind of experimental raiding operation.'[3]

Churchill returned to Washington in June to confer with Roosevelt on the progress of the war, and the two leaders agreed that 'Sledgehammer' in 1942 was impracticable, and that the plans for 'Gymnast', landings in North Africa, later code-named 'Torch', should be resurrected as the best means of taking some pressure off the Russians. Stalin was not told of this until 14 July when he was also informed of the suspension of the aid convoys; the losses during the long summer night of the Arctic Sea having become unacceptably high. As the German offensive in the south was going well and reaping vast numbers of prisoners on the scale of 1941, Stalin's reply was understandably bitter: 'In spite of the agreed communiqué [issued during Molotov's visit in

May] concerning the urgent tasks of creating a Second Front in 1942, the British Government postpones this matter until 1943. I am afraid that the creating of a Second Front is not being treated with the seriousness it deserves. Taking full account of the present position on the Soviet—German front, I must state in the most emphatic manner that the Soviet Government cannot acquiesce in the postponement of a Second Front in Europe until 1943.'[4] A week later Churchill accepted Stalin's invitation to visit him in Moscow. His telegram to Mr Attlee, the Deputy Prime Minister, revealed the purpose of the visit: 'It was my duty to go. Now they know the worst, and having made their protest are entirely friendly; this in spite of the fact that this is their most anxious and agonizing time. Moreover M. Stalin is entirely convinced of the great advantages of Torch [sic] and I do trust that it is being driven forward with superhuman energy on both sides of the ocean.'[5]

Only too soon was the promise of a Second Front nullified by the recommendations of the Chiefs of Staff. Not enough American divisions had arrived in Britain by the end of 1942 and therefore there was no possibility of a second combined operation unless the Mediterranean campaign were brought to a halt which Churchill was loathe to do because of its effect on India and the Far East. But the two Western leaders agreed to set up a planning staff in London for the Second Front, although they hedged it around with significant provisos: the landing would only take place 'if the state of German morale and resources permit'. There were other vague stipulations which made it clear that there were at least significant doubts in their minds, perhaps the most important being the numbers of landing-craft likely to be available. Stalin showed his exasperation with his Western colleagues: 'On the understanding that the decisions you have taken in relation to Germany mean the task of destroying her by the opening of a Second Front in Europe in 1943, I would be grateful to be informed of the concrete operations planned in this sphere and of the intended timing of their execution.'[6]

Two months later, after the loss of Sixth Army at Stalingrad, at a time when Field Marshal von Manstein's brilliant counter-stroke had stabilized the south inflicting great losses on the Red Army, Stalin returned to the subject: 'Therefore the vagueness of your statements regarding the planned Anglo-American offensive on the other side of the Channel arouses in me an anxiety, about which I cannot be silent.'[7]

Shortly afterwards, during the 'Trident' conference at Washington in May, Churchill and Roosevelt confirmed that the shortage of landing-craft precluded a cross-Channel invasion in 1943, and that the planning date for 'Round Up', later renamed 'Overlord' was postponed until 1 May 1944. Stalin was informed by the American Ambassador on 4 June that the Second Front had been postponed for yet another year. He reacted with expected acerbity: 'This decision creates quite exceptional difficulties for the Soviet Union, which has been waging war for already two years under the greatest strain against the main forces of Germany and her satellites. This decision leaves also the Soviet Army, which is fighting not only for its own country, but for the Allies as well, to combat nearly single-handed a still very strong and dangerous enemy.'[8]

Churchill replied sharply: 'It would be no help to Russia if we threw away a hundred thousand men in a disastrous cross-Channel attack such as would, in my opinion, certainly occur if we tried under present conditions and with forces too weak to exploit any success at very heavy cost.'[9] Stalin's reply was even more vitriolic: 'It goes without saying that the Soviet Government cannot put up with such disregard of the most vital Soviet interests in the war against the common enemy.' A cross-Channel invasion would 'save millions of lives in the occupied regions of western Europe and Russia', and would reduce the 'colossal sacrifices' of the Soviet armies, in comparison with which, he reflected, 'the losses of the Anglo-American troops could be considered as modest'.[10]

Later, in 1943, after the successful Battle of Kursk which in reality was the turning-point on the Eastern Front as the German Army was never able again to take more than a local initiative, Stalin agreed to meet Churchill and Roosevelt at Tehran. This was the first occasion on which all three leaders were able to sit round a table to discuss their strategy for the destruction of Nazi Germany and eventually Japan, and to air their views on the post-war structure of Europe. To Stalin's evident satisfaction, the date of 'Overlord' was confirmed as 1 May 1944. Stalin's biographer, General Volkogonov, recorded the occasion: 'At breakfast on 30th November ... Roosevelt said : "Today Mr Churchill and I have taken the decision on the basis of proposals from our combined staffs: Operation 'Overlord' will begin in May, together with a simultaneous landing in southern France." "I am satisfied with this decision," Stalin replied as calmly as he could. "But I also want to say to Mr Churchill and Mr Roosevelt that, at the moment the landings begin, our troops will be preparing a major assault on the Germans."'[11] This was the genesis of the offensive that was to liberate Belorussia and destroy Army Group Centre in the summer of 1944, and inflict the greatest defeat on the German army in its history.

NOTES

1. The main sources used for this prologue were Gilbert, Edmonds, and Volkogonov. Although the translations vary slightly, I have tried to strike a balance between them.
2. Edmonds, Robin. *The Big Three: Churchill, Roosevelt and Stalin in Peace and War*, London, Hamish Hamilton, 1991, p. 242.
3. Edmonds, p. 327.
4. Gilbert, Martin. *The Road to Victory. Winston S. Churchill, 1941-1945*, London, William Heinemann, 1986, p. 435.
5. Gilbert, p. 206.
6. Edmonds, p. 320.
7. Edmonds, p. 321.
8. Gilbert, p. 430.
9. Gilbert, p. 431.
10. Gilbert, p. 436.
11. Volkogonov, Dmitri, *Stalin, Triumph and Tragedy*, London, Weidenfeld and Nicolson, 1991, p. 488.

1
THE GERMAN ARMY

The Army had played a unique part in the fabric of the state of Prussia since the eighteenth century and later in the German Empire. Prussian territory stretched from the Elbe to the borders of Russia, and much of the ethos of the 'Warrior State' came from the Orders of Military Monks who carved out their domain from the Slav countries in the east. After the Thirty Years War, the Prussian Army, under the Great Elector and his son, Frederick the Great, became the dominant institution in Prussia, making the country the greatest military power in northern Europe. Under these two monarchs the army absorbed the nobility of eastern Prussia, the Junkers, material privileges being offered in return for military service. Frederick the Great continued the policy of his father whereby the army should be officered exclusively by the Prussian aristocratic families, the middle classes being left to develop the country's commerce and industry. The Junkers, frequently possessing limited incomes from their small estates, came to dominate all branches of government service.[1]

After the defeat of the Prussian Army at Jena in 1806, the need for a complete reconstruction was recognized and instituted by two military reformers, von Scharnhorst and von Gneisenau. They recognized that the French victory was as much due to the mobilization of the resources of the entire country as it was to Napoleon's skill as a commander in the field. Scharnhorst was responsible for the creation of a standing army backed up by a large militia. Gneisenau was responsible for the system of officer training and the establishment of the Great General Staff.

During the nineteenth century, Prussia became the dominant country in the North German Confederation after the defeat of Austria at Königgrätz in 1866 when the armies of these states were added to the Prussian Army. The final accumulation of strength was the inclusion of the armies of Bavaria, Württemberg and Saxony after the defeat of France in the Franco-Prussian War and the subsequent assumption of the title of German Emperor (*Deutscher Kaiser*) by the King of Prussia. The militaristic Kaiser Wilhelm II led Germany into the First World War which would end with his abdication and his defeated armies marching back to a Germany torn by civil strife.

The Allied powers forced Germany to accept the terms of the Treaty of Versailles in June 1919. These sought to lay the blame for the war on Germany and to remove permanently her capacity for making war. While the navy and the embryo air force were reduced to a derisory level, it was the German Army that was to suffer most. Its size was reduced from its pre-war strength of two million to 100,000 men who were to be volunteers; there were to be no reserves. Regarded as the fount of militarism, the General Staff was abolished, and to prevent military influence on the young the military academies or cadet schools were also proscribed. In order to turn the army into little more than a Home Defence force, it was forbidden to have heavy artillery, tanks or aircraft. Other provisions of the Treaty stipulated the return of Alsace-Lorraine to France and the cession of western Prussia and upper Silesia to Poland, and parts of Schleswig to Denmark. The Rhineland was to remain a demilitarized zone once the Allied Occupation Forces had left. An Allied Control Commission was set up to enforce the provisions of the Treaty.

Germany was stunned by the severity of the stipulations of the Treaty which in essence disarmed the country, leaving it at the mercy of its formerly weaker neighbours, some of whom had old scores to pay off. At first there was a strong move to denounce the Treaty, and risk the threat of invasion by the Allied armies still poised on Germany's borders. Inside Germany the returning soldiers were in many cases mutinous and had been influenced by events in Russia. Most wanted nothing more than to return to their families as soon as possible, but the Soldiers' Councils wanted to control the method of demobilization and tried to impose their own conditions. All distinctions of rank, and saluting were to be done away with, and the Central Soldiers' Council tried to assume overall control over military affairs. General staff officers, concerned at the turn of events, realized that they had no forces at their disposal to uphold government policies or even defend the eastern borders of the country, which were volatile because of the anarchy reigning in Poland and Russia.

This situation was the genesis of the *Freikorps*, volunteer units ranging in strength from a few men to divisional size, and principally made up of former officers and soldiers, although there was a thin sprinkling of students and unemployed. At first the *Freikorps* were ill-disciplined and badly organized, but they fulfilled their original role of providing the government with a modicum of military power. When the *Reichswehr* was set up in 1921, the *Freikorps* formed the basis around which the first units of the 100,000-man army (*Reichsheer*) were organized.

General Hans von Seeckt played a leading role in the development of the new army from 1920 until 1926. He was born into a Silesian military family on 22 April 1886 and was commissioned into the Kaiser Alexander Garde-Grenadier Regimente No. 1. In 1899 he graduated from the General Staff course and from then on distinguished himself in various staff appointments. During the war he served on the Eastern Front, and became Chief of Staff of the Turkish Army. He was a member of the German delegation at Versailles. In appearance he was trim and erect and wore carefully tailored uniforms, and he was very precise in manner, often maintaining long silences broken by short sharp comments. He was nicknamed the 'Sphinx with the monocle'. He was fluent in English and French and had a wide interest in the arts. The British Ambassador to Germany remarked that Seeckt had: 'a broader mind than is expected in so tight a uniform; a wider outlook than seems appropriate to so precise, so correct, so neat an exterior'.[2]

The abdication of the monarchy meant that the army no longer had a mystical figurehead to which it could swear personal allegiance. This left a vacuum, but Seeckt insisted that the Army should not get involved in politics. This became of great importance when the National Socialist Party came to power in the 1930s.

As the political situation became relatively stable, Seeckt set about the development of the *Reichsheer* so that it could serve as a basis for rapid expansion when the time was opportune. Versailles allowed for two army corps, one in Berlin and the other in Kassel, with a total of seven infantry and three cavalry divisions. The General Staff had been proscribed, but Seeckt disguised an establishment with the same responsibilities under the title of *Truppenamt*. The former individual inspectorates that had reported to the Kaiser, such as the personnel directorate and the ordnance department, were grouped under the *Heeresleitung*, which was only nominally the responsibility of Seeckt, but in fact at a very early stage he had achieved total control over the entire army.

Although the *Reichsheer* was formed from units of the *Freikorps* and not from the old Imperial Army, Seeckt preserved the identity and traditions of the old regiments by handing them on to the newly formed units. Thus the traditions of service of the former Hanoverian regiments with the British Army were preserved, such battle honours as Vittoria and Waterloo being worn on their accoutrements. This was swept away with the rise of the Wehrmacht under Hitler, but even then the occasional relic could still be detected, mostly among former cavalry regiments.

The geographical position of the new Weimar Republic faced the *Reichsheer* with potential enemies on both its eastern and western frontiers. Small numbers of reserves were created for frontier defence, and these were supplemented by a special force known as *Grenzschutz Ost*, based on the *Stahlhelm* (an ex-servicemen's organization). Seeckt also supplemented the police beyond the limits allowed by Versailles, with former army officers training large numbers of recruits in basic weapon training skills. Many of those trained in the *Grenzschutz* and the police were to achieve high rank during the war.

At this stage the greatest threat was perceived to be posed by Poland, and to counter this Germany began the negotiations with the Soviet Union leading to the Treaty of Rapallo in 1922, which re-established diplomatic relations between the two countries. This had important military consequences, for the Treaty provided for specialized military training to be carried out in the depths of Russia away from prying eyes. For the army a tank training school near Kazan was set up, as well as a flying school for the embryo Luftwaffe at Lipetsk. These schools were of inestimable value to the *Reichswehr* and continued until 1933.

Although a traditionalist and a supporter of a continuing role for horsed cavalry, Seeckt also encouraged the development of motor transport, initially to lift troops and supplies. He recognized the potential of mechanization as shown by his support for the tank school at Kazan which opened in 1925. The first Inspector of Mechanized Troops favoured experiments with the rudimentary vehicles available to assess their tactical use, and in this he was assisted by one of his staff, a Captain Guderian, later to become the best-known panzer general of the Wehrmacht. Gradually the enthusiasts carried the day, and experiments were carried out in the tactics and organization of an armoured division. Although in the early days agricultural tractors and motor cars disguised by screens were used, these were no more ridiculous as training aids than were the British lengths of string representing infantry sections, and rattles imitating machine-guns. Yet when Hitler came to power, he realized quickly the advantages of this new force in helping to achieve his plans for territorial expansion.

The army retained the same organization until Hitler became Chancellor and concentrated on circumventing the restrictions imposed at Versailles so as to lay down foundations for modern armed forces. In the early days of the Nazi Party, the *Reichswehr* was only too happy to use elements of the SA (*Stürmabteilung*) to help boost manpower on the eastern frontiers. In general there was considerable support for the nationalist aims of the Nazi Party as demonstrated in the so-called 'Ulm Trial' of three young artillery officers accused of trying to promote the spread of National Socialism in the army. In his speeches Hitler used his war service to demonstrate his nationalist feelings and his sympathy with the army in his efforts to win over the *Reichswehr*.

The events surrounding the decision of the President, Field Marshal Hindenburg, to ask Hitler to form a government in January 1933 were confused and depended upon fears and miscalculations. Once Hitler had achieved power, he trod very carefully in his relations with the army. His Minister of Defence, General of Infantry Walter von Blomberg, who had only been appointed one day previous to Hitler, was a convinced supporter of the new regime. He had had a distinguished military career, winning the *Pour le Merite* for his service on the General Staff during the First World War, becoming Chief of the General Staff in 1928. In appearance he was everything that a soldier should be, tall and well turned out, and Hitler liked having him with him on ceremonial occasions to represent the armed forces. Hitler soon dominated him to such an extent that he was nicknamed 'Hitler-Junge Quex' after a film portrait of a Hitler Youth member. His sycophantic attitude to Hitler and the Nazi Party set up the framework which eventually enabled Hitler to dominate the Wehrmacht to a degree that allowed such disasters as Stalingrad and the collapse of Army Group Centre in 1944 to happen.

During the period before the rise to power of Hitler and the Nazi Party there were various proposals for increasing the manpower of the armed forces, but these only came to fruition with the December 1933 decision to treble the size of the army to 21 divisions by March 1938. However, after the French extended the period of military service, following the announcement of the existence of the Luftwaffe, Hitler decided to seize the opportunity to announce in March 1935 the reintroduction of conscription for Germany which he tied to a further increase in the strength of the army to twelve corps of infantry with 36 divisions. This came at a time when the army was still trying to assimilate the earlier threefold increase, and their difficulties were exacerbated when it became clear that these 36 divisions were in addition to the creation of three armoured divisions, a mountain division and a cavalry brigade. All things considered, that this goal was reached represented an incredible achievement.

Hitler expressed great interest in the new Panzer arm and supported the formation of the first three panzer divisions, each of a brigade headquarters commanding two panzer regiments: 1st Panzer Division (Weimar); 2nd

Panzer Division (Würzburg) commanded by Guderian; and 3rd Panzer Division (Berlin). The formation of the first six regiments shows the confusion that existed and was to remain until 1945. Formed from a mix of the original *Kraftfahrkamptruppe* (mechanized) units with cavalry regiments, the regiments themselves were split up within a year to form more regiments for new panzer divisions. The divisions were designed originally to have two rifle regiments as their infantry component in addition to the divisional reconnaissance battalions, but never enough were formed to meet this target. The infantry regiments suffered the same fate as the armoured regiments: 'First create, then split and then split again.' The whole process was made more difficult because the political leadership had not yet decided what tasks the new arm would have to face, and the formations were being created without the opportunity to test in extensive field trials the assumptions upon which they were based.

At the same time as the new panzer divisions were being established, considerable study was being made into the best type of equipment for these revolutionary formations. The first two types of tank issued to the new formations, the Panzer Mks I and II, were out of date by the time they were produced. Both had very light armoured protection unable to stop current anti-tank weapons, and the Panzer I mounted only machine-guns and the Panzer II a very light gun with limited powers of penetration. The first two medium tanks, Panzer III and Panzer IV, were much more substantial machines although still inadequate. The Panzer IV remained in service in different guises until the end of the war. Guderian was basically responsible for two innovations that conferred an incalculable advantage on German formations after the outbreak of the war with Russia. These were the provision of a radio in each armoured vehicle and the equipping of the motorized infantry with its own half-tracked troop carrier which enabled them to keep up with the tanks.

Heinz Guderian (1881-1953) was one of the creators of modern mechanized warfare. Born into a Prussian military family, he was commissioned into an infantry regiment and attended one of the earliest courses on the military application of the radio. At the beginning of the First World War he commanded the Wireless Detachment of 5th Cavalry Division which gave him an early appreciation of the value of good communications for rapidly moving formations. After the war he qualified as a General Staff officer. Guderian saw service with the *Freikorps* in the Baltic states before being accepted into the *Reichsheer* as one of the 4,000 officers allowed by Versailles. In 1922 he was posted to one of the seven motorized transport battalions which at an early stage veered towards tactical experiments and away from their basic role of administrative re-supply. Perceptive reading of foreign manuals, some of them British, convinced him that the tank should not be used in isolation or to support infantry, but should form the spearhead of an all-arms force supported by aerial strikes to supplement the artillery. These fast-moving formations would advance deep into the enemy rear, disrupting their communications and overrunning their headquarters. This was the basis of the Blitzkrieg style of warfare which was used to such effect in Poland and France, and in the opening months of the invasion of Russia.

The process of forming the new panzer divisions was bedevilled with differences of opinion with the infantry, the cavalry and the artillery, all of whom wished to enhance their own arms. But the theoretical organization of the panzer division of a panzer brigade supported by a motorized rifle brigade lasted for five years although it was frequently under implemented. By 1939 there were five panzer divisions in existence, and four cavalry light divisions, each of two truck-borne infantry regiments supported by a tank battalion. In 1940 these became 6th, 7th, 8th and 9th Panzer Divisions, joined shortly by 10th Panzer Division. Later in 1940, there was a basic re-organization of the divisions which lost their second tank regiment in order to form 11th to 20th Panzer Divisions, many of which would appear in Belorussia in 1944. At their peak, some 27 army panzer divisions were in existence. Some were reformed after Stalingrad, others lost in Tunisia were not, while 22nd and 27th were never reformed after their losses in Russia in 1943. For the duration of the war on the Eastern Front, panzer divisions retained their basic organization of a tank regiment and two infantry regiments, one battalion of which was carried in armoured half-tracks with the reminder in an assortment of trucks. The division was supported by its own artillery, and signal, reconnaissance, engineer and anti-tank battalions.

The basic formation of the German Army was the infantry division of three infantry regiments, artillery, engineer and an anti-tank battalion. Except for a motor pool, the division marched on its feet with equipment horse-drawn, known colloquially as 'foot and hoof'. By 1944, the heavy losses that been suffered during three years of heavy fighting resulted in a two-regiment organization with a seventh battalion, sometimes known as a 'Fusilier' battalion, acting as the divisional reserve.

The panzer grenadier divisions were originally designed as truck-borne troops to act in concert with the newly formed panzer divisions, and had the same establishment as normal infantry divisions. By 1943 they had been reduced to two infantry regiments but had a battalion numbering 42 tanks or assault guns as a welcome addition to their strength. The two 'named' army infantry divisions 'Grossdeutschland' and 'Feldherrnhalle' had their own special establishments, making them much stronger than their run of the mill counterparts. They were converted to Panzer divisions late in the war, and Grossdeutschland even became a Panzer corps. Although they play no part in this book, the Waffen-SS panzer and panzer grenadier divisions were stronger than those of the Wehrmacht.

By 1944 artillery support for infantry divisions normally consisted of a heavy battalion of twelve 15cm guns and three battalions of 10.5cm guns, all horse-drawn. A great deal of captured *matériel* was used. The panzer divisions had similar equipment except that it was either towed, or mounted on tracks. Some panzer, panzer grenadier and infantry divisions had been issued with Sturmgeschütze (self-propelled guns) to provide close fire and anti-tank support. These guns were operated by artillery units, and this was a source of contention with General Guderian when he became Inspector of Panzer Troops in 1943 because he had hoped to bring all armoured fighting vehicles under his control.

Having examined the formation of the panzer forces which made the early Blitzkrieg victories possible and, by 1944, provided the framework around which defensive battles were fought, we must look at the command structure that had developed within the Wehrmacht. It was centred upon Hitler, who increasingly insisted on taking all decisions down to the lowest level. The Prussian General Staff system had been developed by the Kaiser with himself at the pinnacle, personally making all decisions and appointments. The Treaty of Versailles tried to introduce safeguards, giving only titular power to the President who was unable to issue military decrees without the concurrence of the Defence Minister who had to be a civilian. Hitler ignored the advice of his Staff with disastrous results.

NOTES

1. The material for this chapter was gathered from many interviews, and supplemented by reference to books by the following authors in the bibliography: O'Neill, Cooper, Goerlitz, Seaton.
2. Lord D'Abernon, British Ambassador to Berlin, as quoted in *Fists of Steel*, Time and Life Books, Alexandria, Virginia, USA, 1988.

2
HITLER AND HIS GENERALS

The men of the German Army fighting on the Eastern Front in the summer of 1944 were very different in attitude from those who had crossed the Russo-Polish border with such élan and high hopes on the morning of 22 June 1941. The command structure had altered drastically and was now centralized in the person of Adolf Hitler with incalculable results. Few generals were strong enough to stand out against his constant interference in operational and even tactical matters, which to some extent was influenced by his experiences in the First World War.

In 1945 those generals who were not either in Russian prisoner-of-war camps or under investigation for involvement in war crimes were put to work by the US Army, initially to provide material to help with the preparation of an official history of the US Army in the Second World War. Subsequently as the Cold War began to threaten, the scope was broadened to cover the Eastern Front. The programme developed and the more historically aware generals were asked to prepare specialist monographs, but unfortunately they had to begin without access to the their documents. But the unifying thread that ran through their writing was that Hitler's personal influence on the higher direction of the war was entirely malignant and contributed to a great extent to the catastrophic military defeat of Germany. To understand how this situation arose, it is necessary to look at the development of the command structure of the armed forces since 1933.

After the First World War, the victorious Allies wanted to ensure that the absolute military power of the Hohenzollern emperors could never be revived to threaten the peace of Europe. Under the provisions of the Treaty of Versailles the President became the titular Commander-in-Chief of the armed forces, exercising this power through a Defence Minister who had to be a civilian. In the main this stipulation was observed until the chaotic closing days of 1932 when, for completely political reasons, the aged President, Field Marshal von Hindenburg, chose General of Infantry Werner von Blomberg to be Minister of Defence.[1] This decision was fatal for the German armed forces because Blomberg from the earliest days was not prepared to stand up to Hitler, and indeed was completely pro-Hitler in his attitude. Blomberg was supposed to resign to fulfil the requirement that the Minister be a civilian, but this was continually postponed.

In the first weeks and months after he came to power, Hitler made a good impression on the senior officers. Here his front line service in the trenches of Flanders and his Iron Cross, First Class, a high award for a private soldier, were very much in his favour. Hitler's Wehrmacht Adjutant at this time, Oberst Hossbach, whom we shall meet later in Belorussia, recorded that Hitler did not interfere with personnel matters or the selection of senior officers for promotion at this stage. Nor did he appear to have an interest in operational planning, but merely wished to see Germany militarily strong once more.[2]

Blomberg chose as the first head of his office an equally fervent supporter of the Nazi Party in Major-General Walter von Reichenau. This had important consequences for the future of politico-military relations, for the alliance of Hitler with Blomberg and Reichenau made the position of the army in relation to the other services very difficult. Blomberg wished to see a unified command in time of war with himself at the top. The army viewed this with disfavour, maintaining that, as Germany was a continental power, the army was the most important service, and the 'Commander-in-Chief of the Army ... must therefore be the principal adviser of the Head of State in all matters concerning the conduct of war, including naval and air matters, and must be his sole adviser on questions of warfare on land'.[3] The navy was not affected by the centralization because of their geographical role, but it was a very different matter with the projected air force under Göring.

The second most powerful man in the Nazi Party, Göring wished to form an independent air force with himself as the final authority. He found it hard to accept a subsidiary role in defence matters, and the conflict became a running battle between Blomberg and Göring. A suggestion that a centralized agency be set up in the Ministry of Defence to control the development and procurement of equipment and resources was rejected by Göring who stated that he 'could not share control of the aeronautical industry with any outside agency, any more than I could share control of my Air Force'.[4] Blomberg's reaction was to emphasize his impulsive personal support of Hitler. For example, he ordered that the armed forces adopt the Party greeting '*Heil*', and, at a later stage, that the Party insignia be worn on all *Wehrmacht* uniforms. After the death of Hindenburg, he authorized the use of a personal oath of loyalty to Hitler replacing one which swore loyalty to the constitution. This was to cause much distress to senior officers when they were considering the alternatives in removing Hitler from power. In his letter of thanks, Hitler told Blomberg that the army was to be regarded as 'the sole bearer of the arms of the nation'. Blomberg responded emotionally by suggesting that the armed forces should now address Hitler as '*Mein Führer*'. Hitler agreed and yet another strand entwining the armed forces with the Party was now in place.

These cosmetic trimmings pale into insignificance beside the main after-effect of the death of Field Marshal Hindenburg – the merging of the office of Reichs President with that of Chancellor in the person of Adolf Hitler. Now he possessed supreme power without any constitutional checks to restrain unwise or illegal measures, and this was to have incalculable results for the history of Germany and Europe. The continuing rivalry over the growth of the Luftwaffe and its role within the structure of the armed forces continued to simmer, stoked by the increasing personal animosity between Göring and Blomberg. The furore caused by revelations about the private life of the newly re-married Blomberg was exacerbated by Göring who, even if he did not arrange the situation, saw in it the possibility of becoming Blomberg's successor as Commander-in-Chief of the armed forces. Fritsch, Commander-in-Chief of the army, was ruled out, being under investigation on charges of alleged homosexuality, again probably master-minded by Göring. Blomberg told Hitler that Göring was next in seniority, but Hitler turned down this recommendation on the grounds that he was too lazy. While this was undoubtedly true, the underlying reason was that Hitler was not prepared to share power with a potential rival. Blomberg then made the fatal suggestion that Hitler should take over the position himself. At this same meeting, Blomberg recommended that General of Artillery Keitel, who 'ran my office' would be the ideal person to run the armed forces staff under Hitler. Few other appointments were to have such dire consequences for the *Wehrmacht*, as the *Reichswehr* had become in 1935, with fatal results for the prosecution of military affairs on the Eastern Front.

General of Artillery Walter Keitel was born in Brunswick in 1882, and commissioned into the artillery in which he served during the First World War. He became a general staff officer and served in the *Freikorps* until he was accepted into the Reichswehr. It was in 1929 that he first came to notice as head of the Organization Department of the *Truppenamt*, the cover name of the General Staff of the Army which was not allowed to exist under the Treaty of Versailles. He became the second head of Blomberg's *Wehrmacht* office in

1935, and in 1938 became head of the *Oberkommando der Wehrmacht* (OKW) as it became after Blomberg's dismissal. Keitel's blind faith in carrying out Hitler's instructions removed any constraints that the army and its once powerful General Staff could have had on Hitler's military fantasies. Professor O'Neill sums up Keitel's attitude on the assumption of his appointment with admirable clarity: 'He abandoned his loyalty to the army in favour of the Party and became, from then on, Hitler's devoted and unquestioning servant.'[5]

After Hitler had decided to appoint himself War Minister, he had to resolve the problem of Fritsch's replacement as Commander-in-Chief of the army. His choice fell upon General of Artillery Walter von Brauchitsch, currently Commander of 4th Army Group at Leipzig. Although he had had a distinguished military career, his Achilles' heel was that he was impecunious. He wished to re-marry but could not do so unless he could make provision for his first wife. Hitler arranged payment of sufficient money for this, and in return Brauchitsch felt able to accept the post of Commander-in-Chief, knowing full well that Hitler intended to increase his own personal control over the *Wehrmacht*.

The leader of the military opposition to Hitler was the Chief of the General Staff, General Beck, who was fiercely critical of plans to commit Germany to war over Czechoslovakia. His arguments to convince Hitler that Germany was not ready for a major war, particularly one for which there was no moral justification, fell on stony ground. Brauchitsch did not support him, and Beck could only resign his appointment. In his retirement he did not waiver in his opposition and played a leading role in the 20 July plot against Hitler. He committed suicide rather than face trial and the certain execution which he knew awaited him.

Brauchitsch selected General Franz Halder to replace Beck in the hope that he would prove more amenable to carrying out the programme of expansion that Hitler wanted to institute. In this he was much mistaken because Halder had already become involved in a plot against Hitler.[6] After the Munich agreement between Hitler and Chamberlain, which allowed Germany a free hand in Czechoslovakia, the military opposition collapsed and Halder remained in his post to plan subsequent military operations. The team that was to plan and carry out the attack on Russia was now in being. Its weakness and lack of cohesion meant that there was no power base strong enough openly to oppose or criticize Hitler, so the conditions conducive to disaster on the Eastern Front were now firmly in place, although in the early stages everything seemed to go well for Hitler.

For the planning of the campaign in Poland, OKH moved from its peacetime headquarters to Zossen, 30 miles south of Berlin, where it occupied a barracks which after the war became the headquarters of the Soviet Forces in East Germany. Hitler moved to the Polish Front in his own train, 'The Führer Special', with a small OKW staff, leaving the remainder at the Bendlerstrasse in Berlin. This proved to be unsatisfactory and was remedied in the French campaign by co-locating OKH's forward HQ with the main OKW at the *Führerhauptquartier*. Relations between the two staffs had deteriorated to a point where the principals were barely speaking to one another; the army general staff at OKH trying to protect its position from the encroachments of OKW.[7]

The planning for the invasion of Denmark and Norway in the spring of 1940 was placed in the hands of OKW, which was reasonable given that it was basically a large-scale amphibious landing operation, but Hitler blurred the picture as he bypassed OKH in the planning of the land battle. He assumed personal responsibility, assisted by the operations staff of OKW. This brought into prominence two members of the OKW staff who were to play a leading part in the military leadership of the Third Reich.

General Alfred Jodl was to serve throughout the war as chief of the operations staff of OKW, maintaining a considerable influence on Hitler. By the end of the war he had been advanced to the rank of colonel-general. He was tried at Nuremberg and, like Keitel, was executed for complicity in war crimes. The operations branch of OKW was run by Colonel Walther War-limont who was a convinced supporter of the idea of the tripartite command structure with a small central staff. He remained at OKW until he was injured in the attempted assassination on 20 July 1944. He was promoted to General of Artillery, and imprisoned by the Allies until 1957. In 1962 he published his account of the war as seen from the lofty heights of OKW. Entitled *Inside Hitler's Headquarters*, it gives an unequalled description of events and the people who were close to Hitler.

Once the campaign in France had been brought to a triumphant conclusion, Hitler's thoughts turned to the east. He reasoned that if Russia could be eliminated, England would soon be forced to surrender, and the uncertainty of a cross-Channel assault would be avoided. Initial planning for the campaign in the east was undertaken by the army, and OKW was not involved until the army had made its first presentation to Hitler on 5 December. A divergence of opinion between Hitler and the planners at OKH developed. Although both agreed on the necessity of crushing Soviet resistance on the border, the general staff believed that Moscow should be the primary objective. Their reasoning was that the Red Army would defend the capital to its last gasp; not only was it the seat of government, but it was also the nodal point of road and rail communications in western Russia. Hitler prevaricated; he wanted a more widely dispersed attack on three axes: in the north to take Leningrad and link up with their allies, the Finns; in the south to deprive the Russians of the Donbas industrial area and eventually the oilfields of the Caucasus; and only a minor thrust on Moscow. This view was encapsulated in Hitler's Directive No. 21, which laid down the framework of the assault, code-named 'Barbarossa'. The army raised no objections, believing arrogantly that events would force Hitler to revert to their plan. This confusion and lack of single-mindedness was to have disastrous consequences; so much depended on the crushing of Soviet resistance before the onset of inclement weather which would inhibit rapid movement, even of armoured formations.

'Barbarossa' opened on 22 June 1941 with total success almost everywhere, with the four Panzer Groups thrusting deep into Russia. After liquidation of the Minsk and Smolensk pockets which yielded more than 500,000 prisoners and huge quantities of *matériel*, Hitler interfered and ordered his generals to turn to the subsidiary objectives on their flanks. Although the attacking formations were halted for more than a month while the arguments raged, at least the weary troops were able to recuperate. Hitler was adamant and on 21 August ordered diversions north and south. Next day he sent a memorandum to Brauchitsch, CinC of the army, as reported by Halder, Chief of the General Staff and a noted diarist: the Führer reproaches the CinC 'for failure to conduct operations on the lines desired by the Führer and tries to show that the shifting of the main weight to south and north is a prime necessity: Moscow is of secondary importance, both as an objective and for the timetable of the campaign.' Later on the same day, Halder noted in his diary: 'I regard the situation created by the Führer's interference unendurable for OKH. None other than the Führer himself is to blame for the zigzag course caused by his successive orders, nor can the present OKH, which is now in its fourth victorious campaign, tarnish its good name with these latest orders.'[8]

In his diary, Goebbels gives the Party view of the depths to which relations between Hitler and his generals had sunk: 'Brauchitsch bears a great deal of responsibility for this. The Führer spoke of him only in terms of contempt. A vain, cowardly wretch who could not even appraise the situation, let alone master it. By his constant interference and consistent disobedience he completely spoiled the entire plan for the eastern campaign as it was designed with crystal clarity by the Führer. The Führer had a plan that was bound to lead to victory. Had Brauchitsch done what was asked of him and what he really should have done, our position in the east would today be entirely different. The Führer had no intention whatever of going to Moscow. He wanted to cut off the Caucasus and thereby strike the Soviet system at its most vulnerable point. But Brauchitsch and his general staff knew better. Brauchitsch always urged going to Moscow. He wanted prestige successes instead of factual successes. The Führer described him as a coward and a nincompoop.'[9]

Army Group Centre's attack on Moscow was renewed at the beginning of October, but it rapidly became evident that it had been left too late in the season. First the mud held up movement of all but tracked vehicles and then the cold weather set in with temperatures dropping to as low as 25°C. The first Soviet counter-offensive opened on 5 December, strengthened by reinforcements well-equipped to operate in bitterly cold weather. After weeks of heavy fighting, the German generals wanted to withdraw to a shorter defensive line in order to assemble reserves, but Hitler insisted that the Army Group hold its positions and with some justification because a withdrawal without defensive positions on which to fall back could have degenerated into a rout which would have been almost unstoppable. Convinced now of his own infallibility, Hitler responded to a request for withdrawal with the following message: 'The Führer has ordered. Larger evasive movements cannot be made. They will lead to a total loss of weapons and equipment. Commanding generals, commanders and officers are to intervene in person to compel the troops to fanatical resistance in their positions without regard to enemy broken through [sic] on the flanks or in the rear. This is the only way of gaining the time necessary to bring up the reinforcements from Germany and the west that I have ordered. Only if reserves have moved into rearward positions can thought be given to withdrawing to those positions.'[10]

General Guderian, commander of Second Panzer Army, refused to hand on these orders. He flew to see Hitler to protest, and en route told the Chief of Staff, Army Group Centre: 'The situation is more serious than one could imagine. If something does not happen soon, things will occur that the German armed forces have never before experienced. I will take these orders and file them. I will not pass them on even under threat of court-martial. I want at least to give my career a respectable ending.'[11]

Hitler took advantage of this parlous state of affairs to remove those generals he thought were opposed to his direction of the war. He replaced von Bock in command of Army Group Centre with von Kluge, and dismissed a number of other generals. The most significant change was the resignation of the CinC, von Brauchitsch, on 16 December, which Hitler accepted without bestowing any of the customary decorations upon the departing field marshal. Hitler then told Halder: 'Anyone can do the little jobs of directing operations in war. The task of the CinC is to educate the army to be National Socialist. I do not know any army general who can do this as I want it done. I have therefore decided to take over command of the army myself.'[12] Having made this decision, Hitler issued a proclamation to the land forces: 'Soldiers of the army and the Waffen-SS! Our struggle for national liberation is approaching its climax! Decisions of world importance are about to be made! The army bears the primary responsibility for battle! I have therefore as of this day myself taken command of the army! As a soldier who fought in many world war battles I am closely tied to you in the will to victory.'[13]

His decision had a number of consequences in the administrative field. Hitler was only really interested in the control of operations and in the senior officers' personnel branch. The remainder of the functions of the army he transferred to the control of the OKW which meant that the army no longer had a senior officer to hold its corner against the other two services and the Waffen-SS for its share of scarce resources. Halder noted on 19 December that there was to be a new style of briefing conference at which such personnel as the directors of transport and of signals, and the Quartermaster-General would be present to support him. Jodl would present briefings to Hitler on the activity of the previous 24 hours, including the Eastern Front, and in the subsequent discussions decisions were often reached before the OKH representatives were called into the room. Two examples from Halder's diary give the tone of these Hitler briefings:

'16 Dec – General withdrawal was out of the question. Enemy has made substantial penetration in only a few places. The idea to prepare positions in the rear is drivelling nonsense.

3 Jan – Another dramatic scene with the Führer, who calls into question the generals' courage to make hard decisions. The plain truth however is

that with the temperature down to thirty below freezing our troops simply cannot hold out any longer.'

The failure to take Moscow was the first major defeat suffered by the Germany Army during the Second World War.

The Führer laid down his policy for 1942 in his Directive No. 41 of 5 April: 'to wipe out the entire defence potential remaining to the Soviets, and to cut them off, as far as possible, from their most important centres of war industry'.[14] Hitler realized that his own lack of resources precluded his attacking in the north towards Leningrad at the same time as he advanced into the Donbas and the Caucasus. He chose to attack first in the south. Although heavy fighting continued in the north and centre for the next two years, no further attempt to take Moscow was made. The main concentration of German operations remained in the south, and this was to have a major effect on the Soviet summer offensive of June 1944.

NOTES

1. O'Neill, Robert. *The German Army and the Nazi Party, 1933-1939*, London, Cassell & Co., 1966, p. 9.
2. *Ibid.* p. 15.
3. *Ibid.*, p. 106; Warlimont, Walter. *Inside Hitler's Headquarters*, London, Weidenfeld and Nicolson, 1964, p.11.
4. O'Neill., p. 109.
5. *Ibid.*, p. 142.
6. *Ibid.*, p. 163.
7. Warlimont, p. 27.
8. Cooper, Matthew, *The German Army, 1933-1945*, London, Macdonald and Jane's, 1978, p. 324.
9. Warlimont, pp. 212-3, quoting Goebbels' Diary.
10. Ziemke, Earl F., *Moscow to Stalingrad: Decision in the East*, Washington, OCMH, 1968, p. 82.
11. Halder, as quoted in Cooper, p. 344.
12. Ziemke, p. 83.
13. *Ibid.*, p. 83.
14. Trevor-Roper, H. R., *Hitler's War Directives*, London, Pan Books, 1966, p. 178.

3
THE TURN OF THE TIDE

Colonel-General Kurt Zeitzler replaced Colonel-General Halder in September 1942. He was a relatively junior officer and had shown much ability and energy in earlier appointments, including a period under Jodl at OKW. On his arrival at OKH he was determined to regain as much as possible of the inroads made by Keitel and Jodl. Warlimont of the OKW operations staff, who detested Jodl, records that on his arrival Zeitzler told the OKH staff: 'I require the following from every staff officer: he must believe in the Führer and in his method of command. He must on every occasion radiate this confidence to his subordinates and those around him.' The new chief of staff arranged to speak first at the Hitler briefings, and persuaded Hitler to agree that plans for the Eastern Front be dealt with at special meetings between him and Hitler with only stenographers present.

The effects of Zeitzler's measures, Warlimont recorded, were to 'make Jodl's exposé of the situation in the east superfluous and thus to remove the opportunity for interference with command of the army that had been the rule ever since the Sudetenland crisis of 1938.'[2] One can now begin to understand the complexities of the command situation that were to contribute to the disaster of the summer of 1944.

The greatest problem facing the new chief of staff was the situation of Sixth Army at Stalingrad. The city had become a symbol for both sides – the original strategic aim having been forgotten. Hitler would not permit a withdrawal and Stalin saw it as an opportunity to deal the German forces in the south a smashing blow. The Soviet counter-offensive began on 19 November, cutting off Sixth Army in Stalingrad, which resulted in its surrender by Field Marshal Friedrich Paulus on 31 January 1943 with an estimated loss of some 200,000 men. The efforts made by Army Group Don, commanded by Field Marshal Erich von Manstein, to relieve the city were nullified by Hitler's categorical refusal to allow the encircled army to break out. In order to avert a disaster of even greater magnitude, First Panzer Army was withdrawn with great difficulty from the Caucasus to join Fourth Panzer Army in the spring counter-offensive, which robbed the Soviets of much of the ground they had won.

The brain behind this decisive counter-offensive was that of Manstein. He was born in 1885 and commissioned into the 3rd Foot Guards in 1906. He was severely wounded in the early days of the First World War and afterwards served mainly in Staff appointments. Hitler accepted Manstein's plan that the main onslaught in 1940 should be made through the Ardennes where the French were least likely to expect it, and its success is history. After that he continued to prove his worth to Hitler who for some time had great confidence in him. He was one of the most successful operational commanders of the Second World War.

Although the surrender of Sixth Army was the most grievous loss suffered by Hitler in the war to date, it was not fatal. This is contrary to the view of the Soviet authorities, who maintain that it was the turning point of the entire war; but the fact remains that Germany retained the initiative and was able to mount a major offensive at Kursk some six months later.

The Axis powers were aware of the impending danger of an Anglo-American invasion in 1943-4 or, at the very latest, 1945, and Hitler and OKH considered that the most effective way of stabilizing the Eastern Front before the landings would be a pre-emptive offensive in the Kursk salient during the spring of 1943. The date of the offensive was continually postponed in order to concentrate more formations and tanks. 'Citadel' opened on 4 July, and there was savage fighting for two weeks and then Hitler called it off because of the need for troops to counter the Allied landings in Sicily.

The Red Army had also considered a pre-emptive offensive but Stalin ruled that the German effort be absorbed before launching his summer offensive north and south of the Kursk salient. 'Citadel' was a decisive defeat for the German Army which finally lost the initiative on the Eastern Front. For the remainder of the war they could only react to Soviet moves, being unable to mount other than local counter-attacks albeit in considerable strength.

By the end of September, the Soviet offensive had regained the line of the Dnieper except in the south. It was along this river line that Manstein had hoped to build the 'East Wall', but little work was carried out because of shortages of materials which were needed for the 'Atlantic Wall'. Colonel Glantz sums up the Germans' dilemma: 'Hitler operated from what he saw as a position of political and economic necessity, while the military commanders looked at the issue of military necessity. That debate between the political and the military would continue throughout the fall of 1943, and of course, throughout 1944 and 1945 as well. Hitler, on the one hand, was reluctant to

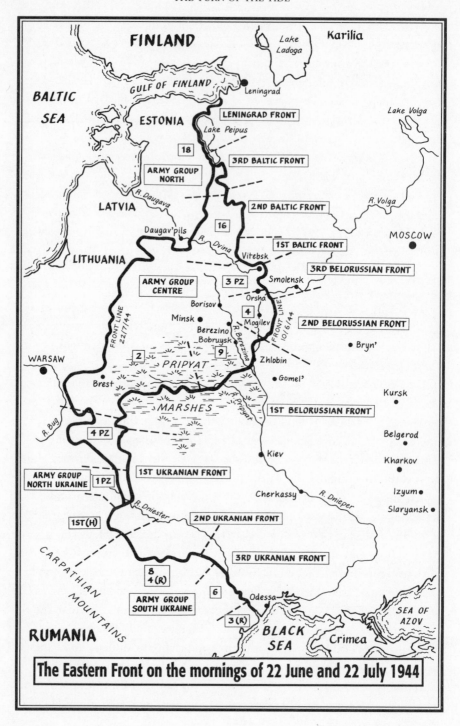

The Eastern Front on the mornings of 22 June and 22 July 1944

trade territory with the Soviets for fear of the economic and political consequences. The German High Command understood the necessity of trading
terrain in order to generate forces capable of halting the inexorable march of
the Soviet forces westward.'

'The potential Dnieper river barrier became a major issue in the fall of
1943. German forces would have liked to have been able to build a strong
defence line along the Dnieper, but Hitler, acting as he had in earlier
instances, had prevented that line from being constructed in advance, Hence,
in September and October of 1943, German forces had to construct hasty
defences along the Dnieper and hope that they would hold the Soviet forces
on its eastern banks. That was the general strategic context for the impending
Kiev operation.'3

In the event, Kiev fell and the German relief attack failed, despite a
masterly display of operational manoeuvre by the panzer divisions which had
demonstrated that they were still tactically superior to their Soviet counterparts. Further Soviet offensives continued along the entire Easter Front during
the winter of 1943 and the spring of 1944 until the Germans managed to halt
the Soviet advance along the line west of Leningrad – Pskov – Vitebsk – west
of Gomel – Kovel – Ternopol – Odessa.

Hitler had lost confidence in Field Marshal von Manstein, who had
stabilized the dangerous situation existing after Stalingrad, and proved himself
a master of mobility on the battlefield. Saying that the days of large sweeping
movements were over, and that stubborn defence was required, Hitler
replaced him as commander of Army Group South, later renamed Army
Group North Ukraine, by Field Marshal Model who had fought defensive
battles in the north. The last word on von Manstein's ability was written by
Liddell Hart after the war: 'The ablest of all the German generals was probably Field Marshal Erich von Manstein ... [He] showed great skill, against
heavy odds, in conducting the step-by-step retreat to the Polish frontier. But
Hitler would not listen to his arguments for shaking off the Russian pressure
by a long step-back. The vigour with which he argued became an increasing
annoyance to Hitler, who shelved him.' General Blumentriit told Liddell
Hart: 'He was not only the most brilliant strategist of our generals, but he had
a good political sense. A man of that quality was too difficult for Hitler to
swallow for long. At conferences Manstein often differed from Hitler in front
of others, and would go as far as to declare that some of the ideas put forward
by Hitler were nonsense.'4 So departed the only general who might have had

enough ability to extricate Army Group Centre from its perilous situation in June 1944, or at least his prestige might have persuaded Hitler to allow limited withdrawals before it was too late.

The German army was now beginning to feel the cumulative effect of its losses: on 1 September its total strength on the Eastern Front fell below 2½ million men excluding Luftwaffe field divisions and Waffen SS, and there were insufficient recruits being mustered to replace the losses – the army was having to compete with the other services and with industry. Great efforts were made to weed-out the rear echelons and training establishments but these failed to produce a significant increase in numbers of front-line troops. Many infantry divisions were under strength, some being based on two rather than the customary three regiments, but this was compensated to some extent by improved anti-tank weapons. Under Albert Speer, Hitler's inspired choice as Armaments Minister, production was dramatically increased, and by 1944 tank and assault gun production was nearing that of the Soviet Union; faults in design had been remedied and they were now superior to their Soviet equivalents.

Previously, after a setback on the Eastern Front, Hitler had replaced worn divisions that needed rest and re-equipping with fresh divisions from the west, but during the course of 1943 it was realized that an invasion was inevitable in 1944 and those troops would be needed where they were. On 3 November 1943, Hitler issued his directive No. 51, which made it clear that reinforcements from the west would no longer be available: 'The danger in the east remains, but greater danger now appears in the west: an Anglo-Saxon landing! In the east, the vast extent of the territory makes it possible for us to lose ground, even on a large scale, without a fatal blow being dealt to the nervous system of Germany. It is very different in the west! Should the enemy succeed in breaching our defences on a wide front here, the immediate consequences would be unpredictable ... I can therefore no longer take responsibility for further weakening the west in favour of other theatres of war ... No units or formations stationed in the west and in Denmark, nor any of the newly raised self-propelled armoured artillery or anti-tank guns in the west will be withdrawn to other fronts without my approval.'[5]

On his return from the Tehran conference, Stalin told Marshal Zhukov: 'Roosevelt has given his word that large-scale action will be mounted in France in 1944. I believe he will keep his word. Even if he doesn't, we have enough of our own forces to complete the rout of Nazi Germany.' There exists some doubt as to whether this was what he actually said, or was what he meant. There were 164 German formations in the east and some 121 in the west and in the Mediterranean theatre. In France and the Netherlands tank and assault gun strength had risen to 1,850 – a not inconsiderable quantity. The truth was that the Western Allies needed the Red Army to tie down German divisions in the east as much as the Soviets needed the Allies to prevent divisions being transferred from the west.

NOTES

1. Warlimont, p. 260.
2. *Ibid.*, p. 261.
3. Glantz, Colonel David, *Art of War Symposium 1985*, US Army War College, Carlisle, Penn., p. 8.
4. Liddell Hart, B., *The Other Side of the Hill*, London, Cassell, 1948, pp. 94-8.
5. Trevor-Roper, p. 221.
6. Zhukov, Marshal G. K. *The Memoirs of Marshal Zhukov*, London, Jonathan Cape, 1971, p. 493..

4
STALIN AND THE STAVKA

Although there were many similarities in the way that Stalin and Hitler directed their war, the machinery of the respective higher commands had developed very differently. While the German system was based on the General Staff as created by von Gneisenau in the early 19th century, the Russians after the revolution had no comparable model, and most of the experience gained since 1917 and the Civil War had been lost in Stalin's infamous purges of 1937-8. As we shall see, the onslaught against the top leadership of the armed forces brought many unqualified and relatively junior officers into posts they were not equipped to fill. This could be compared to the situation in the German army, but for a different reason. Hitler's rapid increase of numbers of front-line and reserve divisions had called for a corresponding increase in the numbers of generals required. It is astonishing that so many of superior quality were available, and so few of them failed to carry out their responsibilities to the high standard expected of them.

In the Red Army and Navy there existed dual military and political control to ensure the political reliability of the officer corps, with commissars appointed at every level to validate military orders. On 30 June 1941 Stalin created the State Defence Committee (GKO) with himself as chairman, Molotov as deputy, and Marshal K. Y. Voroshilov as a council member, although he did not last long. On 8 August Stalin assumed the appointment of Supreme Commander, and the Stavka (Staff) became the Stavka of the Supreme High Commander. Its members became Stalin's personal advisers and were sent to the Fronts to gather information or supervise and co-ordinate special operations. As we shall see, this is what happened in the summer offensive of June 1944.

The Stavka operated from Moscow throughout the war, initially from the Kremlin until German bombers began to raid the city. An operations centre was then set up in the deep underground shelter of the Kirovskaya Metro station. The Chief of the General Staff was General B. M. Shaposhnikov until the end of 1942 when he was succeeded by Colonel-General A. M. Vasilevsky who remained in the post until 1945. His deputy, General A. I. Antonov, was appointed in 1942 and remained until he succeeded Antonov as Chief at the end of the war. The demanding post of Head of the Operations Directorate was filled by General S. M. Shtemenko in May 1943. Military historians are deeply in his debt for the remarkable and full account of the work of the Stavka, first published in 1981, entitled *The Soviet General Staff at War*.

Like Hitler, Stalin was a hard taskmaster. He controlled every detail of the war, and once his command system was working, very little was done without his approval. Some examples from a recent biography give the flavour of his relationship with his generals. Failure was dealt with harshly, the fortunate being dismissed, others were given a summary trial, with no appeal, and executed. Seniority brought no respite from Stalin's wrath, as Vasilevsky, Chief of the General Staff, discovered on 17 August 1943:

'It is already 3.30 on 17 August and you have not yet deigned to report to the Staff on the results of the operations on 16 August and to give your assessment of the situation.

'I have for a long time obliged you as a Staff plenipotentiary to send special reports by the end of each day of operations. Almost every time you have forgotten your responsibility and have not sent reports ... You cannot use the excuse that you have no time, as Marshal Zhukov is doing just as much at the front as you are, yet he sends us his reports every day. The difference between you and Zhukov is that he is disciplined and knows his duty to the Staff. Whereas you lack discipline and often forget your duty to the Staff.

'I'm warning you for the last time that if you allow yourself to forget your duty to the Staff once more, you will be removed as head of the General Staff and will be sent to the front.'[1]

Like Hitler, Stalin made only one, token, visit to the front, though he made much of it to Churchill and Roosevelt. 'Having just returned from the front, I am only now able to reply to your letter of 16 July [1943]. I have no doubt that you are aware of our military situation and will therefore understand the delay. I have to make personal visits to the various sectors of the front more and more often and to subordinate everything else to the interest of the front.' As far as is known, he made only the one visit.

Stalin himself laid down the detailed routine and woe betide any one who stepped out of line. Shtemenko gives a very good picture of what it was like to work him.

'Reports to the Supreme Commander were usually made three times a day. The first came between 1000 and 1100 hours, usually by telephone. This was my job. In the evening, between 1600 and 1700 hours, the Deputy Chief of the General Staff would report. During the night we would both drive to GHQ with the summary report for the day. Before this the situation for each Front had to be entered on 1:200,000 maps to show troop positions, including that of each Soviet division and sometimes even regiment.

'The Supreme Commander would not tolerate the slightest distortion or varnishing of the facts and meted out harsh punishment to anyone who was caught doing so. I well remember how in November 1943, the Chief of Staff of the First Ukrainian Front was dismissed from his post because he had omitted to report the enemy's capture of a certain important populated area in the hope that it might be recaptured.'[3]

Shtemenko describes the procedure at GHQ briefings which were held either in the Kremlin or at Stalin's country dacha: 'A long rectangular table stood in the left-hand part of the room which had a vaulted ceiling and walls panelled in light oak. On this we would spread out the maps, from which we would then report on each Front separately, beginning with the sector where the main events were happening at the moment. We used no notes. We knew the situation by heart and it was also shown on the map.' After this, Stalin dictated the directives to go out to the Fronts. Many were not typed and went out to the Signal Centre in their original form. Directives were signed by Stalin and either his First Deputy, Marshal G. K. Zhukov, or by the Chief of the General Staff, Vasilevsky. If both were out of Moscow they were signed by General Antonov.

Stalin liked to work late at night, as did Churchill, and his staff officers did not return to their quarters until 3 or 4 in the morning. Shtemenko summarizes the effect of working at that pace: 'No one could change the rigorous system of work that Stalin had established for the General Staff. The enormous amount to be done and the urgency of it all made service on the General Staff extremely exhausting. We worked ourselves to breaking point, knowing in advance that we would be severely penalized for the slightest mistake. Not every one could stand the strain. Some of my comrades suffered long afterwards from nervous debility and heart trouble. Many of them retired to the reserve as soon as the war was over, before reaching retirement age.'[4]

Perhaps Marshal Zhukov should have the last word about Stalin's abilities: 'From the military standpoint I have studied Stalin most thoroughly for I entered the war together with him and together with him I ended it. Stalin mastered the technique of the organization of Front operations and operations by groups of Fronts and guided them with skill, thoroughly understanding complicated strategic questions. He displayed his ability as Commander-in-Chief beginning with Stalingrad.'[5]

After the German attempt to take Moscow had been defeated, the Red Army began the process of remedying the faults and omissions that had become evident during the disasters of 1941. A stream of directives concentrating on offensive operations was sent from the Stavka to Front and Army headquarters. On 10 January 1942 the Stavka stated: 'It is necessary that our forces learn how to break through the enemy's defence line, learn how to break through the full depth of the enemy's defences and open routes of advance for our infantry, our tanks and our cavalry.'[6]

During 1942 and 1943 the Red Army devoted much time and effort to devising an organization for their armoured troops that would make them capable of penetrating the German defences and operating in their rear for considerable distances. During the 1930s the Red Army had built up a substantial tank force with four mechanized corps of more than 500 tanks each, but their experiences in Spain had led them to believe that these were too large, and they were reduced to tank brigades. But observation of the German successes with large armoured formations in France in 1940 led the Russians to create first fifteen and then 29 mechanized corps. Most of these formations, equipped with early models of tanks, were destroyed by the Germans. They were replaced by separate tank brigades, but these were not strong enough to effect deep penetration so in turn they were grouped into tank corps. Even these could not create enough momentum to sustain deep operations, so the Soviets formed tank armies of which six were eventually created. These had two tank corps with infantry and supporting units of all types. One such tank army, 5th Guards, took part in the 1944 Belorussian summer offensive.

Of particular significance for this offensive was the creation of the rather strange but very effective formation the cavalry/mechanized group. This consisted of a cavalry corps and a tank or mechanized corps and gave the Soviets the ability to operate across terrain that was unsuitable for tanks and in all climatic conditions. The Red Army also concentrated many of its fire support units into specialized artillery and mortar regiments, and formed engineer regiments with bridging or mineclearing equipment. These were grouped in support divisions which were kept in Stavka reserve to be allotted to armies for particular tasks.

The Red Air Force did not exist as a separate service but was part of the army, but it was represented on the Stavka. The heavy losses that it suffered during the early days of the war when many of its aircraft were destroyed on the ground and in the air by the Luftwaffe meant that it was unable to play a significant role in 1941. Gradually more modern machines came into service, which at low altitude outclassed in speed the latest German fighters. As the Allied strategic bomber offensive gathered momentum, the German fighters were recalled to defend the skies of the Fatherland, and the Soviet aircraft were able to play a major role in the land battle.

Air support was an integral part of Soviet offensive operations and each Front was given tactical support by its own Air Army, which could undertake air defence, ground assault, reconnaissance, and short-range bombing missions. The Air Army commander was a member of the staff of the Front commander, and his aircraft were dedicated to the support of the Front. In addition, units of the Long Range Bomber Force were placed in support of individual Fronts to carry out ground missions.

In essence, the Soviets regarded tactical air support as an extension of conventional artillery. During the attack phase their principal targets were the German artillery positions, their assembly areas and centres of communication. After the breakthrough, aircraft were committed to anti-aircraft protection of the leading armoured formations which had air liaison officers riding in their forward tanks. They were particularly effective in attacking German reserves attempting to move forward to counter-attack.

In the summer of 1944 this was a potentially dangerous situation for the German defences because the majority of the Luftwaffe's fighter aircraft had been withdrawn to the west to oppose the Allied landings in Normandy and the Allied bombing raids.

NOTES
1. Volkogonov, p. 453.
2. *Ibid.*, p. 481.
3. Shtemenko, S. M., *The Soviet General Staff at War, 1941-1945*, Moscow, Progress Publishers, 1981, pp. 182-4.
4. *Ibid.*, p. l86.
5. Ziemke, p. 507; Edmonds, p. 276.
6. Ziemke., p. l42.

5
THE SOVIET ARMY

The Red Army was born out of the Bolshevik Revolution of November 1917 from the old Imperial Army. Many of its first officers and men had served in the Great War and were to know the uncertainties of the Civil War. From the very beginning foreign intervention to restore imperial rule was constantly expected, and the need of strong defence forces was accepted.

The greatest asset that the Red Army possessed was the Russian soldier. A distinguished German staff officer writing after the war, described his virtues: 'He is patient and enduring beyond imagination, incredibly brave and courageous – yet at times he can be a contemptible coward. There were occasions when Russian units, which had driven back German attacks with ferocious courage, suddenly fled in panic before a small assault group. Battalions lost their nerve when the first shot was fired, and yet the same battalion fought with fanatical stubbornness on the following day ...

'A feature of the Russian soldier is his utter contempt for life or death, so incomprehensible to a Westerner. The Russian is completely unmoved when he steps over the dead bodies of hundreds of his comrades; with the same unconcern he buries his dead compatriots, and with no less indifference faces his own death.'[1]

The Red Army of Workers and Peasants was formed during the Revolution and its structure as a political force was maintained during the inter-war years. Its first task was to eliminate the threat to the new government from the 'Whites', the representatives of the combination of anti-Communists and those who remained loyal to the old regime. Although the government realized that it needed the skills of the former officers of the former Imperial Army, it was not convinced of the political reliability of these converts, called 'military experts', and instituted the system of political commissars which lasted until well into the 1941-5 War. Their original task was to ensure that there was no 'back-sliding' or treachery. No military order was valid unless it was counter-signed by the appropriate commissar, and this gave them considerable power in all aspects of military life, sometimes to a stultifying degree.

The great majority of the peasants were much more interested in looking after the land they had acquired during the Revolution, than they were in military service and so a system of conscription had to be introduced. The political content was increased by the formation of Communist Party cells to form a backbone in units of doubtful reliability. During the fighting with the 'Whites' who were supported by the Western Allies in an endeavour to maintain a viable Eastern Front to keep up pressure on Germany which in 1918 was still unbeaten, the controversial figure of Tukhachevsky first appears.

M. N. Tukhachevsky was born into an impoverished aristocratic family, and because his family could not afford a university education for him he entered the army and was commissioned into the élite Semenovsky Guards. He was taken prisoner shortly after the outbreak of war and was released in 1917. In 1918 he volunteered to be a 'military expert', and served with great distinction in Poland. At the age of 26 he was appointed Commander-in-Chief of the Southern Front until he was called upon to deal with the threat to Russia's borders with Poland. At the end of the war he was appointed Deputy to the Chief of the General Staff, his close friend General M. V. Frunze, and succeeded him after his death. They worked together to form a new Red Army as an up-to-date modern force in line with concepts of mechanized and armoured warfare.

After the conclusion of the Civil War in 1922, there was fierce discussion about the type and size of army required by the Soviet Union. Frunze was the principal architect of this new force which was established at seventeen rifle corps and two cavalry corps, each corps having two or three divisions under command. Similar reorganization was carried out in the air force and navy. After Frunze's death in 1926, Stalin appointed Voroshilov Commissar of the Army and he retained this position until after the disastrous showing of Soviet forces in the Finnish War.

In its earliest days the Soviet Union was regarded as a pariah by the developed countries of the world. The only exception was Weimar Germany, still treated as having been responsible for the First World War and therefore emasculated by the Treaty of Versailles. The Treaty forbade Germany to possess or carry out research into armoured warfare or aircraft for military purposes. The 1922 Treaty of Rapallo between Germany and Russia had secret provisions for joint training and development of tanks and military aircraft. This provided a basis for extensive co-operation between the armed forces of the two countries until Hitler came to power in 1933.

As early as 1930 the Soviets had formed an experimental tank brigade which developed into the mechanized corps of 1936. A mix of foreign-bought prototype tanks and indigenous tanks developed under the Five Year Plan were tested in these formations: by 1935 the Red Army possessed 7,000 tanks, mostly T-26 and T-27 light tanks and the T-35 heavy tank. The basic formation was the mechanized corps, renamed in 1938 as tank corps, which had two tank brigades, a rifle/machine-gun brigade with supporting units, and a total of 560 tanks. However the experiences of the forces that the Red Army sent to support the Loyalists in the Spanish Civil War questioned the size of these formations, and tank numbers were cut. But the success of German armoured formations in France in 1940 caused the Soviet military authorities to try to rebuild an armoured force structure. At first there were to be nine new mechanized corps, but this figure was increased to 29, scheduled to be formed by the summer of 1942. These new formations were to be equipped with the latest KV heavy tanks and the workhorse of the Soviet tank formations, the legendary T-34, thought by some to be the best medium tank of the war.

While the Red Army was developing its armoured formations, the regime it served dealt it a body blow from which it had not really recovered by the outbreak of war with Germany. The cause of Stalin's purge of his generals is not clear. Some authorities ascribe it to his relentless drive towards liquidation of potential rivals, others maintain that there was a genuine military plot led by Marshal Tukhachevsky. The evidence against him consisted of documents promising strategic secrets to Germany for support for his coup against Stalin, although these may have been fabricated by Stalin in pursuance of a long-standing grievance. Tukhachevsky was tried in closed court on 11 May 1937, found guilty and shot next day. This unleashed a purge throughout the senior ranks of the armed forces. The final list of those shot or imprisoned numbered some 35,000, or 50 per cent of the officer corps. Perhaps the worst aspect was that so many were holding very senior appointments. They included: 3 out of 5 marshals; 14 out of 16 army commanders; 8 out of 8 admirals; 60 out of 67 corps commanders; 136 out of 199 divisional commanders; 221 out of 397 brigade commanders. In addition, all eleven deputy commissars of defence and 75 out of 80 members of the Supreme Military Council were executed.[2] These bare figures give no idea of the horror of these men's end. One temporary survivor wrote: 'Death in battle is not frightening. One moment and it is all over. But the consciousness of close, inevitable death is horrifying, when there is no help, when you know that nothing can halt the approaching grave, when until the frightful moment there remains less and less time, and finally when they say to you, "Your pit is ready".[3]

Those officers fortunate enough to survive led a life overshadowed by constant fear that their turn would come. Internal confusion in the army was extreme. One officer who arrived at a division to take over the appointment of Chief of Staff found that the most senior surviving officer was a captain. Perhaps one of the most disastrous effects was the loss of large numbers of forward-thinking officers who had been responsible for the technical and organizational advances of the 1930s. Although opportunities were created for promotion for promising younger officers, the remaining senior officers were often Civil War cronies of Stalin's, and ill-suited to take advantage of the new mechanized formations.

The loss of Marshal Tukhachevsky, the leading military theoretician, was particularly severely felt. He had been responsible for the issue of the 1936 Field Service Regulations which advocated the use of massed armoured formations supported by the firepower of the artillery. Those who came to power after him did not have the foresight to continue with his innovative measures which would have had a considerable effect during the opening battles in 1941. Before that the Russians had an embarrassing rebuff when they attacked Finland in 1941 in order to seize a buffer zone around Leningrad. Despite overpowering superiority, the Red Army could not break through the Finnish lines, and suffered a number of defeats at the hands of numerically inferior forces who were able to use the terrain, despite the bitter cold, to their advantage. Eventually Soviet superiority in numbers began to tell in their favour and the Finns, having suffered enormous losses and running short of ammunition, could no longer continue their resistance and agreed to an armistice.

The manifest shortcomings of the Red Army in the Finnish War were subjected to close examination. The eminent Russian historian General D. A. Volkogonov states that Stalin decided to replace Marshal Voroshilov after reading his report on the lessons to be learned from the Finnish war. Voroshilov described 'the inadequacies of Red Army intelligence, poor technical supply, cumbersome communications organization, poor winter clothing and food for the troops'. He emphasized that 'Many top commanders were not up to the task. Headquarters had to remove many senior officers and staff chiefs not merely because their leadership was not doing any good, but because it was doing positive harm.'[4] Although Stalin was in overall command, there was a complete reshuffle of the top posts in the military hierarchy. Perhaps one of the most far-reaching results of the war was the poor impression of the capabilities of the Red Army given to other countries. Germany formed a low opinion of Soviet forces with a general staff evaluation which stated: 'In quantity a gigantic military instrument ... Organization, equipment and means of leadership unsatisfactory ... Communication system bad, transportation system bad, no personalities'. The assessment concluded: 'Fighting qualities of the troops in a heavy fight, dubious. The Russian "mass" is no match for an army with modern equipment and superior leadership.'[5] Such reports confirmed Hitler's opinion that he could defeat the Russian forces in one campaigning season. This led to his enormous gamble which he so nearly won. Failure brought about his eventual defeat.

Soviet intelligence monitored the assembly of German forces following Hitler's decision to invade Russia. This was augmented by warnings received from American, Japanese and British sources. For many years the official Soviet line was that the invasion on 22 June 1941 had come as a complete surprise to Stalin and the Soviet high command, who hoped that the Germano-Soviet Non-Aggression Pact of August 1939 would be maintained so as to allow Russia time to re-arm. Documents released during the last few years question this view.

Evidence of Soviet awareness of German preparations is found in a hand-written note sent by Zhukov, then Chief of the General Staff, to Stalin: 'As Germany is now fully mobilized, and with her rear organized, she has the ability to surprise us with a sudden attack. To avert this, I think it essential that we deprive the German command of the initiative by forestalling their forces during deployment, by attacking them at the moment they are at the deployment stage and have not had time to organize a front or co-ordinate their forces.'[6] There is no record of Stalin's reaction.

However, many preparations for war were being implemented in the summer of 1941. Partial mobilization had been set in motion with formations being brought up to their wartime establishments. These preparations were made at the strategic level, but not at a lower level because Stalin was still hoping to avoid provoking the Germans. The four Fronts that would be formed out of the peacetime border military districts had instructions to prevent enemy incursions and basically to buy time for mobilization of the main forces.

In June 1941 the Red Army had 303 divisions, 170 of which were facing the Germans in the border military districts: Leningrad, Baltic, Special

Western, Special Kiev, Odessa and Crimea. Also, 20 of the 29 mechanized corps were in the west. The formation of these new mechanized formations had been set in motion after the success of the German panzer forces in France. The new tanks, the KV and T-34s, were only present in appreciable numbers in eight of the mechanized corps. There were considerable problems with the older tanks, many of which were inoperative because of shortage of spare parts. Numerically the Soviets possessed more tanks than the panzer divisions, but only the new tanks would have any significant effect upon the forthcoming battle.

On 21 June, deserters confirmed that the Germans would attack early the next day, and the Politburo assembled. Zhukov read out an order to put all troops in the border districts on full alert. Volkogonov records that Stalin broke in to say that the situation might still be solved by peaceful means. He was woken later to be told that the invasion had begun.

NOTES

1. Von Mellenthin, Friedrich-Wilhelm, *Panzer Battles*, London, Cassell, p. 350.
2. McCauley, Martin, *The Soviet Union, 1917-1991*, London, Longman, p. 106.
3. Moynahan, Brian, *Claws of the Bear*, Boston, Houghton Mifflin, 1989, p. 73.
4. Volkogonov, p. 365.
5. Moynahan, p. 87.
6. Volkogonov, p. 398.

6
1944 – A YEAR FOR DECISIONS

Although Stalin had told Churchill and Roosevelt at Tehran in November 1943 that the 'Overlord' landings in Normandy would be followed by a 'major assault on the Germans', there is no evidence to suggest that any planning had begun.[1] It is possible that the Stavka had commenced feasibility studies, and that these were discussed at the meeting of the State Committee for Defence with members of the Stavka present which Zhukov attended in December. But no decision was recorded as it was too early to tell how the winter and spring offensives would prosper.[2] The options that the Stavka examined were wide-ranging, but all had their difficulties. Four main options emerged.

The first option was to continue their advance through Roumania into the Balkans. While this was politically highly desirable and would threaten Germany's dwindling fuel supplies, an advance on this axis would leave strong German forces on their flanks. Moreover all six Soviet tank armies were in the south, engaged with the major concentration of the panzer divisions, and needed rest and replenishment.

The second was to launch a major offensive from the northern Ukraine across Poland to the Baltic. But to sustain an advance of this magnitude was adjudged beyond the capabilities of Soviet forces in the area. It too would leave strong German formations on their flanks.

The third was to attack in the north, but this was rejected because of the many natural obstacles that would hamper movement.

The fourth option was to cut off Army Group Centre in the Belorussian 'balcony' or salient which barred the shortest route to Warsaw, and provided airfields from which Moscow could be bombed. It also had great symbolic importance, being the last area of Russia to be occupied by the Germans. Finally it would have the advantage of clearing the forces that would threaten an advance to the Vistula from the Lvov area.[3]

The Stavka weighed up the advantages and disadvantages of each option, particularly bearing in mind that the Western Front had already failed in Belorussia during their winter and spring offensives. As it was considered that the failure was more the result of Soviet organization and conduct of the

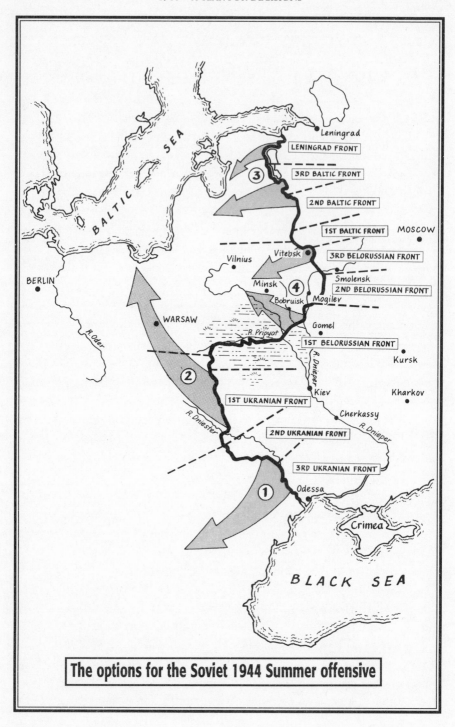

The options for the Soviet 1944 Summer offensive

offensive rather than the strength of the German positions, it was decided by Stalin and the Stavka on 12 April that the destruction of the German forces in Belorussia should have priority. The Stavka now began planning the details of the sequence of operations for the forthcoming summer. The timing and sequence of the offensives were critical so that the enemy would not have time to move reserves into the threatened sectors.

Zhukov was summoned from First Ukrainian Front where he had assumed command after the Front commander had been killed by Ukrainian partisans, to discuss the summer and autumn offensive operations. At this meeting Stalin stated that: 'In June the Allies intend at last to carry out a major landing operation in France. The Germans will have to fight on two fronts. This will increase their difficulties still further and they will not be able to overcome them.' Zhukov was sent away with Antonov to produce a draft plan in much the same way as students at the Staff College are told to: 'Go away and make your plan and come back and show it to me!'

By late April the Stavka had produced the sequence of operations for the summer. In the north an opening diversionary offensive in Karelia and the Lake Ladoga area would begin in early June. When German attention had been drawn northwards, the main offensive would be launched against Army Group Centre in Belorussia later in the month. After German reserves had been drawn in, Soviet forces in western Ukraine would attack towards Lvov and the River Vistula in eastern Poland. After the successful conclusion of these offensives, the Soviet forces would attack in the south, which by then it was hoped would have been denuded of German reserves.

The main offensive in Belorussia was code-named Operation 'Bagration' after the Russian Marshal mortally wounded before Moscow in 1812.

The terrain was crucial in shaping the course of the forthcoming operations. The front of Army Group Centre ran for about 1,000 kilometres from Kovel through Pinsk – west of Mozyr' – Zhlobin – Mogilev – Orsha – Vitebsk to a point fifteen kilometres north-east of Polotsk.

The southern sector of the lines ran through the Pripyat Marshes, home of myriads of wildfowl and mosquitoes, and virtually impassable for armoured vehicles. The ground between the front and Minsk was wooded and swampy and only in some places suitable for tanks. It was good open country in the triangle formed by Zhlobin – Rogachev – Bobruisk. The rivers ran generally north to south: the Dnieper, Drut, Berezina, Svisloch and Ptich were all potential obstacles.

Communications were very important and canalized the Soviet attacks once the initial penetrations had been made. Communications between the cities of eastern Belorussia: Bobruisk, Mogilev, Orsha and Vitebsk, were good but the overwhelming rapidity of the Soviet attack prevented their use for troop movement. The firm ground between Orsha and Vitebsk had played a conspicuous role throughout history – during the Napoleonic Wars and in 'Barbarossa' in 1941. The Soviets had tried with everything at their disposal to break through at this point during the winter of 1943/4.

Minsk was an important nodal point of road and rail communications, with two important corridors along which ran the railway tracks and roads linking up with the lateral links at Molodechno and Baranovichi. There was a further critical lateral link from Vilnius to Brest-Litovsk along which reinforcements could be moved.

The difficult terrain influenced the Soviet decision to use one tank army and a cavalry/mechanized group in the north and to employ another specialist cavalry/mechanized group in the south. The geography virtually dictated the objectives for the phases of the offensive. The first were the four cities along the eastern edge of the German position: Vitebsk, Orsha, Mogilev and Bobruisk. The next obstacle was the River Berezina with its important crossing at Borisov followed by the two corridors leading to Minsk. From then on the restrictions of terrain confined the Soviet forces largely to corridors leading from Minsk to the west.

Security was extremely strict. In the early stages operational details were known only to Stalin and five others: Marshal Zhukov, First Deputy; Marshal Vasilevsky, Chief of the General Staff; General Antonov, his Deputy; General Shtemenko, Chief of the Operations Department and one unnamed staff officer. During May, they produced a plan for the operation: to attack with four Fronts with the aim of encircling and destroying the German forces in the areas of Vitebsk, Orsha, Mogilev and Bobruisk; to liberate Minsk and then develop the offensive westwards. To co-ordinate the immensely complex operations, the Stavka appointed two Special Representatives: in the north, Marshal Vasilevsky was assigned to First Baltic Front and Third Belorussian Front; in the south, Marshal Zhukov was assigned to Second Belorussian Front and First Belorussian Front. Both Representatives closely supervised the development of the plan and its implementation in conjunction with the Front commanders.[4]

The final timetable for the summer offensives was:

Karelia:	10 June – 9 August
Belorussia:	19 June – 29 August
Lvov – Sandomierz:	13 July – 29 August
Lublin – Brest-Litovsk:	18 July – 2 August (technically part of the Belorussian operation, but in reality a link to the Lvov–Sandomierz operation)
Yassy – Kishinev:	20 August – 7 September

The outline plan for the Belorussian offensive was signed by General Antonov on 20 May and after confirmation by Stalin was sent to the Fronts on 31 May. In the north First Baltic Front would launch their attacks against Third Panzer Army around Vitebsk. Two main attacks would take place, one north and north-west of Vitebsk by 6th Guards and 43rd Armies; one south of Vitebsk by 39th and 5th Armies. An additional attack would be launched by 11th Guards Army on the axis Orsha – Borisov. The Armies were to be supported initially by their own armoured formations. Fifth Guards Tank Army and a cavalry/mechanized group were kept in Stavka reserve for use within these two Fronts as the situation demanded.

Second Belorussian Front would deliver a secondary attack by 49th Army against the German Fourth Army in the Mogilev area. The second main strategic thrust would be launched by the right wing of First Belorussian Front with 65th and 28th Armies supported by a cavalry/mechanized group and by 3rd Army attacking the German Ninth Army in the Bobruisk area.

In order to achieve the superiority required to break into the German defences, a considerable reinforcement of the four Fronts was required. In addition, the left wing of First Belorussian Front and First Ukrainian Front both had to be reinforced for their role in the Lvov–Sandomierz offensive which was timed to begin once 'Bagration' was well under way. The offensive necessitated a strategic redeployment of troops involving a move into Belorussia of five combined-arms armies, two tank armies, one air army, First Polish Army, five tank, two mechanized and four cavalry corps – a force of more than 400,000 men with 3,000 tanks and 10,000 guns and mortars. Two armies came from as far away as the Crimea, which had been liberated in early May.

Where possible, the infantry divisions marched on their feet, the limited railway rolling stock being required for moving ammunition and fuel. Some divisions marched 250 kilometres in twelve nights to reach concentration areas 15-20 kilometres behind the front line, moving forward to assembly areas only a short time before H-Hour.

An offensive on this scale required a supreme effort from the Red Army's logistic services, which had to rely upon primitive roads and a rail network only recently recaptured from the Germans after heavy damage. Shtemenko tells of the Stavka concern: 'While we were regrouping and building up the supplies we needed for the offensive, we were constantly worried about the railways. They were badly overburdened and might let us down. The need to complete our rail transport programme on time was the constant concern of the Operations Department of the General Staff. Our misgivings on this score had been reported to Stalin more than once, but the Supreme Commander relied on the People's Commissar for Railways and, as was soon to be seen, clearly overestimated his potentialities.' Zhukov reported on 11 June: 'The movement of trains with ammunition for First Belorussian Front is extremely slow. Only one or two trains a day ... There is reason to believe that the Front will not be fully provided for on time.' Although at Stalin's insistence the railway timetable was revised and trains were speeded up, the operation had to be postponed from the 19th to 23 June.[5]

The amount of ammunition and fuel required for an operation on this scale was prodigious. Stavka had laid down that Fronts should have five first and second basic loads of ammunition, 10 to 20 refills of fuel, and 30 days' rations, but in many cases these targets were not met. One of the greatest difficulties with ammunition was the transportation forward from the railhead to the gun positions where dumps were formed. This caused a problem when the artillery advanced because the ammunition had to be left behind and brought up later. Sergeant M. Fukson, a technical sergeant in an artillery brigade supporting First Baltic Front, tells how this was done: 'For this we got on Lease Lend sixteen Studebakers from America for transporting shells. The Studebakers were powerful vehicles which could travel over marshland and all types of ground. The Soviet roads just couldn't be compared with European ones. There were muddy swamps and so on, but the Front doesn't run along a main road! So the Studebakers helped a lot.'[6]

Great care was taken over medical arrangements. Before the offensive opened dressing-stations and hospitals were cleared as far as possible of wounded. Dressings-stations and field hospitals were formed in the forward administrative echelons, to be moved forward as the troops advanced. Wounded were evacuated to the rear in empty logistics vehicles returning to pick up new loads, and from the leading mobile and cavalry/mechanized groups they were flown out by light aircraft. Those requiring hospital treatment were evacuated by ambulance or by temporary hospital trains. Soviet authorities maintain that prompt evacuation and skilled treatment made it possible to return 50 per cent of the sick and wounded to duty during the offensive.

The logistical system was the responsibility of the Deputy Commander of Rear Services and his staff. In particular they had to work out a flexible scheme to ensure that the fast-moving armoured and cavalry/mechanized groups were kept supplied with fuel, ammunition and food and forage. They had considerable powers and when fuel ran low, they could even order trains to be sent direct to the Caucasus to collect fuel.

The administrative services gained great practical experience in moving forward supplies to rapidly advancing formations during the offensive, an experience which was to stand them in good stead in the subsequent offensives of 1945.

On 6 June, D-Day in Normandy, Stalin wrote to Churchill and Roosevelt: 'The summer offensive of the Soviet troops, to be launched in keeping with the agreement reached at the Tehran Conference, will begin in mid-June in one of the vital sectors of the Front. The general offensive will develop by stages, through consecutive engagement of the armies in offensive operations. Between late June and the end of July the operations will turn into a general offensive of the Soviet troops.'[7]

NOTES

1. Volkogonov, p. 588.
2. Zhukov, p. 489.
3. Shtemenko, p. 296; Glantz,. 1985 Symposium, p. 303.
4. Glantz, David, *Soviet Military Deception in the Second World War*, London, Frank Cass, 1989, p. 365 and Appendix 2.
5. Shtemenko, pp. 3l6, 332.
6. Interview with Mr Fukson at Tel Aviv.
7. Shtemenko, p. 317.

7

MASKIROVKA (DECEPTION)

By this stage in the war, the Red Army had developed *maskirovka* or military deception into a fine art. It can exist at three levels: strategic, operational and tactical. It means much more than the literal translation of the word, which is 'camouflage'. The official Soviet definition of *maskirovka* is: 'The means of securing combat operations and the daily activities of forces; a complexity of measures, directed to mislead the enemy regarding the presence and disposition of forces, various military objectives, their condition, combat readiness and operations, and also the plans of the command ... maskirovka contributes to the achievement of surprise for the actions of forces, the preservation of combat readiness, and the increased survivability of objectives.'[2]

The corollary of successful deception measures is that there must be impeccable security about one's own plans or the deception measures are negated.

During the virtual collapse of the Red Army in the first months following the German invasion of Russia, Soviet military thought was devoted to survival and little attention was given to formulating a concept for *maskirovka*. German tactical intelligence, particularly their radio interception units, were able to reap rich harvests as Soviet units appeared to be unable to grasp the principles of radio security. During the battle for Moscow, however, German strategic intelligence was inadequate because it did not detect the presence of three new armies arriving to take part in the first major Soviet counter-offensive at a time when the Germans were confident that the Soviets had little left in the way of reserves. It is not clear whether this was the result of a definite *maskirovka* plan or whether it was a combination of coincidence and the appalling conditions, but it did have the effect of alerting the Soviet High Command to the advantages of deception.

In the summer of 1942, the Germans successfully deluded the Soviet forces into believing that their summer offensive would be a continuation of their attack upon Moscow. The German plan was characteristically thorough: maps of Moscow were issued down to a low level, planning conferences were held and prisoners of war interrogated about the defences of the city. In an effort to draw troops away from the Moscow axis, the Soviets mounted an offensive in the Kharkov area where the real German operation was being prepared. The Red Army losses were high.

Some of the Stavka's deception operations had proved successful and the principles are mentioned in the systematic studies, known as the Soviet War Experience Studies, which eventually totalled 60 volumes. They were all highly security classified and most are only now becoming available. Instructions were given on how to create false units and how to construct dummy tanks and guns. It was also at this time that a special *maskirovka* staff was created at Front and army headquarters and a reference to *maskirovka* became an integral part of operational plans.

A Soviet commentator wrote in the 1980s: 'The experience of force operations showed that when commanders devoted serious attention to maskirovka, as a rule success accompanied them; and on the other hand, when the enemy succeeded in discovering our plans, then the forces often suffered great losses and did not fulfil their assigned missions.'[2] Although Soviet forces began to use improved methods of *maskirovka* to hide the place and timing of an attack, using darkness and bad weather to achieve surprise, their efforts brought little success, while German air reconnaissance could fly at will.

The Soviet counter-attack at Stalingrad in November 1942 was the first major example of this newly found confidence in conducting *maskirovka* operations on a large scale. The extent to which the Soviets had been able to conceal their preparations is confirmed by the Chief of the German General Staff, General Zeitzler, who stated in early November: 'The Russians no longer have any reserves worth mentioning and are not capable of launching a large-scale attack. In forming any appreciation of enemy intentions, this basic fact must be taken fully into consideration.' Just over two months later Sixth Army surrendered and the German Army suffered its greatest defeat so far in the war.

The Red Army learnt many lessons from Stalingrad, one of which was how to develop a *maskirovka* plan, which included the following headings:

a. The aims of the operation restricted to a very limited number of staff officers.
b. Verbal orders, given out to lower echelons as H-Hour approaches.
c. Concentration of forces at night with strict camouflage on arrival; no movement by day.
d. Exclusion of unauthorized visitors to concentration areas.

e.   Reconnaissance to be carried out only by units already in the forward area.

f.   Radio silence of incoming units, especially tank units.

g.   Movement and engineer preparations only at night.

h.   Probing of enemy positions to determine any weak points.

k.   No artillery registration.

l.   Air strikes against enemy headquarters and administrative areas before D-Day.[4]

All these basic ingredients will be found to be present in the *maskirovka* planning for 'Bagration'.

Maskirovka played a significant role in the successful Soviet Orel–Belgorod counter-offensives after Kursk, and in the Kiev operation where an entire Tank Army was secretly moved into the bridgehead.

Once the Stavka had decided upon the strategic plan for their 1944 summer offensive, they began to consider how the Germans could be deceived about the aims and scale of the offensive. Soviet offensive action during the previous winter and spring had concentrated upon the south of the front, and the key to the *maskirovka* operation was to reinforce the German conviction that operations would continue along this axis. In early May the commander of the Third Ukrainian Front in the south was ordered to carry out a large-scale *maskirovka* operation to misinform the enemy. The assembly of eight or nine rifle divisions with supporting armour and artillery was to be simulated. Anti-aircraft guns were to protect the assembly area with additional air cover provided. These measures were to be checked by staff officers flying daily over the area in light aircraft.[5]

The question immediately arises, how could the Stavka be sure that German attention was directed to the south and remained there. The NKVD was responsible for strategic intelligence and until their wartime files are available for study by historians, we shall remain uncertain about their sources. There has been speculation whether the Russians had the ability to read German military radio traffic (Enigma) at any time during the war. There is no doubt that they had the opportunity to capture a number of Enigma machines, possibly as early as January 1942 after Moscow, but certainly after the surrender of Sixth Army at Stalingrad it has been calculated that more than 20 machines could have been captured. Although it is possible the accompanying encoding material may have been captured at the same time, it is not certain whether the Soviets had the ability to construct the 'bombe' required to decipher the daily settings. This is one of the last surviving secrets of the Second World War.[6]

Much has been written about the existence of Soviet spies or sympathisers within the German command system. The best known being the three operating from Switzerland, the '*Rote Drei*'. There is a suggestion that this was a means adopted by British intelligence to pass on Ultra information without revealing its source, but this has been categorically denied in the British official history of wartime intelligence. There is no doubt, however, that the German radio intercept service listened to more than 400 messages from the '*Rote Drei*', almost half of them coming from an agent code-named 'Lucy', alias Rudolf Roessler, who appears to have been a Swiss double agent as well as working for Soviet intelligence. The German historian Paul Carell alleges that 'Lucy' controlled 'Werther', a very highly placed source, probably at OKW, who was able to supply information for the duration of the war. His identity has remained one of the best kept secrets of the Second World War. One of the most uncanny aspects of his work was that he was able to provide answers to questions posed by Moscow in a relatively short period of time which seems to preclude the theory that it was based on British 'Ultra' information. According to the official history, this appears to have completely dried up after Kursk in 1943, probably because the Russians were not prepared to share the results of their own intelligence, such as the characteristics and performance of captured Luftwaffe aircraft.[7]

Whatever the source of this information, it was vital to the Stavka to know that the Germans were convinced that the main Soviet effort would be in the south. The *maskirovka* plan was designed to keep the German reserves to the south of the Pripyat Marshes until it was too late for them to intervene in Belorussia. It succeeded because it reinforced the appreciation made by Hitler and OKW, as we shall see in the next chapter.

As part of the deception plan the forces facing Army Group Centre were made to appear to have gone over to the defensive. Shtemenko relates: 'The troops were set to work on perfecting their defences. Front, army and divisional newspapers published material only on defence matters. All talks to the troops were about maintaining a firm hold on present positions.'

Simultaneously with the deception manoeuvres, the concentration of the troops began. Those troops lucky enough to travel by train found that they were only able to leave at halts in controlled groups, and while aboard the trains were cordoned off from the public. Railway workers were given the identification number of the train but no details of its final destination. When they arrived in their concentration areas the formations had to be thoroughly camouflaged and this was checked from the air by staff officers. All but the most essential reconnaissance was forbidden and even the officers taking part had to dress as private soldiers. To preserve the fiction that the tank formations were remaining in the south, tank crews were not allowed to wear their distinctive black uniforms.

In the areas where activity was to be simulated, namely the south and, to a more limited extent, in the north, an aggressive attitude was assumed. An attack was launched by 27th Army and 2nd Tank Army across the River Prut near the Roumanian border. This was the one of the first occasions in which the Grossdeutschland Division met the new Josef Stalin heavy tanks, but although the Soviet forces suffered a reverse, in reality it was a success for the *maskirovka* plan because the Germans thought that they had defeated a major Soviet thrust. It is also interesting to note that this reverse, known as the Battle of Targul-Frumos, was regarded by NATO forces in the early 1980s as an ideal example of the handling of armour in the defensive battle.

In other areas the Soviets simulated traffic movement, empty trains moving out by day and returning full by night. This also happened with marching troops. Major V. Vilensky was a battalion commander in an infantry division used in the deception plan: 'The troops would be moved out during the night, and then to give the impression that ten divisions had built up, our division would actually have moved backwards and forwards for ten nights. We'd move out at night, come back in the morning, sleep the whole day, and then repeat it all over again.' Many other ruses were employed: the Russians became masters of improvising dummy equipment. If there were not enough inflatable rubber tanks, they made them of wood and even turf. These dummy concentrations were protected by anti-aircraft guns, and air cover was provided to enhance the deception.

The basic *maskirovka* plan was issued by the Stavka on 29 May and passed to the Fronts next day. As the date of the offensive drew near, activity increased. Perhaps the most critical moves were those of the two tank armies from the south to concentration areas behind the attacking Fronts. Shtemenko records that 5th Guards Tank Army faced difficulties of a different kind. It was discovered that Second Ukrainian Front, to which it had previously been attached, intended appropriating some of its tanks and regiments of self-propelled artillery before its departure. This did not fit in with the

General Staff's plans, and Second Ukrainian were told sharply that the two corps of 5th Guards were to be sent off at full strength in men and *matériel*, the two corps to have not less than 300 tanks in total.

The final deception measure consisted of reconnaissance in force along the front so that the actual area of attack could not be isolated. However as June passed it was obvious that a major offensive was imminent. Stavka hoped that although the Germans were aware of the intense activity behind the Soviet lines, they would still be unaware of the objectives and the scale of the offensive.

Notes

1. This chapter was based on the work of Colonel David Glantz, US Army (Retd.). His book on Soviet Military Deception is the basic source on the subject. I am extremely grateful to him for permission to quote extracts.
2. Glantz, p. 103.
3. Glantz, p. 117.
4. Glantz, p. 130.
5. Glantz, p. 355.
6. Carell, Paul, *Scorched Earth*, London, George G. Harrap, 1970, pp. 95ff.
7. Glantz, David, *Soviet Military Intelligence in War*, London, Frank Cass, 1990, p. 88, quoting Mulligan.

8
THE GERMAN VIEW

After nearly three years of war on the Eastern Front which had seen near victory pass to almost stalemate, the German Army was still extremely powerful. There were four Army Groups: North, Centre, North Ukraine and South Ukraine. At the beginning of May, Army Group Centre had 38 divisions, of which one was Hungarian, with three panzer or panzer grenadier divisions and two infantry divisions in reserve, and three Hungarian and five security divisions in the rear areas. It held a front of 488 miles. Army Group North Ukraine held a front of 219 miles but had a strength of 35 German and ten Hungarian divisions, including eight panzer divisions. Army Groups North Ukraine and South Ukraine together had eighteen panzer or panzer grenadier divisions, as opposed to Army Group Centre's meagre three.

Army Group Centre was commanded by Field Marshal Ernst Busch, who had served as an infantry officer in the First World War and had taken part in some of the most hard-fought battles on the Western Front. He had been awarded the *Pour le Merite*, an unusual distinction for a relatively junior officer (Lieutenant Rommel received the same award). Those who knew him thought that he had his merits as a leader of men, but that he owed his promotion to his strong affinity with the Nazi Party. Colonel Peter von der Groeben, at that time his senior general staff officer or '1a', said: 'I was present at some of the discussions in which he attempted to dissuade Hitler from a particular course of action. If he failed, he considered himself committed to carrying out the decision. He often said to me: "Groeben, I am a soldier. I have learnt to obey." Then against his better judgement, he would carry out the order.' Army Group Centre had four armies to defend its long front. In the north, Third Panzer Army, commanded by Colonel-General Hans Reinhardt, had three corps with nine infantry divisions in forward positions and two in reserve, but, despite its name, no panzer divisions. Its armour consisted of 86 self-propelled guns. Four of its divisions garrisoned the Vitebsk area designated by Hitler as a '*Fester Platz*'. This was intended to be the cornerstone of the army group's defensive position.

Southwards the next army was Fourth Army whose three corps of nine divisions were commanded by Colonel-General Gotthard Heinrichi, one of the most skilful of all German generals and a master of the defensive battle. He was on leave in Germany and his deputy, the very able General of Infantry Kurt Tippelskirch, a distinguished historian who later wrote a very comprehensive history of the war, had taken over.

Ninth Army with ten divisions held the angle around Bobruisk under the command of General of Infantry Hans Jordan, perhaps the most exposed of the four forward '*Feste Plätze*'. The southern flank of Army Group Centre was held by Second Army commanded by Colonel-General Walter Weiss, but it played little part in this phase as it did not lie in the path of the Soviet offensive which, though there was still little firm intelligence, every one felt was overdue to support the Anglo-American landings in Normandy which had taken place on 6 June.

In the spring of 1942, the highly capable Colonel Reinhard Gehlen had been appointed Chief of the intelligence branch of OKH dealing with the Eastern Front – *Fremde Heeres Ost* (FHO). He remained in the appointment with the rank of major-general for the remainder of the war. After the war, with the help of microfilms of his wartime files and documents, he set up the Gehlen Organization in conjunction with the Americans to continue to gather information about the Eastern Bloc. In 1956, the organization was transferred to the Federal Republic of Germany and became the *Bundesnachrichtendienst* (Federal Intelligence Service) with Gehlen as its first chief.

At the time of 'Bagration' Gehlen was producing regular intelligence summaries. As early as November 1943 he predicted that: 'The main effort of the enemy overall operations at the time is undoubtedly directed against the southern half of the Eastern Front. The mass of the operational armoured units is assembled against Army Group South and here obviously a decisive assault is sought, primarily directed toward the Balkans and to the southern part of the 'General Government', or occupied Poland'. Some six months and several Soviet offensives later, this remained the view of OKH. In May FHO forecast two possible offensives, one from the area of Army Group North Ukraine to Warsaw and on to the Baltic, or in the south towards the Balkans. The second option was thought to be the most likely as the Soviets were not considered to have the ability to sustain an advance to the Baltic. FHO thought that the area to the north of the Pripyat Marshes would remain quiet, so the bulk of the German reserves were kept in the south.[1]

Unfortunately for the Germans, their intelligence gathering was now restricted by the unfavourable military situation. The now considerable Soviet air superiority placed considerable limits on aerial reconnaissance. The stable situation on the ground restricted ground reconnaissance and very little signal intelligence was available because the Soviets had imposed strict radio silence. Therefore it was very difficult to observe the Soviet concentrations for the offensive. The FHO estimate coincided with OKH's views although there was concern about a build-up in the area facing Army Group North Ukraine. On 12 May FHO revised its estimate, stating that although the main offensive would be in the south, a subsidiary offensive would take place in the Army Group North Ukraine area directed towards Brest and Lublin.

This was not unwelcome news to OKH because they could bring powerful reserves to bear in this area. LVI Corps was taken away from Army Group Centre to create a reserve to strike a pre-emptive blow. The Army Group lost heavily as a result, for although it gave up 6 per cent of its front, it lost 15 per cent of its divisions, 88 per cent of its tanks, 23 per cent of its SP guns, 50 of its anti-tank guns and 33 per cent of its heavy artillery. A devastating blow as the date of the offensive approached.[2]

The intelligence picture was also beginning to change. As May passed, there were indications that some of the Soviet armour was moving northwards. Although General P. A. Rotmistrov, commander of 5th Guards Tank Army, was spotted in the Smolensk area by a Russian prisoner of war, no tanks were seen and therefore it was not deduced that his army had moved into the area facing Army Group Centre. There were strong indications that rifle divisions and artillery were concentrating opposite the army group's area, and heavy rail traffic was observed. Other indicators confirmed this, particularly the results of interrogation of prisoners of war and defectors.[3]

This produced a certain disquiet among some officers at OKH. Colonel J. A. Graf von Kielmansegg, '1a' or senior general staff officer in the Operations Branch at OKH, records that the head, Lieutenant-General Adolf Heusinger, who after the war became a senior NATO general, shared his increasing doubts about the accuracy of the FHO forecast that the offensive would be directed towards the Balkans. At this stage they considered that it would be Army Group North Ukraine which would bear the main brunt of the Soviet offensive.

During late May and early June, the picture changed as the four armies of Army Group Centre detected Soviet reinforcements opposite them. As a result the pre-emptive strike by Army Group North Ukraine was cancelled, but the divisions of LVI Corps were not restored to Army Group Centre.

However 20th Panzer Division was re-allocated to the army group as late as 16 June to be its only panzer reserve.

Third Panzer Army had detected a major effort south of Vitebsk, but was not impressed by a similar attack on the north of the city. Fourth Army forecast an attack along the '*Rollbahn*' (main highway between Smolensk and Minsk) and another east of Mogilev based mostly on the deployment of artillery units. Ninth Army recognized as early as 30 May that there would be two major thrusts designed to envelop Bobruisk. Second Army along the Pripyat Marshes reported that all was quiet and that the preparations for the offensive were complete. Therefore Army Group Centre had identified all the major thrust lines except that north of Vitebsk. The armies of Army Group Centre were now convinced that the full weight of the Soviet offensive would fall upon them. In their final summary, which was very detailed, Army Group Centre suggested that the OKH appreciation was no longer valid. However their summary ends: 'But the OKH has informed us that there is no reason to suppose this.'

The last Army Group Centre Intelligence Summary was dated 19 June and stated categorically: 'The enemy attacks to be expected on Army Group Centre's sector – on Bobruisk, Mogilev, Orsha and possibly south-west of Vitebsk – will be of more than local character. All in all the scale of ground and air forces suggests that the aim is to bring about the collapse of Army Group Centre's salient by penetrations on several sectors. On the other side the Red Army order of battle, so far as it is known or can be estimated, is not yet indicative of a deep objective like Minsk.'[4]

The extent of the success of the Soviet *maskirovka* operation can be summarized by saying that the German side were aware of the forthcoming offensive, but as they had not determined the whereabouts of the Soviet reserves, they could not assess the weight of the blow that was about to fall upon them.

The army group realized at an early stage that its resources were insufficient for it to defend its present front and investigated possibilities of improving the situation. There seemed to be two options: a withdrawal to shorten the defensive position and create reserves, or, once penetration had taken place, mobile defence, at which the German Army had proved itself to be such a master, moving back to prepared positions to prevent being surrounded and defeated. Hitler rejected both these options out of hand on 20 May when he told Field Marshal Busch that he never thought that he was another of those generals who spent their whole time looking over their shoulders. As a result, on 24 May Busch exhorted his troops to improve their present positions to the best of their ability.[5]

Major Heinz-Georg Lemm was the commander of 1st Battalion, Fusilier Regiment 27 of 12th Division and had served in the same division throughout the war on the Eastern Front. He later served as a lieutenant-general in the Bundeswehr. His battalion was sited on the River Pronja east of Mogilev, and was part of Fourth Army's XXXIX Corps. He gave his impression of the days before the offensive: 'The position was semi-circular but with an open right flank. It was an area of water meadows which we were able to cover with machine-gun fire by day and with standing patrols by night. The main position was on a small hill running down to the river with trenches dug on the reverse slope. I practised my soldiers in the procedure to be followed when the Russians began to fire: the forward positions would be held with observation posts and the remainder would withdraw to the reverse slope position.

'Roughly ten days before the Soviet attack, we observed activity on the Russian side. In the forests, wood was being cut to make access tracks for tanks. Occasionally we heard guns registering from previously unknown positions. Also Russian patrols were trying to reconnoitre fords and possible bridging sites over the river. We were also able to establish that there was a distinct increase in the level of Russian telephone traffic. When we reported this, we were told at both Corps and Division that this was merely decoy action and that the main Soviet attack was expected in the south.'[6]

It is appropriate at this point to mention another of Hitler's obsessions which contributed so much to the impending disaster; that is his practice of designating a city or town as a 'Fester Platz'. His Order dated 8 March 1944 established the concept, which was that they would 'fulfil the function of fortresses in former historical times. They will ensure that the enemy does not occupy these areas of decisive operational importance. They will allow themselves to be surrounded, thereby holding down the largest possible number of enemy forces, and establishing conditions favourable for successful counter-attacks.'[7]

Graf von Kielmansegg explains the background to this decision: 'As a concept, the Fester Platz was an invention of Hitler. It had been in his mind for some time and arose from his personal philosophy. We must not forget that Hitler had very vivid memories of the First World War – trench warfare –

and at that time every inch of ground really counted, to put it bluntly. This stuck in his mind, and his idea was to hold the German front by this policy until the end of the war.'

In Army Group Centre's sector, Vitebsk, Orsha, Mogilev, and Bobruisk were designated as '*Feste Plätze*' in the forward area, as well as Slutsk, Minsk, Baranovichi and Vilnius in the rear. These centres were established with the intention of breaking the momentum of the Soviet attack, tying down their forces and blocking their supply routes. The idea might have worked had the Soviets been less mobile and had there been sufficient German forces available to make an effective resistance, or to relieve them after they had been surrounded. As a result of this policy, about six divisions were encircled and captured in the '*Feste Plätze*' near the front. Most of those in the rear were evacuated in sufficient time, often in direct contradiction to orders, but even so, many installations containing badly needed stores and equipment fell into Soviet hands.

Along the German front line the troops worked on their positions and awaited the forthcoming offensive with considerable apprehension. Perhaps the situation can best be described in the words written by General Jordan, commander of Ninth Army, on 22 June: 'Ninth Army stands on the eve of another great battle, unpredictable in extent and duration. One thing is certain: in the last few weeks the enemy has completed an assembly on the very greatest scale opposite the Army, and the Army is convinced that that assembly overshadows the concentration of forces off [*sic*] the north flank of Army Group North Ukraine ... The Army has felt bound to point out repeatedly that it considers the massing of strength on its front to constitute the preparation for this year's main Soviet offensive, which will have as its object the conquest of Belorussia.

'The Army believes that, even under the present conditions, it would be possible to stop the enemy offensive, but not under the present directives which require an absolutely rigid defence ... there can be no doubt ... if a Soviet offensive breaks out the Army will either have to go over to a mobile defence or see its front smashed ...

'The Army considers the orders establishing "*Feste Plätze*" particularly dangerous.

'The Army therefore looks ahead to the coming battle with bitterness, knowing that it is bound by orders to tactical measures which it cannot in good conscience accept as correct and which in our own earlier victorious campaigns were the causes of the enemy defeats – one recalls the great break-through and encirclement battles in Poland and France. 'The Commanding General and Chief of Staff presented these thoughts to the Army Group in numerous conferences, but there, apparently, the courage was lacking to carry them higher up, for no counter arguments other than references to OKH orders were given. And that is the fundamental source of the anxiety with which the Army views the future.'[8]

NOTES

1. van Nes, Colonel Harald, *1985 Art of War Symposium*, p. 57. 2. Ziemke, pp. 313-14
3. Van Nes, *Symposium* , p. 262.
4. Niepold, Lieutenant-General Gerd, *Battle for White Russia: The Destruction of Army Group Centre June 1944*, London, Brassey, 1987, p. 23.
5. *Ibid.*, p. 14.
6. Interview with Leutnant-General Lemm.
7. Trevor-Roper, H. R., p. 233. Reproduced as Appendix VII.
8. Ziemke, *op. cit.*, p. 316, quoting General der Infanterie Hans Jordan.

9
THE PARTISANS

The Red Army had one great asset that was largely denied to the German side – the partisan movement. Their wide-ranging use was incorporated into the planning for the Belorussian offensive at a very early stage. The background for this popular uprising goes back to the ideological miscalculation made by Hitler in the early days of his invasion of Russia. Instead of harnessing the cauldron of national hatred bubbling below the surface of the apparently monolithic structure of the Soviet Union, he unleashed his terror squads who rapidly extinguished the warm welcome extended to the forces originally seen as liberators from the Soviet yoke.

The problem of nationalism in the Russian state had existed long before the Revolution of October 1917 and is still very much in evidence today. Its origins go far back into Russian history when most of the country was overrun by the Tartars, except an area in the north-west which developed its own customs and language. This became known as Belorussia and retained strong Polish and Lithuanian influences in its language which remained quite separate from Russian, although the area was re-absorbed into the Russian state during the dismemberment of Poland in the 18th century. The Ukraine had a similar separate development with its own language and in the Uniate Church its own version of the Russian Orthodox religion.

The 1917 Revolution brought the issue of nationalism to prominence. While at first the Baltic republics, Lithuania, Latvia, and Estonia, were allowed to become independent, as initially were Belorussia and the Ukraine, after some years of troubled independence, both the latter were re-absorbed into the Union of Soviet Socialist Republics. There was no lessening of nationalist fervour which was made more intense by the Soviet programme for the collectivization of agriculture, rigidly enforced to the detriment of the peasants. Thus when the German troops arrived in June 1941 they were regarded in many areas as liberators who would help them throw off the yoke of Soviet imperialism. There are many reports of the welcome extended in the early days to the German 'liberators' in the hope that they would assist the peasants to repossess their land. An officer of 7th Panzer Division recorded: 'I found time and opportunity to make contact with local people, in the course of which my knowledge of Russian came in useful. I was astonished to detect no hatred among them. Women often came out of their houses with an icon held before their breast, crying, "We are still Christians. Free us from Stalin who destroyed our churches." Many of them offered an egg and a piece of dry bread as a "welcome". We gradually had the feeling that we really were being regarded as liberators.'[1]

To show that this was not just a flash in the pan, one can quote the legendary General von Mellenthin who was in the Ukraine as '1a' of 11th Panzer Division: 'During the spring of 1943 I saw with my own eyes the German soldiers were welcomed as friends by Ukrainians and White Russians [Belorussians]. Churches were reopened. The peasants who had been downgraded to *kolkhoz* workers were hoping to get their farms back. The population was relieved to have got rid of the Secret Police and to be free of the constant fear of being sent to forced-labour camps in Siberia ... There were thousands of Ukrainians and White Russians (Belorussians) who, even after the numerous and disastrous setbacks the German armies suffered during the winter of 1942/3, took up arms to free Russia from the yoke of Communism.'

This was confirmed to me by a former Soviet officer who fought in the same regiment and then division for the duration of the war, eventually rising to be Chief of Staff of the division. He defected to the West after the war, giving as his reason the poverty, and the brutality against his own people during the collectivization of the peasants' farms. The benefits of utilizing the anti-Soviet fervour were completely negated by the racist policies followed by Hitler and his henchmen. Their view of the role of the various nationalities of eastern Europe was uncompromisingly simple with no scope for moderation. Hitler's New Order foresaw the total overthrow of the Soviet state, accompanied by the exploitation of its labour and natural resources. Hitler and those of his associates who shared his interest in the development of Nazi policy did not differentiate between the various nations of the east, regarding them all as 'Slavs'. The only exception was Alfred Rosenberg, the Reichsminister for the Occupied Eastern Territories, who wanted to recruit the population of the Ukraine and Belorussia as allies in the fight against the Soviet Union. In this he was supported by a small coterie of like-minded individuals in the foreign ministry and armed forces. However they were powerless against the overwhelming influence of such men as Himmler and Bormann, both of whom had intentions of extending their own influence in the east. Therefore no effort was made to woo the Ukrainians and Belorussians and a golden opportunity was lost.

OKW prepared special orders for the troops in dealing with the threat of opposition from the civilian population. The first three sections of the order set the framework:

'1. Until further notice the military courts and the courts-martial will not be competent for crimes committed by enemy civilians.

2. Guerrillas will be relentlessly liquidated by the troops, while fighting or escaping.

3. Likewise all other attacks by enemy civilians on the armed forces, its members and employers, are to be suppressed at once by the military, using the most extreme methods, until the assailants are destroyed.

4. Where such measures have been neglected or were not at first possible, persons suspected of criminal action will be brought at once before an officer. This officer will decide whether they are to be shot.'[2]

Orders such as these were responsible for the draconian measures which were adopted against the civilian population and in their turn encouraged the formation of partisan units. The first irregular bands were formed from soldiers of the Red Army left behind when the Germans advanced deep into Russian territory. As large areas were not occupied by German forces, these bands were given time and space to develop their strength and organization.

On 3 July, Stalin made his emotional broadcast to the Soviet people and among other measures called for the formation of partisan bands to fight for 'Mother Russia'. The concept of partisan warfare stretched back far into Russian history. It came into its own during the Civil War of 1917-21 when partisans were used by both the Reds and Whites with incredible savagery on both sides. The efforts of the Whites were reduced by the savagery of the Bolsheviks in their own rear areas. The Red partisans are lauded by recent Soviet military commentators: 'The selfless heroic struggle of the workers, under the leadership of the Communist Party in the rear areas of the interventionists and White Guardists, played an important part in the successful outcome of the Civil War.'[3] Although there was some military study of the principles of partisan warfare during the inter-war years, this came to a halt after the purges of the higher military command. Stalin held the view that war should be conducted on enemy territory, therefore planning for partisan activity was irrelevant. In addition the areas most threatened were those where there was the greatest danger of nationalist feeling taking root, as it would be folly to arm potential opponents of the Soviet leadership. Within a month of the German invasion detailed instructions were given for partisan detachments to be formed to sabotage bridges, roads and railway lines and blow up German supply dumps. A regional organization was to be established in areas already overrun and preparations were to be set in hand where a German advance was threatened. Eventually a special department in the Central Committee was set up to deal with partisan affairs, with special cells at Front and army level.

The formation of the first partisan detachments was haphazard, often depending upon the Red Army soldiers left behind by the German panzer thrusts or survivors of the large encirclements of the first months of the war. Frequently short of equipment, particularly radios to communicate with Red Army units, as well as weapons and even rations, they were able to make their presence felt to the extent that the problem was mentioned in OKH communiqués, which stated that there had been some derailment of trains and ambushes on road traffic. In Belorussia the inhabitants of the small towns and villages were still hopeful that the German invaders might still act as liberators, and were not yet prepared to throw in their lot with the partisans.

The Soviet success in defeating the German attempt to take Moscow and the subsequent stabilization of the lines of the opposing armies led to conditions which allowed the partisans to put their detachments on a better footing. The German attitude to the hitherto friendly population was beginning to show itself in its true colours and this produced increasing support for the partisans. The barbaric treatment of Soviet prisoners and the increasing activities of the SS *Einsatzgruppen* in exterminating Jews and Commissars all had an effect on the civilian attitude towards resisting the German invaders. In February 1942, Field Marshal Günther von Kluge, the commander of Army Group Centre, gave the Chief of the General Staff, General Halder, his views on the situation: 'The steady increase in the numbers of enemy troops behind our front and the concomitant growth of the partisan movement in the entire rear area are taking such a threatening turn that I am impelled to point out this danger in all seriousness. While formerly the partisans limited themselves to disruption of communications and attacks on individual vehicles and small installations, now under the leadership of resolute Soviet officers with plenty of weapons and good organization, they are attempting to bring certain districts under their control and to use those districts as bases from which to launch combat operations of a large scale. With this the initiative has passed into the hands of the enemy in many places where he already controls large areas and denies these areas to the German administration and German economic exploitation.'[4]

The Soviets set up training schools for partisans as soon as the initial shock of the invasion had subsided. These were designed to train Party members and Young Communists (Komsomol) in how to organize partisan activity; a second course trained partisan leaders and a third, one of the most vital components, radio operators. Gradually these courses produced large numbers of trained personnel ready to go into the field to organize partisan detachments to replace the groups that had been formed by chance. At first the groups had difficulty in reaching the minimum viable strength which was fifty men, but by the spring of 1942 in some areas where the front line had broken down detachments numbering thousands were formed into regiments and brigades. Through gaps between the German positions, convoys of food, weapons and ammunition supplied the detachments which increasingly became more conventionally military in their outlook. It was this re-alignment away from the Party that resulted in the partisans being removed from NKVD responsibility and placed firmly under the various levels of military command. Marshal Voroshilov was appointed commander-in-chief and the movement now ranked as a separate service of the armed forces.

The partisans fared best where there was good cover and poor communications, and in these areas they controlled wide tracts of countryside. The forests and swamps of Belorussia were particularly suitable for partisan activity. Large areas behind the German lines lived under a form of Soviet rule with the re-establishment of collective farms and even a rudimentary mail service to the remainder of Russia. Senior German officers were concerned at this rise in partisan activity and realized that repression would never produce a satisfactory answer. In areas where German discipline was strict and good relations were maintained with the local population, encouraged by the abolition of collective farms, partisan activity did not flourish. As soon as the front line troops moved on to be replaced by the military government, which imposed harsh conditions, co-operation broke down and the local inhabitants welcomed the arrival of the partisans.

In vain, German senior commanders tried to convince senior officials in the Ministry for Occupied Eastern Territories that they were missing golden opportunities to influence the native population in favour of their liberators. Giving them back their land and allowing the restoration of their religion would turn them permanently against their former Soviet masters. But

Hitler would accept no compromise and would not even agree to the formation of local police or militia units. Gradually the more intelligent among the officials began to realize the extent of the opportunity they were missing. Even Goebbels noted in his diary: 'Basically, I believe we must change our policies essentially as regards the people in the east. We could reduce the danger from partisans considerably if we succeeded in winning some of these peoples' confidence.'

German measures to counter the growing partisan threat were at first 'passive' to protect their ever-lengthening and vulnerable lines of communication. With the successful end of the war thought to be in sight, regular panzer and infantry divisions would be available to subdue the partisan dominated areas. Lightly armed security divisions (*Sicherungsdivisionen*) were formed to safeguard the roads and rail links upon which the German forward troops depended for their supplies. Some of these divisions were to play an important role in the fighting in Belorussia in the summer of 1944.

More active measures against partisan detachments on their own ground proved unsuccessful – they just melted into the countryside. This provided the impetus for the set-piece large-scale anti-partisan operation involving divisions extracted from the front line for the purpose. In Belorussia, the triangle bounded by Nevel in the north, Orsha and Minsk held the greatest concentration of partisan forces: at one time part of this area rejoiced in the name of the Usachi Partisan Republic. Several vital road and rail links passed through the area, and these were under constant attack by partisan detachments. An initial attempt was made by 12th Panzer Division to clear the area late in 1942 but this had no notable success. Another, even larger operation, 'Cottbus', was mounted in June 1943, but despite its scale, few confirmed partisans were killed, though civilian losses were high. Similar operations were mounted during the remainder of 1943 and in early 1944 with varying degrees of success.

Throughout the period the partisans continued their attacks on the communications systems, concentrating on mining and ambushing troop and supply trains. Increasingly sophisticated demolition charges were placed on joints in the rails and on bridges and tunnels and sections of the line such as cuttings or embankments where it was difficult to make repairs. Frequently the demolitions were accompanied by ambushes with anti-tank weapons and machine-guns. German railway repair teams were also harassed while trying to repair the permanent way, and their casualties were high.

The German forces instituted measures to try to mitigate the effect of these attacks. Ground was cleared for considerable distances on either side of the tracks, and inter-connecting blockhouses were constructed as bases for patrols. Guard positions ringed all important railway installations, particularly water towers which were vital for the steam locomotives.

On the trains defensive measures were taken in accordance with the importance of the load carried. The basic defence was a detachment of infantry with a machine-gun mounted to give a good all-round field of fire. In the early days individual obsolete tanks were used in this role. Trains were preceded by ballast trucks to detonate any explosive charges, and there even some armoured trains to patrol stretches of line passing through centres of partisan activity. Train commanders instructed troops being carried in specific drills to ensure a quick reaction if the train were attacked. The effect on the railway system was considerable although the partisans were only able to bring traffic to a complete halt on very few occasions and then only for a relatively short period of time.

Attacks on road traffic were much more limited because the railways were used to carry the bulk of reinforcements and supplies for the simple reason that the road system was rudimentary in the extreme. Apart from the highway from Moscow to Minsk, there were very few made up roads and these could be repaired with comparatively little effort. Bridges were the weak spot and they were always well guarded against sabotage. German vehicles had to travel in convoy with strong escorts who searched carefully for mines and for signs of partisan ambushes. Cutting telephone wires was a nuisance activity which sometimes offered the possibility of ambushing the line parties sent out to repair the breaks. One of the most valuable functions of the partisans, although not as dramatic as more direct intervention, was the gathering of information about German dispositions. This was relayed to the appropriate staffs who passed it back for collation to help form the overall picture of German dispositions. This was particularly valuable to intelligence officers trying to evaluate the extent to which the Germans had been deceived by *maskirovka*.

Very rarely did the partisan forces engage in open battle with the Germans, and if they did they usually came off worse. However this did not apply when German formations and units had lost their cohesion. We shall see that the units of Army Group Centre suffered greatly at the hands of the partisans as they withdrew across Belorussia. There were instances quoted where partisan detachments seized bridges and important road junctions and held them until regular Soviet forces arrived, but these were very much the exception.

By the summer of 1944, the partisan movement had reached its peak of development and efficiency. Post-war accounts state that in Belorussia there were 374,000 partisans divided among 199 brigades and that they had in addition some 400,000 reserves to call upon. They were controlled by the Central Committee of the Communist Party of Belorussia in conjunction with the military staffs of the Fronts responsible for meeting their administrative requirements. The areas controlled by the partisans were now large enough to have landing strips able to take even aircraft the size of Dakotas (C-47s), which could bring in substantial payloads of ammunition and supplies. Most brigades had regular Red Army officers in command assisted in key areas by personnel trained on Soviet courses and these had a beneficial effect on training and discipline. Although the disruption of German communications increased, partisans failed to divert front line German formations except on the rare occasions when a major anti-partisan operation was planned.

Army Group Centre decided to mount three such operations during the spring and early summer of 1944 against the particularly strong formations that had grown up right across its area but were strongest behind the sectors held by Third Panzer and Fourth Armies. The aim of the two inter-related operations, 'Regenschauer' and 'Frühlingsfest', was to destroy the area of the Usachi Partisan Republic to the west of Polotsk, Vitebsk and Orsha. The partisans were holding strong positions behind minefields and even had substantial air support, but this was of to no avail against steady German pressure. Some brigades collapsed after the first attack and their members vanished into the trees and swamps. Others fought valiantly and were only overcome with great difficulty. By mid-May the Usachi network of detachments had been smashed.

In mid-May the final anti-partisan operation of the war, 'Kormoran', began against various detachments in the large area bounded by Lepel, Senno, Borisov, Minsk, and Molodechno. It was almost as if there were a premonition of what was about to happen. The partisan defence was unco-ordinated and they were forced into an ever-smaller pocket which the Germans attacked repeatedly. Before final success was achieved, however, 'Kormoran' had to be shut down as the Soviet offensive opened all along the front of Army Group Centre.

The Soviet High Command included attacks made by the partisans in the German rear areas as an integral part of the plan for 'Bagration'. On 8 June, the Belorussian Communist Party issued instructions to all its partisan detachments for Operation 'Rail War' to commence on 19 June, three days before the main offensive. An all-out attack was to be launched against German rail communications with the particular aim of impeding the bringing forward of reinforcements. Soviet accounts make much of the success achieved in this operation, and mention is made of 40,000 demolitions, but this is probably an exaggeration. However, it is an indisputable fact that both 5th and 12th Panzer Divisions were able to be brought up to the front line without undue delay less than a week later. An explanation of this may be that the highly efficient repair teams concentrated on the most important lines to the front. A Soviet account confirms this: 'Owing to continuous attacks of partisans, a line which was of vital importance for the German Third Panzer Army was completely put out of operation for a distance of 53 kilometres by June 27. The German Command took urgent and resolute measures to restore it and summoned several specialized units. But the partisans foiled the enemy's attempts to restore the railway.' The same Soviet account quotes an apparent German source: 'Twenty-four hours before the Russian offensive was launched the partisans conducted an action of tremendous scope on the night of June 19. There were 10,500 instances of damage to the tracks ... The outcome was that the traffic was "nearly" [Author's emphasis] completely paralysed for more than 24 hours, on the supply lines above all. The material losses were so great that it was necessary to dismantle without delay the second line to produce enough rails for at least a single track.'[5] An authoritative account written after the war by Major-General Otto Heidkämper, Chief of Staff, Third Panzer Army, stated that as a consequence of the anti-partisan operations carried out earlier in the summer, partisan activity was negligible in the area of Third Panzer Army.[6]

The other aspect of partisan operations during 'Bagration' was their tactical co-operation with regular Red Army units during the offensive. The German accounts give the impression that this was most effective when the Germans were withdrawing to escape encirclement. There are no German accounts of partisans holding positions or seizing bridgeheads over rivers but this undoubtedly happened.

An article written in 1984 gives a very detailed account of partisan operations in the area of 65th Army on the right wing of First Belorussian

Front. They were given tasks for the immediate future, namely the capture of specific crossings over rivers, the prevention of the arrival of reserves and to assist the advance of Red Army units. To quote two examples: 'The partisan detachments of the Minsk and Pripyat formations destroyed several enemy rear and security sub-units and on 27 June, having seized crossings over the River Ptich to the south of Glusk, held them until the arrival of the forward sub-units of 15th Rifle Division.' Another four brigades of the Minsk formation captured a crossing and bridge over the River Ptich near Berezovka, and in another area assembled and concentrated 40 boats which were used for the crossing of the forward detachments of 48th Guards Rifle Division. ... The commanders of the partisan brigades sent out guides to meet the forward sub-units of the armies and they led the units to the crossing seized by the partisans.'

To summarize: the partisans of Belorussia co-operated closely with the advancing units of the Red Army. They disrupted the work of the enemy rear areas, supplied information to the staffs at all levels, and helped the regular units by seizing crossings and bridges, rebuilding roads and providing guides through difficult terrain. The Soviet view was that they played a significant role in assisting the Red Army to achieve its objective of liberating Belorussia.[7]

Once that objective had been achieved the partisan movement had outlived its usefulness and was disbanded, often to the dismay of individual partisans. German agents reported that instead of the gratitude the partisans expected, they were given a short leave and then co-opted into regular units. Dedicated partisans who had suffered much at the hands of the Germans were fortunate if they were not forced into punishment battalions. Those who survived the political interrogations lived to enjoy the considerable publicity given to the achievements of the partisan movement both during and after the war.

As a postscript to this chapter it is interesting to look briefly at the fortunes of the partisans who wished to break free from the shackles of Soviet Communism. Given the complexity of the nationalist issue, it is hardly surprising that partisan bands were set up by Ukrainian and Belorussian Nationalist Movements. However they were uncertain allies for the Germans because they were so virulently anti-Russian that they made no distinction between those on the Soviet side and those working for the Germans. As there were increasing numbers of 'Hilfwilliger' or 'Hiwis' (auxiliaries who were serving the Germans in a non-combatant role), this attitude became rather a liability.

One of the most notorious of these bands was that formed by Bronislav Kaminski which eventually reached a strength of 9,000 men who fought under the tsarist emblem, the Cross of St George. Almost impossible to control, it was given its own semi-autonomous area in the Bryansk forest. As the German Army withdrew to the west, the Kaminski Brigade followed, accompanied by more than 20,000 camp-followers. It was described as 'Undisciplined and haphazardly armed and uniformed, the brigade resembled a 16th or 17th-century band of mercenaries rather than a modern military unit.' It was employed to horrifying effect in the suppression of the Warsaw Rising. Kaminski became so flagrantly disobedient of his orders that the Germans had him shot.[8]

Anti-Soviet partisan groups developed in both the Ukraine and Belorussia, but on occasions they also fought against the Germans as well, once they had realized that they were to be denied a separate and independent state of Ukraine. It is very difficult to establish details of their achievements because the Soviet Union adopted a policy of largely ignoring this aspect of the war. Moreover anti-Soviet partisan warfare continued into the Cold War period, and the story remains murky. Two short accounts give some indication of the extent of the wartime activities of these anti-Soviet partisans.

In March 1944 General N. F. Vatutin, the commander of First Ukrainian Front, drove through snow covered fields to visit one of his subordinate armies. Without warning the partisans opened fire on the General's car which was in the lead. His car and one of the escort vehicles was set on fire and a fight began between the partisans and the escort. During this exchange of shots the General was wounded in the hip, and he was carried away for medical attention. Despite the care of the best available surgeons he died on 15 April at the age of 42.

The last word on the effectiveness of partisan activity behind Soviet lines is given by Marshal K. K. Rokossovsky in his memoirs where he states that to visit the southern formations of his Front, he had to travel in an armoured train 'as the forests were still infested with bands of Bandera men and other fascist hangers-on'. 'Bandera men' was what the Soviets called the Ukrainian Liberation Movement. Taking no chances, the Marshal returned to his headquarters in a light aircraft. When the Soviet archives are finally opened to public scrutiny, the achievements of these brave men will make an interesting story.

As might be expected, the Soviet authorities dealt harshly with these nationalist partisan movements after the war. A defector recalled in 1986:

'After the war, our division returned on foot. Beginning in September 1945 until the following July, there was a struggle with Ukrainian nationalist partisans, the so-called Bandera organization that wanted to create Ukrainian independence. We crushed this movement in the most cruel way. By night MVD vehicles approached the villages and in 3 hours would clear out the entire village. On one occasion in March 1946 in the village where I served, the commander of the artillery regiment, who was the son of the famous Chapayev [one of the victims of the pre-war purges], had an officer killed in one of the villages. He gave ten soldiers signal flares, and they went to the village and set the straw roofs on fire.'[9]

NOTES

1. Von Luck, Hans, *Panzer Commander*, New York, Praeger, 1989, p. 56.
2. Cooper, Matthew, *The Phantom War*, London, Macdonald & Jane's, 1979, p. 167.
3. Glantz, David, *The Military Strategy of the Soviet Union*, London, Frank Cass, 1992, p. 27.
4. Ziemke, p. 103.
5. 'Bagration', collection of Soviet articles, undated, p. 29.
6. Heidkämper, Otto, *Witebsk, Kampf und Untergang der 3 Panzerarmee*, undated.
7. Soviet account of the operations of 65th Army.
8. Ziemke, p. 344, Note 77.
9. Author's interview with a defector in 1986.

10
FINAL SOVIET PREPARATIONS

During May and early June, the Soviets completed their concentration and planned the final details of 'Bagration'.

In the north, First Baltic Front was commanded by General I. Kh. Bagramyan, an Armenian protégé of Marshal Zhukov's. During the first year of the war Bagramyan had served in various staff appointments until he was appointed to command Western Front's 16th Army under Zhukov. His army, redesignated 11th Guards Army, played an important role at Kursk, and Stalin promoted him to full general in command of First Baltic Front in November 1943.[1] The Front had three armies: 5th Shock (the northernmost), 6th Guards and 43rd Army. Its task was to destroy the northern wing of Third Panzer Army, cut communications between Army Groups North and Centre, and cover the northern flank of the operation. The left-hand army, 43rd, was to encircle Vitebsk from the west, in co-operation with the right flank of Third Belorussian Front.

Third Belorussian Front was to destroy the enemy forces between Vitebsk and Orsha and then advance towards Minsk, Molodechno and Vilnius. The Front's mobile group consisted of General N. S. Oslikovski's cavalry/mechanized group. The 5th Guards Tank Army, which was to exploit success, was still in Stavka reserve 30 kilometres west of Smolensk, having only just arrived from the Ukraine. This Front was commanded by the newly promoted Colonel-General I. D. Chernyakovsky who was only 38 years old and was of Jewish origin. He had commanded 60th Army with distinction at Kursk and afterwards in the Ukraine.[2]

Second Belorussian Front was to launch what Marshal Zhukov called a secondary attack towards Mogilev. It too was commanded by a newly appointed Front Commander, General G. F. Zakharov. He was a veteran of the Civil War, having joined the Petrograd Red Guards in 1917. He joined the Red Army artillery and served in various high profile staff appointments until 1944 when Stalin appointed him to succeed General I. E. Petrov who was alleged by Mekhlis, the 'political member' of the Military Soviet, to be always sick and not capable of holding his present appointment.[3]

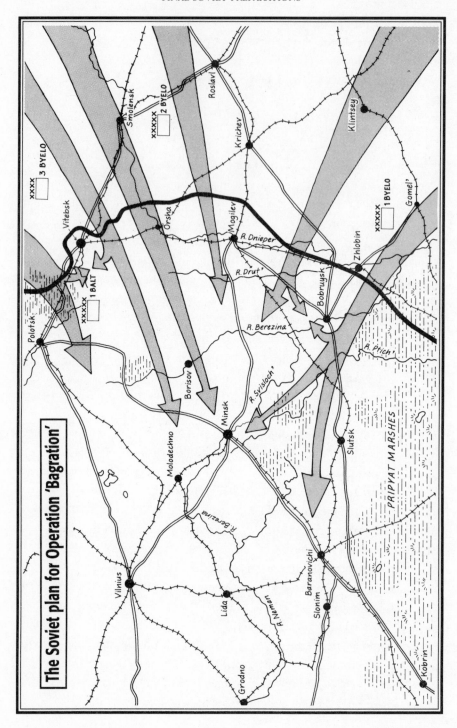

The Soviet plan for Operation 'Bagration'

82

In the south, the decisive formation was First Belorussian Front commanded by one of the most competent Soviet commanders, Marshal K. K. Rokossovsky. He was of Polish extraction and spoke Russian with a strong Polish accent. He served in the Imperial Army during the First World War and was highly decorated for gallantry on several occasions. He continued to serve in the cavalry of the Red Army. In 1941, he commanded a mechanized corps on the Kiev axis, before being promoted to command an armoured group of several divisions. From then on he commanded an army and then a Front, playing crucial roles in the battles for Stalingrad and Kursk.[4] Only the right wing of his Front was involved in 'Bagration', and was itself divided into two thrusts, both initially aimed at the encirclement of Bobruisk. Once this had succeeded, the right thrust was directed towards Minsk and the left to the east towards Baranovichi. The Front's mobile group consisted of General A. I. Pliyev's cavalry/mechanized group.

The overall aim of the first phase of the offensive was to destroy a significant proportion of the German formations as quickly as possible, denying them time to bring forward their reserves. The second phase envisaged a deeper envelopment aimed at the city of Minsk by the mobile forces of Third and First Belorussian Fronts. The third phase was to be the continuation of the advance to the east Prussian and Polish frontiers. The orders for this phase would only be issued when the first two phases neared completion, further exploitation depending on the initial successes achieved.

As the formations assembled for the offensive, a rigorous training programme was entered upon to prepare them for the tasks ahead, although no details of the plan were disclosed.

General Shtemenko was sent to help the new commander of Second Belorussian Front, General Zakharov, settle in to his new command – with rather surprising results: 'The object of the conference was to hear the commander's reports and set certain tasks for preparing the troops ... for the offensive.

'We assembled in a large marquee. Everyone was watching the new commander with more than usual interest. Zakharov realized this and began the conference with a detailed account of his own career, laying particular stress on the fighting side ... Then came a harangue that started as follows: "I'm the one who does the talking here and it's your job to listen and take note of my instructions."

'He then insisted on seeing what people were going to take their notes on. Hands were raised holding tattered notebooks and scraps of paper.

Zakharov had some exercise books which he had obviously been keeping for this purpose; he had them given out and explained at some length what they were for.

'Thus equipped, everyone naturally made ready to take down his instructions, but no instructions were forthcoming. Instead, the commander made people stand up and questioned them in turn on army regulations and field combat tactics. Many were nonplussed and gave muddled answers. Zakharov grew more and more impatient until he was downright rude. Something had to be done to relieve the tension. Since the conference had been going on for some time already, I suggested an interval.

'While the commanders were outside, smoking and exchanging their impressions in reserved tones, Zakharov and I had a showdown. I tried to convince him that he could not go on in this manner. After the interval he became much more practical and actually gave some useful pointers on how to prepare for breaking through the enemy defences.'[5]

The co-ordination of fire support was of concern to all levels from the Stavka representative and Front commander down to company and battery commanders. The best way of dealing with individual targets was examined and then included in the plans for air support, tanks and infantry. In particular, commanders were intensely worried that the Germans might withdraw a considerable distance and the artillery barrage would fall on empty ground. The entire offensive would then have to be replanned. This of course would have been a sound tactic, but it was forbidden by Hitler.

Shtemenko gives an account of training: 'On June 11 and 12, Zakharov and I attended some exercises of the 32nd and 290th Divisions. It all looked good enough on the surface. The men camouflaged themselves well, did some very effective crawling, then rushed at the "enemy", cheering lustily. But the real atmosphere of battle was missing. Not a shot was fired; there were not even any targets. Zakharov gave orders that such exercises in future must be carried out with live ammunition. Under front-line conditions this was not so easy. There were no firing ranges ... The biggest difficulty was to simulate the actual situation as closely as possible without giving away our real intentions to the enemy.'[6]

In some areas, particularly the swampy wooded terrain near the Pripyat Marshes, new techniques had to be learned and practised. Marshal Rokossovsky records: 'Our officers and men were faced with the extremely arduous task of fighting their way over this difficult ground. This was a feat that required special training. Men learned to swim, cross swamps and rivers with any available means and find their way through woods. They made special "swamp shoes" to cross the bogs, and built boats, rafts and platforms for trundling machine-guns, mortars and light artillery. The tankmen also underwent training in the art of marsh warfare.[7]

There was also considerable activity in preparing the ground for the assault. In the First Belorussian Front area engineers cleared 34,000 mines and constructed 193 access roads for tanks and infantry. They also made bridges and fords over the Rivers Drut and Dnieper and laid many miles of new roads.

Rokossovsky also tells of the final preparations at the higher level: 'We conducted several field exercises for the commanders of the large units and studied relief maps of the terrain on which we were to operate. Shortly before the attack we held staff exercises and war games on the subject of "Penetrating enemy defences and committing mobile formations to action." As GHQ representative with the special task of co-ordinating the operations of the First and Second Belorussian Fronts, Zhukov took an active part in this work.' In some cases where a unit had a critical role to play, the Marshal went through the plans with individual battalion commanders.[8]

At this time arrangements were also being made to co-ordinate a major operation by the partisans behind the German lines to dislocate rail traffic and disrupt the defensive deployments. This was regarded as an integral part of the offensive and had been one of the factors in choosing Belorussia for the major summer offensive. Soviet sources allege that there were as many as 370,000 men operating in the area behind Army Group Centre.

On 10 June a German radio station intercepted an order to the partisans to step up their activity against the railways in Fourth Army's area, particularly from 20 June. During the night of 19/20 June, more than 10,000 demolitions were reported; the Germans were able to render many attempts harmless as a result of warnings received. The extent of this activity can be judged by the fact that it was only with some difficulty that two panzer divisions were able to be brought forward by rail some days later. (See Chapter 9.)

The scene was now set for the opening of the Soviet offensive which was to lead to a German defeat even greater than Stalingrad. Soviet superiority was awesome. The four armies of Army Group Centre had a total strength of 800,000 men of whom only half were front-line troops. They had five hundred tanks and self-propelled guns. The Red Army had amassed 2,500,000 men, with a front-line strength of 1,250,000. They had 4,000 tanks and self-propelled guns, 22,000 guns and mortars and 2,000 Katyusha multiple rocket-launchers. This represented an overall superiority of 3:1 in men and 10:1 in tanks, although in key areas this superiority was increased dramatically by concentration of force. Although the morale of the German front line troops was high, they would have been far less confident if they had been aware of the vastly superior numbers of tanks and men poised to attack them.

NOTES

1. Shukman, H. (ed.), *Stalin's Generals*, London, Weidenfeld and Nicholson, 1993
2. Erickson, John, *The Road to Berlin*, London, Weidenfield and Nicolson, 1983, p. 197.
3. Shtemenko, p.242.
4. Shukman, *ibid.*, 'Rokossovsky' by Woff.
5. Shtemenko, p. 322.
6. *Ibid.*, p. 329.
7. Rokossovsky, K., *A Soldier's Duty*, Moscow, Progress Publishers, 1970, p. 236.
8. *Ibid.*, p. 238.

11
IN THE NORTH

The offensive was scheduled to commence on 23 June, having been postponed from the 19th because of congestion and difficulties of bringing forward troop and supply trains. At this stage in the war Soviet practice was to carry out wide-ranging reconnaissance to confirm that the Germans had not abandoned their forward positions and that their dispositions had not undergone any major change. First Baltic and Third Belorussian Fronts carried out their reconnaissance in strength on 22 June, the third anniversary of 'Barbarossa'.

Colonel Glantz gives an outline of the opening moves of the attack: 'The Soviets used assault detachments to lead the attack. These units were composed of infantry and sappers reinforced by mortars, heavy machine-guns, and several self-propelled guns or tanks. Often these assault detachments destroyed specific strongholds in the German defences in close co-ordination with supporting artillery. Advanced battalions followed the assault detachments and were also supported by self-propelled gun and tank battalions.'[1]

At 0500 hours on 22 June, General Bagramyan gave the orders for the opening barrage to support the reconnaissance and this lasted for a mere 16 minutes. Within hours reports were coming in that advanced battalions were engaged in fierce fighting along the fronts of 6th Guards and 43rd Armies. Army Group Centre's War Diary notes: 'The major attack by the enemy north-west of Vitebsk has taken the German command completely by surprise. Up till now the intelligence picture had not indicated any concentration on this scale (six or seven divisions) there.'

During the day IX Corps on the left of Third Panzer Army had been forced back some 7 kilometres from Sirotino on a 12-kilometre-wide front. As a precautionary move, OKH transferred 24th Infantry Division with an assault gun brigade to Third Panzer Army to restore the situation. In the Vitebsk area, LIII Corps was able to repulse the reconnaissance attacks, but in the south of the Army's area limited penetrations were made. In view of this success General Bagramyan decided not to fire the main barrage except in areas where the defences had not been penetrated.

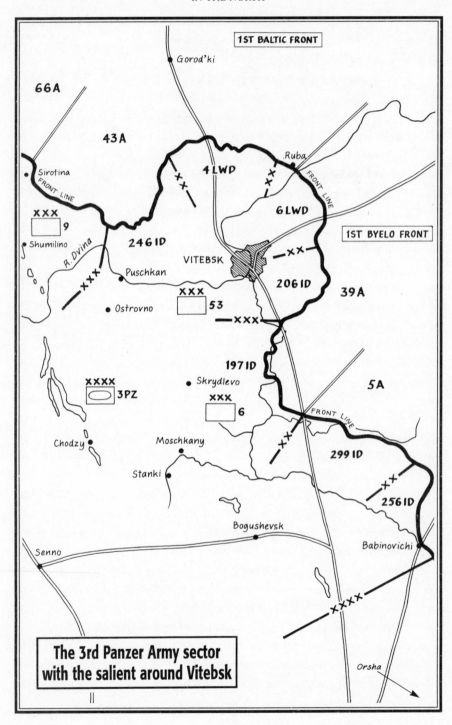

**The 3rd Panzer Army sector
with the salient around Vitebsk**

The main artillery bombardment had been scheduled to last for varying lengths of time; in First Baltic Front's area, for example, for 2 hours 15 minutes, the first 90 minutes being devoted to the destruction of defensive works. The assaulting infantry were to be supported by a rolling barrage until they had captured the first and second lines. Some guns were always reserved for counter-battery work. It was a sophisticated and flexible system that could be integrated with air support, and was used on all the other Fronts with varying refinements.

General Bagramyan describes his Front's attack: 'Early at dawn on 22 June I arrived at my observation post with a group of commanders to direct the operations of the reconnaissance detachments. At 0500 hours our artillery opened fire. On the 16th minute it reached its peak. General I. M. Chistyakov, Commander of 6th Guards Army and General A. P. Beloborodov, Commander of 43rd Army, reported that the battalions had gone into the assault. Several minutes later prisoners were brought to the observation post. The information they gave at the interrogation confirmed our own data on the enemy dispositions and the outlines of his defence positions. The prisoners said that they thought the artillery attack and the assault of the leading battalions which followed it, was the beginning of the general offensive by the Soviet forces.

'By 0800 hours the Nazis had recovered from the blows and a fierce fire battle started for the forward positions. The enemy's resistance did not weaken even as it grew dark. He used both fire and counter-attacks to force the Soviet elements out of his positions. The Front Command realized that this fierce resistance might be intended to camouflage the withdrawal of the main body to positions organized in advance in the depth of the enemy defence zone.'[2]

A member of a Russian signals unit who was checking the lines to an artillery observation post states: 'We reached the observation post and the artillery were still firing. I had been a forward observer before and so I was allowed to watch. The whole line was burning from the shell bursts. The enemy was giving very little answering fire because of the weight of our bombardment. It was a well-thought-out attack, and almost all the positions could be seen to be blazing. Then the aircraft appeared, Ils – Ilyushins. They were ground-attack aircraft with heavy calibre machine-guns and rockets and they added their bit. The enemy just kept silent and the aircraft flew past firing their guns.'[3]

Army Group Centre's War Diary records: The major attack by the enemy north-west of Vitebsk has taken the German command completely by surprise. Up till now the intelligence picture had not indicated any concentration on this scale.' This is illustrated on Third Panzer Army's intelligence map of 24 June, two days after the beginning of the offensive, which still shows only 4th Shock and 43rd Armies facing them. In 43rd Army's sector only 154th and 156th Rifle Divisions are shown, and they are seen as occupying a wide sector. In reality the entire 6th Guards Army of four rifle corps supported by a tank corps had moved into the area previously occupied by 154th Rifle Division during the three days and nights before the offensive began. This was a classic example of a successful '*maskirovka*' operation.[4] An additional element of surprise came when 43rd Army attacked over swampy ground instead of across the firmer ground on their left as might have been expected. This was confirmed by a captured German general.

During the day, IX Corps on the left of Third Panzer Army was forced back for some 7 kilometres in the Sirotino area on a front of twelve kilometres. During the night General Bagramyan had to decide whether to mount the full set-piece attack, or continue the attack with the advanced battalions. 'Towards morning on 23rd June the intelligence officer reported to me that the Nazis were withdrawing from their positions in separate sectors of the breakthrough area. We were again confronted with the alternatives of carrying out the artillery bombardment we had planned or, taking advantage of the enemy's confusion, to attack with all forces available, supporting the move with massive artillery fire and air strikes. At 0400 hours we decided to carry out the artillery bombardment where the enemy defences remained intact. In the sectors where our soldiers had penetrated the enemy defences we decided to continue the assault without further loss of time, supporting this with artillery and air strikes.'[5]

This same decision faced General Chernyakhovsky, whose Third Belorussian Front had begun the reconnaissance phase of the offensive on the same day. Its mission was to attack initially westwards with two armies, 39th and 5th, with the 39th turning to the north to complete the encirclement of Vitebsk and the 5th attacking to the west. The 11th Guards and 31st Armies would attack towards the Orsha area. This left wing of the Front's offensive will be dealt with in Chapter 12.

The only sizeable gain made on 22 June was on the boundary between 39th and 5th Armies. Elsewhere in Third Belorussian Front's area the full artillery preparation was to be fired and the planned attack mounted on the next morning.

The German formations had fought hard against odds of more than 10:1 in men and about 7:1 in tanks and SP guns, the Soviets having a great superiority in guns, mortars and ground-attack aircraft. The Army Commander, General Reinhardt, asked Field Marshal Busch if he could give up some small salients, particularly in the area of Sirotino, but was told they were only to be given up under enemy pressure. However, a regiment of 95th Infantry Division would be moved north to cover the gap to the west of Vitebsk, and 24th Infantry Division and an assault gun brigade, both from Army Group North, would be placed under command of Third Panzer Army to counter-attack south- eastwards from Obol.

On the 23rd, the joint offensive of 6th Guards and 43rd Armies continued in the Sirotino area, forcing their way to the lakes near Shumolino which were swollen from recent rain. In the late afternoon, IX Corps was ordered to withdraw to the line of the River Dvina. Around Vitebsk, in LIII Corps' sector, everything remained quiet, but there were signs of offensives being prepared from both flanks to close the corridor leading to the city.

The Commandant of *Fester Platz* Vitebsk was the Commander of LIII Corps, General of Infantry Friedrich Gollwitzer, an experienced infantry soldier who had commanded a division on the Eastern Front before being promoted to command this Corps in March 1943. He was no respecter of rank and seems particularly to have disliked Field Marshal Busch. He was appointed Commandant of Vitebsk in April 1944, and was summoned to Army Group Headquarters to be briefed on his responsibilities, together with eleven other generals, none of whom he noted wryly had any other command responsibilities as he had. Then followed the most amazing display of bad temper by the Field Marshal:

'Q: Where does the Commandant get his Staff?

FM: That's your business. Apply to your Army.

Q: The strength of the garrison is not sufficient for all-round defence.

FM: More troops are not available. Take them from units withdrawing from the front.

G. Goll: Who can build the Vitebsk defences as there are no civilians who can do the work, and combat troops cannot be used?

FM: Staff personnel, administrative troops and Hiwis.

G.Goll: If there is an attack threatened, can the Corps expect any reserves to prevent the encirclement of its flanks?

FM: No! Put the strongest part of your defences at the junction with your neighbours!

G.Goll: The junctions of my LIII Corps are with my neighbouring Corps, VI and IX. Presumably they will halt the first attacks and must build up strong defences at these points.

FM: Everything will be as I have said! The Führer has ordered it!'

What General Gollwitzer most feared was about to happen. The Soviet forces were about to break through at the junction with the Corps on his right and left. He asked for permission to withdraw from this extremely vulnerable salient before he was surrounded, and the Field Marshal put this request to Hitler. All that Hitler would agree to was for the Corps to withdraw into the *Fester Platz*, thus ensuring its destruction. General Gollwitzer did not write his account of events until after he had returned from being a prisoner of war in Russia in 1955, but he obviously harboured bitter resentment against those responsible for the losses suffered by his men. It is also an interesting example of Hitler's obsessive insistence on making tactical decisions down to a relatively low level even when he was far away from the front on the Obersalzberg.

The Soviet reconnaissance in force had not succeeded everywhere on the right wing of Third Belorussian Front's area. The 39th Army made little progress against the southern and eastern defences of Vitebsk, but on their left 5th Army was more successful.

In order to gain an idea of what these statements meant at a lower level, we will look at the right-hand rifle division of 5th Army attacking westwards. The 63rd Rifle Division had three infantry regiments supported by an artillery regiment, and a separate tank destroyer battalion. Prior to the offensive it had been reinforced with a regiment each of self-propelled guns, tank destroyers, light artillery, rocket-launchers (Katyushas), and two regiments of heavy howitzers. A formidable force!

The Division was to attack on a 3.3-kilometre front to break through the German tactical defences and cross the Vitebsk-Bogushevsk railway. The German 299th Division was facing them with two regiments in the first line of defence and a third regiment in depth behind the artillery positions. It was a formidable position with strongpoints sited in depth.

The Divisional Commander, General Laskin, decided to attack with two regiments on his right and one on the left; one of the battalions of this regiment was in brigade reserve. Two batteries from the tank destroyer battalion and two from the self-propelled artillery regiment were detailed as an anti-tank reserve, the remainder being attached to individual regiments.

The reconnaissance in force began on the afternoon of the 22nd after a 25-minute artillery bombardment. The advanced battalion quickly took the first German positions, and the Divisional Commander then attacked with the infantry regiments. By the end of the day, after heavy fighting, units of the division had captured one of the German strongpoints and seized a bridge over a river which ran along their front. A bridgehead was formed which would allow the deployment of the division's main forces. In this action, the division crossed two water obstacles, almost completely destroyed five infantry battalions and captured a large number of weapons.[6]

The 5th Army was supported by a number of tank units to help penetrate the German positions, and by coincidence we have a vivid account by a platoon commander in 2nd Guards Independent Tank Brigade. Professor Yon Degan was then a lieutenant commanding a platoon of four T-34 tanks newly equipped with the long and powerful 85mm gun. When I interviewed him he was living in Tel Aviv, and he told me: 'We had the feeling that something was about to begin, but we had no idea that we were going to attack until 40 minutes before the start of the offensive. We were ordered to our initial positions and waited for the artillery barrage to start. When the barrage had finished we were shown on maps where we were to make the breakthrough and what our objective was.

'We were hidden in a pine wood near the guns and could not be seen. Just before the start we came out of the wood and went straight into the attack. We attacked in the usual way, a line of tanks. The company attacked with ten tanks with the company commander in the line with his tanks. Our task was to break through to Bogachevsk. We broke through the German positions but our tank losses were enormous. It took us three days to reach our objective. By that time our Brigade was almost finished.

'My Battalion had very few tanks left [only 5 out of 65]. We were no longer capable of carrying out our task of advancing to the west. We were then tasked to support the infantry which were trying to destroy the German units coming out of the woods where they had hidden. It must be said that they were fighting like mad. They did not realize what had happened and that the front had been breached. They still thought that they would succeed in getting out.'[7]

On the 23rd, at the end of the day, in IXth Corps' area, Soviet forces were closing up to the River Dvina, but the tanks of 1st Tank Corps were finding it difficult to make much ground because the heavy rain had made what tracks that existed almost impassable. At this point air reconnaissance reported a large column of German vehicles moving from the south-west towards the river, and the staff of First Baltic Front assumed that the Germans were intending to hold the Dvina. General Bagramyan saw that there was a great danger that the Germans would be able to stabilize the situation if they could use the river as an obstacle. As the tanks were making such slow progress, he ordered the two armies to send their infantry ahead to seize bridgeheads over the river.

On the southern flank of Third Panzer Army, penetrations had been made along the front of VI Corps, but although they were largely contained, the last reserves were at the end of their tether. The 299th Infantry Division was smashed and 197th Infantry Division was penetrated and forced to the north-west, but a 20-kilometre corridor to Vitebsk remained open. By that evening even Field Marshal Busch was telling OKH that he could see no way to restore the situation in Third Panzer Army.

On the 24th, the situation began to deteriorate even more. North of Vitebsk the two corps were being forced into smaller groups, with large gaps between them. By midday the leading elements of 6th Guards Army were across the Dvina, having crossed by rafts, trees and anything that came to hand. The bridging equipment arrived later so that tanks and heavy weapons could cross. The reason for their haste was that signal intercept teams had picked up vital information. The Stavka representative, Marshal Vasilevsky, explained: 'We have information that the Fascist command has twice sought Hitler's permission to withdraw from the Vitebsk "bag"... but it is not Hitler, but us who must decide the fate of this concentration of troops. In any case we must not let go of the Fascists. That depends on rapid operations on the part of Comrade Beloborodov.'[8]

General Beloborodov's 43rd Army was having great difficulty in getting the artillery across the Dvina, and therefore he was promised full air support by the Front Commander. This enabled the Soviet 60th Rifle Corps to defeat the counter-attack made by the German 246th Infantry Division from the north, in an attempt to keep the Vitebsk corridor open. This was the exact situation envisaged by General Gollwitzer in his question to Field Marshal Busch at the meeting on 7 April.

The corridor to LIII corps around Vitebsk was getting narrower by the hour. General Gollwitzer asked for permission to break out. Both the Army and Army Group Commanders supported this and tried to get permission from OKH, but at 1905 hours General Reinhardt was told: 'My request has been turned down yet again. There are quite special reasons which make it essential to hold Vitebsk [the effect on the Finns, who might have broken off their alliance with Germany]. One division is to stay there; this will be 206th Infantry Division and its commander, General Hitter, is to assume local command of the battle. The need for compliance with this order is to be impressed on the Corps Commander. He is to conduct the breakout. No other decision can be expected.'[9] But at least steps could be taken to save the remainder of the Corps.

That evening Busch returned to the fray to try to get permission to evacuate all troops from Vitebsk and to withdraw westwards, thereby creating reserves while there was still time before Third Panzer Army collapsed completely. The Field Marshal's failure to win his case with Hitler made the ensuing disaster inevitable. At 20.25 hours, LIII Corps was given orders by radio: '206th Division is to hold firm under General Hitter. Remaining divisions are to re-open the road from Vitebsk to the west.'

On the morning of 25 June, the first attempt of LIII Corps to break out from Vitebsk failed. General Reinhardt sent a moving message to the Corps Commander: 'To General Gollwitzer. Best of luck to you and your men in fighting your way out. You must do this soon, but I am convinced you still have a good chance of success. My best wishes to General Hitter and his division, who for the moment must stick to their guns and if needs be, sacrifice themselves for you.' At 1400 hours the Corps reported: 'Situation fundamentally changed. Complete encirclement by enemy who is growing steadily stronger. 4th Luftwaffe Division now non-existent. 246th Division and 6th Luftwaffe Division heavily engaged on several fronts. Several penetrations, bitter fighting.' At 1833 hours the Corps announced: 'Overall situation compels us to concentrate all our forces and break out south-westwards. H-Hour 0500 hours. Air cover south-west Vitebsk.'

This last message caused consternation because the Field Marshal knew that Hitler wanted Vitebsk held for at least another week and had ordered that a staff officer be parachuted into the '*Fester Platz*' to ensure that General Gollwitzer understood the situation and the importance of his orders. Major-General Heidkämper, Chief of Staff of the Army, relates what transpired.

General Reinhardt said firmly: 'Field Marshal, please inform the Führer that only one officer in Third Panzer Army can be considered for this jump and that is the Army Commander. I am ready to carry out his order.' No more was heard of this, but a further message was sent to LIII Corps in answer to theirs of 1833 hours: 'Your intention agreed. Renewed order from Führer, 206 Inf Div with General Hitter must hold firm. Reinhardt.'

During the day the Corps Commander had driven back into Vitebsk to conclude the final details for the breakout. On his way there, his party was attacked from the air and had to take to the ditches while the staff cars were driven into a nearby cornfield. In the city he found that there was fierce fighting as the Soviet troops tried to take the thinly held centre. He found the Commander of 6th Luftwaffe Division, Lieutenant-General Walter Peschl, in the Command Post with Lieutenant-General Alfons Hitter. He recalled that Peschl was deeply dejected and seemed close to a nervous breakdown; one of his regiments had only advanced 50 metres in one attack and the survivors were still lying out in the open. The Luftwaffe field divisions, having been for the most part employed in defensive positions, had received no training in offensive operations. Despite their bravery and willingness, Peschl feared that they would be massacred in the open during the breakout.

Despite his own considerable misgivings, General Gollwitzer tried to reassure his subordinate. He then told General Hitter of his decision to save as much as possible of 206th Division, and give up the '*Fester Platz*' despite the Führer Order. He added that he had taken this the most difficult decision of his life with perfect confidence in the fighting ability of the Division. For this reason he would site his own Command Post in the Divisional area and would accompany the men in their attack during the breakout.

On returning to his Command Post he saw with horror that the sole remaining railway bridge, that was critical for the withdrawal of 246th Infantry Division that night, was being prepared for demolition by railway troops who were not under his command. To prevent disaster, he ordered the Corps Chief Engineer to place an 'energetic' officer at each end of the bridge, to ensure on pain of death that the bridge was not blown before the Division had crossed. But these precautions came to nothing because shortly after midnight, while the General was crossing the Dvina in an assault boat, there was a tremendous explosion and the bridge went up just as the leading unit of 246th Division, an artillery battalion, was approaching. In the pitch-black night the sounds of a fierce fire-fight in the narrow streets gradually died

Army Group Centre

Right: Field Marshal Ernst Busch. Appointed 12 October 1943, dismissed 28 June 1944.

Below right: Field Marshal Walter Model. Tasked by Hitler to restore the situation in the East, he was moved to the West in August 1944.

Soviet Stavka Representatives

Left: North. Marshal A. M. Vasilevsky, 1st Baltic and 3rd Byelorussian Fronts.

Below left: South. Marshal G. K. Zhukov, 2nd and 3rd Byelorussian Fronts.

German Army Commanders
Above left: 3rd Panzer Army. Colonel General G. H. Reinhardt.
Above right: 4th Army. General of Infantry K. von Tippelskirch.
Below left: 9th Army.General of Infantry H. Jordan. Dismissed by Hitler for his handling of 20th Panzer Division.
Below right: 9th Army. General of Panzer Troops N. von Vormann. When he was appointed, his command had ceased to exist.

Soviet Front Commanders
Above left: 1st Baltic. General I. Kh. Bagramyan.
Above right: 3rd Byelorussian. General I. D. Chernyakhovsky.
Below left: 2nd Byelorussian. General G. F. Zakharov.
Below right: 1st Byelorussian. Marshal K. K. Rokossovsky.

Commanders, 3rd Panzer Army

Above left: LIII Corps. General of Infantry Friedrich Gollwitzer seen as a prisoner marching through Moscow on 17 July. He survived more than 10 years' captivity in Russia.

Above right: VI Corps. General of Artillery G. Pfeiffer. Killed during an air attack outside Mogilev on 28 June.

Below left: 206th Infantry Division. Lieutenant-General A. Hitter. Captured during the attempted breakout from Vitebsk. He remained in captivity for more than 10 years.

Below right: 6th Luftwaffe Field Division. Lieutenant-General R. Peschl. Killed after the breakout from Vitebsk.

3rd Panzer Army
Above: German transport destroyed during the breakout from Vitebsk.
Below: A party of German soldiers trying to break out from Soviet encirclement.

Commanders, 4th Army
Above left: XXVII Corps. General der Infanterie P. Volckers. Captured and died in Soviet captivity in 1946.
Above right: 78 Sturm (Assault) Division. Generalleutnant H. Traut. Captured near Minsk and released in autumn 1955.
Below left: 57 Infantry Division. Major General A. Trowitz. Captured near Minsk.
Below right: 267 Infantry Division. Lieutenant General O. Drescher. Killed in August 1944 near Memel.

4th Army
Above left: 12th Infantry Division. Lieutenant General R. Bamler. Recently appointed to command the Division, he was ordered to take over as 'Fester Platz Mogilev' commander on the day that the city was stormed.
Above right: Commander Mogilev. Major General G. von Erdmannsdorff. He was captured on the day he handed over and was later executed for war crimes. Seen marching through Moscow.
Below: Generals Bamler and von Erdmannsdorff marching as Soviet prisoners shortly after their capture.

In the South
Above: Soviet troops advancing into Bobruisk.
Below: German demolition guard looking out over a river bridge in Byelorussia.

Commanders, 9th Army

Above left: XXXV Corps. Lieutenant General Freiherr K-J. von Lützow. Taken prisoner after the breakout from Bobruisk.

Above right: XXXXI Panzer Corps. Lieutenant General E. Hoffmeister. Captured during the breakout from Bobruisk as acting Corps Commander.

Below left: 36 Infantry Division. Major General A. Conrady. Captured during the breakout from Bobruik when he was near the relief by 12th Panzer Division.

Below right: Commander Bobruisk. Major General A. Hamann. Captured and executed for war crimes in 1945. Seen during the march through Moscow, 17 July 1944.

Soviet Army Commanders
Above left: 65th Army. Colonel General P. I. Batov.
Above Right: 49th Army. Lieutenant General Grishin.
Below: General G. F. Zakharov giving out orders to his Army Commanders, amongst them
General Boldin, 50th Army, sitting on the Front Commander's left.

Panzer Commanders
Above left: LVI Panzer Corps. General of Infantry F. Hossbach.
Above Right: XXXIX Panzer Corps. Lieutenant General D. von Saucken. Given command of a Task Force which included 5th Panzer Division.
Below left: 5th Panzer Division. Lieutenant General K. Decker.
Below right: 20th Panzer Division. Lieutenant General M. von Kessel.

Veterans
Above left: HQ Army Group Centre. Colonel P. von der Groeben.
Above right: 12th Panzer Division. Colonel G. Niepold, with Model (wearing hat).
Below left: 5th Panzer Division. Colonel von Plato, wearing the Ritterkreuz he won in Byelorussia.
Below right: 12th Infantry Division. Major Lemm also wearing the Ritterkreuz, but with the additional distinction of the Oakleaves.

Captivity
Above: Lieutenant General V. Muller being interrogated by General Boldin. Shortly afterwards General Muller issued orders for the surrender of those units of 4th Army that he could still contact.
Below: The Soviet Victory March through Moscow on 17 July 1944.

Minsk

Above: German road sign denoting the end of the Smolensk–Minsk Highway.

Below: Soviet T-34/85 tank driving along the main boulevard of Minsk. This tank is similar to that commanded by Guards Lieutenant Frolikov during his triumphant entry into the city.

A Ruckkampfer
Dr Rolf Hinze, now an International Arms Control lawyer, and during the Byelorussian campaign an artillery observer, after his epic journey back to German lines.

away. After that there was silence. The demolition of the bridge would ensure the destruction of the greater part of 246th Division. There was now no communication with the north bank of the Dvina and it was not until dawn that the situation in Vitebsk became clearer and the Corps Commander could take personal control of the situation.

To add to the confusion of the night, the orders concerning the silent withdrawal and forbidding demolitions did not reach everyone. Shortly after nightfall a shower of flames and demolitions erupted in the city. Someone had started to destroy the vast dumps of fuel and ammunition that had been built up in accordance with Hitler's Order No. 11: 21 days' supplies of food and ammunition went up in a series of tremendous explosions, aggravated by the detonation of bombs stored on the airfields. According to Hitler's Order anything that might be of use to the enemy was to be destroyed. Gas and electricity installations, water mains and even civilian bakeries all went up in flames. Any hope of getting away without detection had vanished. As General Gollwitzer remarked rather dryly: '*Die Kesselschlacht beginnt sehr dramatisch!* [The battle to escape from the pocket is beginning very dramatically!]'.

General Gollwitzer described the scene as he left the city which he had defended for so many months: 'The Old Town on the hill with the old Tsar's palace blazing and the ruined towers of the cathedrals and churches, surrounded by brightly burning ruins of houses surmounted by thick black smoke gave a ghostly silhouette in the night sky. Surrounded by the sounds of machine-gun fire, the cracks of bursting grenades, and the flashes and detonations of our demolitions, we took our farewell of a city which we had successfully defended for so many months at the cost of so many lives. Now our own fate called!'

That morning the Corps began its attempt to break out towards the remainder of Third Panzer Army, at the nearest point some 70 kilometres away. During the morning, General Gollwitzer reported that 206th Infantry Division was outside the perimeter of the *Fester Platz* and as only two battalions remained inside, it was impossible to carry out the Führer's order. Even at this stage, with the breakout under way, Field Marshal Busch repeated that there was no freedom of decision and that the *Fester Platz* must be held as ordered. As we have seen, General Gollwitzer had decided to ignore this order and all that was left of 206th Division had been ordered to break out with the remainder of the Corps.

During the morning of 27 June the Corps reported that its breakout was going well, that they were now 10 kilometres south of Vitebsk, and requested continuous air cover. The message was signed by General Goll-witzer. It was transmitted over the only remaining radio set, the General's own Tactical Headquarters set. One more message was sent off at about 0900 hours saying that they had advanced another 3 kilometres and were under heavy air attack. During transmission of this message the radio truck slid off the track into a ditch and almost immediately was hit by a Soviet anti-tank gun. The last contact with the outside world had gone.

At midday General Gollwitzer and some of his staff officers met General Hitter in a small Russian village. He reported that his leading regiment had probably advanced some kilometres farther but he had no contact with it. The following combat group had halted under constant air attack. The leading battalion was held up by a bunker, probably held by partisans, which dominated the road. They had already lost numbers of men in trying to take the bunker but it was impossible without artillery support. Therefore the advance could not be continued until nightfall. As a result of the breakout, regiments had been reduced to battalion strength and battalions to companies. The considerable number of wounded were being brought along by the combat groups on their vehicles, but losses among medical staff and lack of supplies meant that very little could be done for them. Ammunition and supplies were very low.

In view of the seriousness of the situation, it was decided that contact must be re-established with the leading combat group. The Corps commander decided to go himself accompanied by General Hitter and some staff officers to guide the breakout in the best direction. They had to make a detour around the bunker through overgrown woods thick with partisans. They passed bodies of German soldiers murdered by partisans. They found that the leading combat group had taken the wrong direction and was heading towards columns of Soviet tanks which the generals had seen and heard during their journey. New orders were given for the night march towards the next objective.

The night was fine and clear. Despite the exertions of the day, they had little sleep. The two generals sat discussing the various possibilities of reaching the remainder of the army which they imagined by now would be back on the line of the Beresina, some 100 kilometres to the west. They considered it likely that both Luftwaffe divisions and the attached elements of 197th Division had been destroyed. At least they could hear elements of 246th Division fighting to the north, but they recognized the shattering fact that LIII Corps had ceased to exist, and that their wider responsibilities were at an end. Towards midnight they decided to make one last effort to establish contact with the remnant of 246th Division. As they had lost maps and compasses during the breakout, they had to steer by the stars during a long march through swampy woods. In the early morning, they reached the western edge of the wooded area only to find that it was sealed off by Soviet troops. After dawn there were bursts of firing from the area where the remnant of the troops were thought to be. After that, silence, followed in turn by the sounds of motor engines and the rattle of tracks. The mobile columns of Russian troops following by their supplies were all moving westwards.

While the other corps of Third Panzer Army withdrew leaving a large gap between them and the right-hand corps of Army Group North, no more was heard of the fate of LIII Corps in its withdrawal from Vitebsk. As the Soviet forces advanced they reduced the main groups of survivors into smaller and smaller groups which were mercilessly harried from the air, by artillery fire and by partisans. Eventually some survivors found their way back to the German lines, by now far to the west. Many thousands were captured: the Soviet estimate of 20,000 men killed and 10,000 prisoners may be an exaggeration. General Gollwitzer wrote after the war that 28,000 men were originally encircled, and that 22-23,000 were taken prisoner and only 5,000 killed. Probably as in most history the truth lies somewhere in the middle.

General Gollwitzer remained a prisoner in Russia until 1955. On his return he wrote a full account of the battles and suffering of his LIII Corps, and laid the blame fairly and squarely on the higher leadership and, in particular, on Hitler personally. As an indication of the severity of the fighting, the fate of the senior commanders should be recorded. Of the two corps commanders, one was killed in action and the other taken prisoner. Of the six divisional commanders, three were killed in action, two were taken prisoner and one was reported missing.

By this time Soviet forces had advanced far to the west and were approaching Lepel, opposed only by the remnant of Third Panzer Army. A wide gap had opened between Third Panzer Army in the north and Fourth Army in the south. Through this gap were advancing 3rd Guards Mechanized Corps in brigade columns along different routes, with 5th Guards Tank Army operating to the south of them, striving to reach the River Berezina.

NOTES

1. Glantz. *1985 Art of War Symposium*, p. 556.
2. Bagramyan in *Bagration*, p. 2l.
3. Interview with Mr Fukson at Tel Aviv.
4. Bagramyan, p. 21.
5. Gollwitzer, MS, '*Der heldenmütige Kampf und dramatische Untergang des LIII Armeekorps in der Kesseischlacht von Vitebsk – 22 bis 28 Juni 1944*, November 1958. This manuscript was used extensively in the preparation of this chapter. General Niepold was kind enough to lend me his own copy.
6. Ogaryov, 'A Division breaking through enemy defences', in *Soviet Military Review*, 1979, (1), p. 79.
7. Interview with Professor Degan at Tel Aviv.
8. Erickson, p. 218.
9. Niepold, Lieutenant-General Gerd, *The Battle for White Russia*, London, Brassey, 1987, p. 89.

12
TO THE BEREZINA

On 23 June, the first day of the main offensive, the left wing of 3rd Belorussian Front, 11th Guards Army, came up against strong German opposition from 78th Stürm (Assault) Division, and 25th Panzer Grenadier Division of XXVII Corps, the left-hand formation of General von Tippelkirch's Fourth Army. One source suggests that the reason why the opening artillery bombardment did not hit the German defensive positions or their gun lines was that the Germans had plotted the new gun positions of the incoming units, whose standard of camouflage was poor, and were able to move to alternative positions when the opening bombardment began.

The 11th Guards Army was more successful on its right where the ground was extremely swampy; in order to reinforce success Colonel-General K. N. Galitsky moved divisions from his two left-hand corps to the right. This is an extremely good example of the degree of operational flexibility which the Red Army had achieved by this stage of the war. This marked ability to switch formations at short notice to take advantage of a changing situation is also shown in the handling of the corps' mobile group which consisted basically of 2nd Guards Tank Corps.

The 2nd Guards Tank Corps commanded by Major-General A. S. Burdeiny was one of the most experienced armoured formations of the Red Army. It had three Guards tank brigades and a Guards motorized rifle brigade as its infantry component. It numbered 11,132 men, with 252 tanks and SP guns, and 112 field guns and mortars. In all a considerable force. Their overall mission was to help 11th Guards Army complete its breakthrough of the defensive positions on the first day of operations and 'create favourable conditions for introducing 5th Guards Tank Army into battle'.[1]

This élite formation had prepared for all possible variants of its role. Once it had received its mission, the corps commander made reconnaissance's with his brigade and regimental commanders and they did the same with their battalion and company commanders. Presumably they had abandoned their distinctive black tank overalls and wore the uniform of infantry soldiers as part of the '*maskirovka*' measures! Special liaison posts were set up in the first echelon divisions so that they could feed back information on the progress of the infantry formations for the moment when the army commander released his mobile group to combat.

Political preparation of the men was considered an important part of their training for the offensive. 'The challenges for Communists and Young Communists [Komsomol] members in the forthcoming battle were discussed at Party and Komsomol meetings. Making use of the cases of savagery, torture and mockery by the fascists against local inhabitants, activists told the soldiers, sergeants, and officers about the conditions under which the Belorussian people were living and fighting and how impatiently they were awaiting liberation.' Presumably no mention was made of the large numbers of Belorussians who were preparing to flee to avoid coming under the Soviet yoke again!

There is another fascinating insight into the Red Army given in this account of preparations of 2nd Guards Tank Corps: 'Special attention was given to the young soldiers arriving as replacements shortly before the fighting began. A ceremony was held when the corps received the Sibiryak tank column, which was formed at the expense of the working people of Irkutskaya Oblast. The powerful combat vehicles and weapons were handed over to the newcomers in front of a parade with the Guards banner flying. The transfer of tanks whose crews had died heroically in earlier fighting was especially significant. Specifically, the young fighting men were given the tanks formerly driven by deceased Heroes of the Soviet Union. The tank troops vowed to perform their duty to the Motherland with honour.'[2] One wonders whether the provenance of these tanks would have acted as incentive to higher morale for Western tank crews!

The success of 78th Assault Division in holding up the left flank of 11th Guards Army prevented the release of 2nd Guards Tank Corps on the first day of combat as planned, and it was not until the late evening of the 24th that the right flank had made sufficient progress to consider the release of the armour. One of the reconnaissance patrols reported to the corps commander that they thought that it was possible to get tanks through in this sector. After ordering an engineer battalion to be ready to move at short notice, he went to see for himself whether this were possible. He found that the swampy ground was crossed by the embankment of an old narrow- gauge railway, and if this were reinforced in a few places and brushwood were put down in some of the swampy sectors, his Corps could advance on this axis. He then went to the command post and gave the welcome news to General Galitsky, who quickly saw the considerable advantage in employing this strong armoured force to attack the enemy from an unexpected direction on their flanks and rear areas across terrain thought by the Germans to be impassable to tanks.

During this same evening, in 5th Army's area the cavalry/mechanized group was launched towards Senno on the inter-army boundary, with the objective of crossing the Beresina north of Borisov. Originally Marshal Vasilevsky had planned to commit 2nd Guards Tank Corps through 11th Guards Army on the first day of battle, to achieve a 'clean breakthrough' for 5th Guards Tank Army to break out on the same axis on the fourth day. But the determined resistance of XXVII Corps in front of Orsha upset this plan, with the result that 2nd Guards Tank Brigade had to be sent through the swamps in the north as we have seen.

On 24 June, the Front commander, General Chernyakhovsky recommended to the Stavka Representative, Marshal Vasilevsky, that 5th Guards Tank Army should move north and enter the battle through 5th Army rather than 11th Guards Army as had been planned. The 5th Guards Tank Army with 524 tanks and SP guns was released from Stavka reserve to Third Belorussian Front at 1700 hours. Against the advice of its Commander, General Rotmistrov, his two corps had been ordered to move up behind 11th Guards Army during the night of 23/24 June. He had recommended that they be left in their assembly area until it was certain on which axis they were to be committed. He now received orders to assemble in an area behind 5th Army by 1200 hours next day. As there were no suitable lateral roads, the two corps had to turn about to return to their concentration area west of Smolensk and then drive another 60 kilometres to the new assembly area.[3]

On the 24th, XXVII Corps were still holding a strong position east of Orsha, with 78th Assault Division and 25th Panzer Grenadier Division fighting hard against greatly superior odds. But the odds were not quite so unequal as elsewhere because both formations had different establishments from conventional infantry divisions: 78th Assault Division had 31 assault guns; 25th Panzer Grenadier had 45, whereas conventional infantry divisions had fourteen on establishment and by this stage in the war they varied between ten and six.

At 1120 hours General von Tippelskirch asked Army Group Centre if he could pull back to the Dnieper position. This was turned down brusquely: 'The mission is still crystal clear —to hold firm and support the blocking positions. To this end forces are to be switched from the divisions which have not been attacked, for example 260th Infantry Division.' This was followed later in the morning by an order to pull back the left flank to the 'Tiger' line (Bogushevsk – Orekhovsk) and to take under command 14th Infantry Division and the remnant of the badly shattered 256th Division. A further limited withdrawal was allowed during the evening.

On the 25th the fierce fighting on the northern flank of Fourth Army continued, but General von Tippelskirch realized that his weary troops could not hold out much longer and gave a warning order to withdraw that night. At 2135 hours he told Army Group that his position had deteriorated and that he had issued orders for a general withdrawal to the Dnieper position. While the Army Commander was explaining the situation to the Army Group Chief of Staff, the Field Marshal broke in on the conversation and said that this was in contradiction of orders, and that the main position was to be re-occupied at once as the permission granted only referred to 31st and 12th Divisions in front of Mogilev. One version has it that von Tippelskirch replied: 'I will not execute this order and my divisions will retreat behind the Dnieper, in order to maintain contact with neighbouring formations.' However he issued a subtle order to his two commanders that troops were only to withdraw when attacked, otherwise they were to hold firm. He did not mention the Field Marshal's order to reoccupy the main defensive positions, but reported back that he had issued orders that the corps were to withdraw only when they were attacked. An entry in the War Diary gives an indication of what was going on: 'C of S – With all respect to the old man, watch what you say on the rear link!' From this time on, the practice of issuing timely orders and afterwards justifying them with false situations reports, spread in all lower level headquarters. The loyalty of the commanders in the field was to their men battling against such odds, rather than to stupid and unrealistic orders. At 2300 hours, Chief of Staff, Army Group Centre informed General von Tippelskirch that Hitler had agreed to the complete withdrawal suggested earlier in the day. [4]

Although Field Marshal Busch at his conference in April had airily dismissed a questioner who stated that the strengths of the *Feste Plätze* were insufficient, by saying take them from the units withdrawing from the front, General Traut, the commander of *Fester Platz* Orsha, found that he really did not have any troops. He had already reported this up the chain of command as early as 23 June. His own division, 78th Assault Division, which had fought so valiantly from the beginning of the offensive, had fallen back on 26 June and was in the north-western suburbs of Orsha under attack from two Soviet divisions. A request to cancel Orsha as a *Fester Platz* had been refused and Corps orders for the 27th included holding it. On the 26th, 2nd Guards Tank Corps crossed the Vitebsk—Orsha highway and then turned south, cutting also the Orsha—Minsk road. It detached a brigade to enter Orsha from the west, thus completing its encirclement. That night an attack by rifle units of 11th Guards and 31st Armies supported by the tanks of 25th Guards Tank Brigade succeeded, and the important rail junction fell into Soviet hands. The last trains carrying wounded managed to steam out of the city just before it fell, only to be destroyed by Soviet tanks a few miles outside the city. [5]

The exploitation forces were now pressing on towards the River Beresina, in order to seize the crossings and trap as many German divisions as possible. The cavalry/mechanized group and the two corps of 5th Guards Tank Army were advancing in brigade columns, sometimes separated by as much as 20 kilometres, all striving to get to the river. At this stage in the war, mobile formations were led by forward detachments consisting of a separate tank brigade with its own infantry, engineers, artillery and Katyusha rocket-launchers, and its own anti-tank capacity. Very often the brigade commander had an aviation officer beside him in his tank to call up air support. They operated well in advance of the main body, destroying any enemy they met, preferably by attacks from the flanks. If the enemy had set up a defensive position, they tried to go round it, leaving it to be reduced by other forces following on. Of particular importance was the seizure of river crossings and road defiles. One forward detachment leader, a battalion commander, decries his own particular method of operating: 'I was in the first tank at all times and the battalion followed me. The reconnaissance patrol was in visual contact. So, I did not fight in accordance with regulations which said the reconnaissance patrol should be 5, sometimes 10 kilometres in front. It is better if you yourself are forward with the reconnaissance patrol so that you can see for yourself what is going on. So, I always did it that way. There was no other choice.'

Lieutenant Degen tells of what it was like to travel in the rear: 'Byelorussia is nothing but a swamp and so we had to use the roads. If the German Air Force had been operating as they had in the past, they would have been able to wipe out much of the Red Army, because everything was piled up and crowded on the roads. There were terrible traffic jams. This might seem funny, but the traffic controller at a crossroads might be a full Colonel. Imagine, a full Colonel standing holding little flags and directing traffic on the road! Not a little female soldier but a full Colonel directing traffic. However, we moved forward. There is a march discipline for tanks with 20 metres in between tanks, but the trouble was that other vehicles got in between. Once when I was just a junior lieutenant, I went up to this Captain and said: "Comrade Captain, you are hindering our march discipline." He told me to go to hell, but I didn't like that so I got into my tank and pushed the Captain, together with his Studebaker, right off the road. Then the Captain began to realize what march discipline is all about.'[6]

The 5th Guards Tank Army had moved into their new assembly area behind 11th Guards Army by midday on the 25th, and early on the 26th attacked south-west along the main road from Smolensk to Minsk towards Tolochin, where they arrived during the evening. On the 27th they resumed their advance along the main road towards Borisov, where 5th Panzer Division was unloading and preparing to move eastwards to cover the remnant of Fourth Army as it struggled to get back to the Beresina. When 3rd Guards Tank Corps on the left flank of 5th Guards Tank Army arrived at Bohr, they found 5th Panzer's 89th Engineer Battalion taking up positions just in front of them to cover the unloading of the Division at Nemanitsa, six kilometres north-west of Borisov. Thus the hard-fought battle between 5th Panzer Division and 5th Guards Tank Army was about to begin. This will be covered in Chapter 15.

NOTES

1. Skorodumov, 'Wartime Tank Corps Operations Described', in Voyenno-*Istoricheskiy Zhurnal*, No. 6, 1979, p. 29.
2. *Ibid.*, p. 32.
3. Niepold, p. 98.
4. *Ibid.*, pp. 125-6.
5. Buchner, 'The Defensive Battles on the Eastern Front', in *Schiffer Military History*, West Chester, PA, USA, 1991, p. 161.
6. Professor Degan, interview Tel Aviv.

13
FOURTH ARMY AND MOGILEV

The full artillery preparation fell on German Fourth Army opposite the left wing of Third Belorussian Front and Second Belorussian Front for upwards of two hours in the early morning of 23 June. General von der Groeben describes the method of a full artillery preparation as opposed to that accompanying the reconnaissance of the previous day: 'The Russians had assembled a tremendously great amount of artillery and rocket projectors of all calibres at their points of main effort. The numbers of guns and great quantities of ammunition enabled the Russians to keep up a heavy artillery concentration for hours, covering the whole main battle position, and extending in depth as far back as divisional command posts. A new tactical procedure, of lifting fire for a considerable period of time so as to create an impression that the fire preparation had been concluded, was successful. Its purpose was to trick local German reserves into leaving the cover of their trenches and dugouts, and to destroy them through a renewed fire concentration. In many instances, this procedure, which then was still unknown to us, achieved considerable success.'[1]

One of the most unwelcome surprises to the German troops was the part that Soviet ground-attack aircraft would play in the forthcoming battle. This was emphasized by the almost total lack of German air cover, the Luftwaffe fighters being needed to try to defend German cities against increasing air attack, as well as in Normandy against the Tactical Air Force.

Two major attacks developed: one thrusting against Fourth Army's left wing north of Orsha, the other opposite Mogilev. There were only what appeared to be holding attacks in XII Corps' area in the south. In order to try to re-establish the position, XXVII Corps in the north was reinforced by an assault gun brigade and a security regiment with an engineer battalion in support. XXXIX Corps was allocated Panzer Grenadier Division 'Feldherrnhalle' which was at very low strength, having suffered heavy losses. It had only 28 Mk IV tanks. Despite its name, commemorating Hitler's confrontation with the police in Munich in 1923, it was an Army division, although it had a high proportion of SA volunteers. It was not to be used for counter-attacks but was to be stationed in the rear to give some stability.

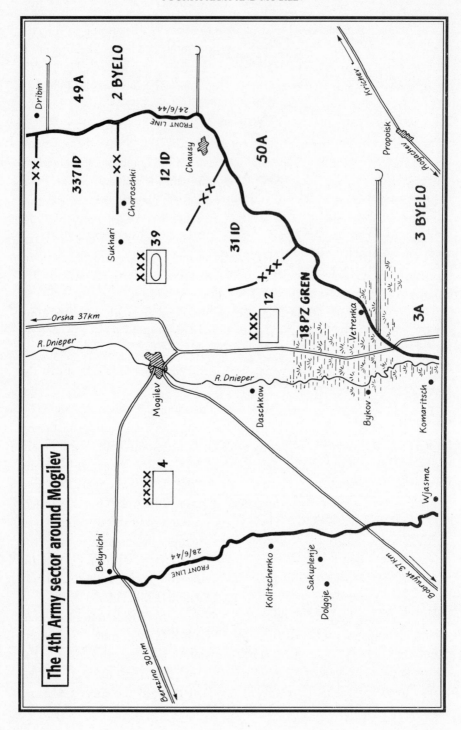

The 4th Army sector around Mogilev

The penetration north-east of Mogilev was now beginning to threaten the left flank of 12th Infantry Division, which so far had been able to retain its well-prepared positions. The 12th Infantry Division was established in 1935/6 in Mecklenberg, one of the northern regions of Germany on the Baltic. In Poland and France the division had fought with three infantry regiments consisting of three battalions each. After the bloody battles of the first Russian winter, one battalion of each regiment was disbanded so that the regiments were left with two only. Each battalion had an anti-tank company and an infantry gun company, together with reconnaissance, signal and engineer platoons. An infantry division had an engineer battalion, a reconnaissance battalion, one signal battalion and an anti-tank battalion. At the beginning of 1944, the division received a company of 10 assault guns, lightly armoured self-propelled 7.5cm guns, which were very useful as anti-tank guns and for engaging targets such as bunkers and machine-guns. Last but not least, the division had its own administrative units as well as medical and veterinary support.

The 12th Infantry Division had a very high reputation in the Army and had proved itself on the northern part of the Eastern Front. There were still many professional soldiers among its NCOs. Most of the soldiers came from Mecklenberg and Pomerania, and orders were given in a dialect that the men could understand.

Major Lemm commanded the 1st Battalion of Fusilier Regiment 27, on the right flank of the division's position along the Pronja River. The careful preparation of the positions was paying off, as the troops could withdraw to their shelters along communication trenches. Only two men were slightly wounded. Very heavy fire fell on the empty trenches on the forward slopes. On the first day tanks were seen advancing through the woods but as yet there had been no infantry attacks. These began on the second day when there was again very heavy artillery fire supporting attempts by infantry to cross the river. The battalion was again successful in beating them off from the forward positions. The Soviets penetrated one of the company positions and was ejected by the reserve company led by the battalion commander.

Somewhat unusually, there is a corresponding Soviet account written by the Commander of 121 Rifle Corps, General D. Smirnov. 'During the night of June 23/4 the 139th Infantry Division in full strength crossed to the west bank over bridges launched in advance. At 1500 hours units of the division supported by tanks, artillery, and aircraft engaged the enemy, breaking his resistance, and forced it on the move.'[3]

On the 24th Major Lemm heard in the late afternoon that the Regimental Headquarters behind was under attack and that the Regimental Commander, Lieutenant Colonel Engel, a former Army Adjutant to Hitler, had been wounded. Major Lemm decided to withdraw as it was obvious that the battalions on their flanks had already retired. Major Lemm describes the scene: 'We move past evacuated artillery positions and supply trucks which seem to have been destroyed by air attacks. Several stragglers, line parties of a signals unit, dispatch riders, and even an artillery supply vehicle, join us ... At noon we are attacked by fifteen tanks with mounted infantry. Although we have no anti-tank weapons, we repel this and another enemy attack in battalion strength, destroying two enemy tanks. After three days of battle without sleep and the night march, during which all weapons, radio sets and ammunition had to be carried by the Fusiliers, our soldiers were exhausted. Artillery fire can be heard north-east and south of us. We do not know where our neighbours are.'

Major Lemm tells how he sorted out a problem of morale: 'The Second Company was attacked supported by fighter-bombers. The Company Commander was killed and one of the platoon strong points cut off by Soviet tanks. The situation in the Company became critical and some of the soldiers began to panic and to run away. As soon as I heard this I got into a motorcycle side car with a driver and my Adjutant and drove forward. Then I suddenly saw a straggling group of soldiers of the Company approaching saying: "All is lost. The Company Commander is dead and we are all that is left!" The first thing I did was to try to calm them down. Then I sent my Adjutant to a nearby hill to watch out for the Russians. I then made the soldiers fall in as on parade. I called them to "attention" and inspected their arms and ammunition. I quite deliberately went from man to man saying a few words to every single one and made him smarten up his uniform. This calmed them down. I told them that I would get them to the Dniepr but if they tried to make a run for it they would be definitely spotted by Russian tanks and shot dead. After that, I had not the slightest difficulty with that Company.'

Later that afternoon the Battalion was ordered to break off the battle. They were ordered to move the four self-propelled guns they had taken under command and the trucks they had acquired, taking the wounded with them. They approached the Dniepr bridge covered by the SP guns. 'As soon as the last vehicle of our small convoy had crossed the bridge, the engineers fired the demolition charges and the wooden bridge collapsed into the river. When I asked the engineer officer standing next to me, "Why are you in such a hurry?" he handed me his binoculars and pointed across the river where, at a distance of approximately 1,000 metres, I saw a tank column of at least sixty Russian T-34s moving quickly towards the point on the eastern bank where the bridge was. Only five minutes later my battalion would not have been able to reach the western bank.'

General Smirnov takes up the story again: 'The main forces of the 238th and 139th Infantry Divisions reached the Dnieper, captured Lupolovo [on the east bank] and started crossing the Dnieper on the move, using what ever means they had: barrels, gates, logs tied into rafts, fishing boats, or simply swimming. By noon units of the two divisions with machine-guns, battalion and regimental mortars and artillery had crossed the Dnieper but could not advance any farther, the enemy meeting them with heavy artillery, mortar and machine-gun fire. Unfortunately we were unable to ferry across artillery or tanks to support the infantry. But in order to give fire support to the units which had crossed we placed tanks and guns along the highway near the Dnieper in positions for direct fire.

'By 1700 hours units of both infantry divisions and the anti-tank artillery had taken up jumping-off positions for the assault on Mogilev. The artillery attack started at 1730 hours. Fire was brought to bear on the trenches and the outskirts of the city where the enemy had concentrated his main forces. As soon as the last artillery salvoes had died down, the infantry went into the attack supported by the corps and army artillery and the direct fire of the tanks from the east bank of the Dnieper. At first the attack developed successfully. Our units seized individual houses on the outskirts of the city, but their further advance to the centre was stopped by enemy machine-gun and mortar fire. The battle had to be organized anew. The units received fresh supplies of ammunition, tasks were given to artillery and tanks. At 2100 hours, following a short artillery barrage, the 238th and 139th Infantry Divisions repeated the attack. By then units of the 330th Infantry Division had also effected the assault crossing of the Dnieper. This time the attack was a success. Troops of the three infantry divisions burst into the centre of Mogilev. Fierce street fighting continued the whole night in the city.'

During the afternoon of 27 June, Major Lemm arrived at Mogilev, an old wooden city which had been Imperial Headquarters for some time during the First World War, he was taken to the '*Fester Platz*' commander, who had only been appointed that afternoon. It was his own divisional comman-

111

der, Lieutenant-General Rudolf Bamler who had been with the Division for only three weeks, having come from a staff appointment in Norway. He had no experience of warfare on the Eastern Front, and had made himself very unpopular during the short time he had been with the Division. Having walked through the burning streets, Lemm was told that there was no ammunition for the heavy weapons and that there were more than 1,000 wounded men for whom there was no transport. When he reached the Governor's Residence he found General Bamler in the cellar, almost a nervous wreck, talking of nothing save fighting to the last man and to the last round. 'He said that he had no orders for me. I decided to break out with my Battalion, and asked General Bamler to give me orders to do so. He replied that he had received a personal order from the Führer to hold the "*Fester Platz*". I replied that surely the Führer would not want to lose a complete division which had no ammunition. He called for the Divisional Legal Advisor and asked him what would be the result of ordering a breakout contrary to the Führer's orders. The advisor said it was quite clear – he would be court-martialled and sentenced to death.' Lemm made a remark to the effect that it would be better to have one dead general than 8,000 men in captivity. Then the General said: 'Do what you will,' and left the room. After his capture, Bamler was one of those generals who collaborated with the Russians. It is interesting that another prisoner noted that General Bamler was always looking out for his own welfare.' He not only did everything that the Russians asked him to do, but anything he thought they might like. He was not just interested in getting home, but was ambitious to play a leading role in the government of East Germany.'[4]

Later that evening, Major Lemm led his battalion out of Mogilev after hand-to-hand fighting with Russian infantry. They made their way along by-roads and tracks, destroying three Soviet tanks with close-combat anti-tank weapons, and eventually reached the Beresina. The last message received from Mogilev at 2200 hours stated that only the city centre was in German hands. After that, silence.

General Smirnov reported that the city had been completely cleared and that over 3,000 officers and men had been taken prisoner, including the *Feste Plätz* commander, General Bamler and the staff of the German 12th Infantry Division. The former commander, Major-General Gottfried von Erdmannsdorff was also taken prisoner and was executed by the Russians in 1946 for war crimes.

General von Tippelskirch, understood the position quite clearly and ordered his Army to withdraw in bounds to the west. The overriding priority now was to prevent the encirclement of his Army by the main Soviet thrusts to the north and south, and in order to do this the Army had to withdraw over the Beresina before the Soviet mobile formations could take the vital river crossings. The first trains carrying 5th Panzer Division were arriving in the area west of the Beresina, Hitler having agreed to transfer the Division from Army Group North Ukraine on 24 June. Its arrival was timely.

NOTES

1. HQ USA REUR MS T.31. Von der Gröben, *Collapse of Army Group Centre, 1944*, p. 62.
2. Glantz, *Art of War Symposium 1985*, pp. 36lff; supplemented by interviews with Lieutenant-General Lemm.
3. Smirnov, D. *In the Mogilev direction*, abridged from *The Liberation of Belorussia, 1944*, Moscow, 1970.
4. Knappe, Siegfried, *Soldat: Reflections of a German Soldier, 1936–1949*, London, Airlife Publishing, 1992, p. 336.

14
IN THE SOUTH:
NINTH ARMY AND BOBRUISK

On 23 June, First Belorussian Front began the reconnaissance phase of the offensive, using battalion-strength attacks to confirm the German positions in preparation for the attack on the following day. All but two of the limited penetrations were cleared up by German local reserves. The artillery preparation for the main attack began at 0400 hours. An author who endured such a bombardment describes what it was like: 'Shells of countless guns of every calibre pounded the German positions. Metre after metre of ground was torn up, giant craters changed the landscape, everywhere were shell-holes and crater after crater. In this howling, crashing, roaring, exploding inferno individual shell bursts could not be distinguished. Obstacles were torn apart, bunkers and dugouts were flattened and buried, whole trenches were levelled, direct hits struck machine-gun and mortar positions. Artillery positions disappeared under grey-brown-black clouds of smoke, guns were tossed into the air, ammunition being kept at readiness exploded. Dead, bloody and dying men lay among the fountains of earth and muck which constantly sprang up. Those who survived cowered in their battered trenches and half-destroyed positions, scarcely aware of what was going on around them. Aircraft bearing the red star roared overhead, dropping sticks of bombs and leaving behind them walls of fire. Then the Soviet rifle divisions attacked.'[1]

The two northern armies did not fare too well on the first day, which Soviet sources put down to inadequate reconnaissance, marshy ground, poor preparation of the crossings over the Drut, and wet weather with poor visibility.

Colonel-General A. V. Gorbatov's 3rd Army made an initial penetration of 10 kilometres along the boundaries between the German Fourth and Ninth Armies. Although Lieutenant-General P. L. Romanenko's 48th Army made little progress, Army Group Centre agreed to the proposal made by the Army Commander, General Jordan, that the only armoured reserve, 20th Panzer Division, should move up behind XXXV Corps. But the situation to the south of Bobruisk deteriorated even more as Colonel-General P. I. Batov's attack south-east of the city with 65th Army went so well that he was able to release his 1st Guards Tank Corps to develop the situation, and by the end of the day had penetrated the German positions to a depth of 8 kilometres on a front of 24 kilometres. However, XXXXI Corps still hoped to restore the situation and it may be for this reason that Army Group agreed to the committal of part of 20th Panzer Division to the north.

The 20th Panzer Division had been formed in 1940 after the fall of France. It was an experienced division, having fought on the Eastern Front since June 1941, its commander, Lieutenant-General Mortimer von Kessel, having taken part in many battles including Kursk. Although the 2nd Battalion of its Panzer Regiment was not present because it was converting to Panzer Vs (Panther), the 1st Battalion had a strength of 71 Panzer IV Long Gun tanks. The Division was organized into an armoured group and an infantry group, both having some artillery support. The armoured group attacked in the afternoon, due east from Podsely, on the boundary between Fourth and Ninth Armies, to support 134th Division. While this attack was in progress and the infantry group were moving up, Ninth Army ordered the division to disengage and move to the south of Bobruisk to counter-attack an even more dangerous enemy penetration.

Colonel Fricke, adjutant of Panzer Grenadier Regiment 59, the infantry component of the armoured group, describes what happened: 'The attack started with the Panzer Grenadiers on foot supported by the tank guns, but in the middle of the attack it was called to a halt ... The orders were to disengage ourselves immediately and to head back south in order to check a serious enemy attack.

'I am sure you can picture the situation. If during a battle the unit receives a new order to disengage from the enemy, this presents a major problem. To free oneself from the clutches of a powerful force of enemy armour is incredibly difficult. Those units and companies could not march in peace-time formation. The roads and tracks were jam-packed with administrative vehicles and civilians fleeing from the Russians; there were constant air attacks; detours were through swampland. In other words the whole march was extremely difficult. Above all we were determined to take our wounded comrades with us, and in that situation this proved to be extremely hard.'

Leaving one tank company behind to support 134th Division, 20th Panzer carried out a night move under appalling conditions. At 0600 hours the Divisional Commander reported to XXXXI Corps and was ordered to attack with his leading group – the infantry, to be joined by the armoured group on arrival – the enemy forces that had advanced into the area to the west of Slobodka. These consisted of 1st Guards Tank Corps which was making good

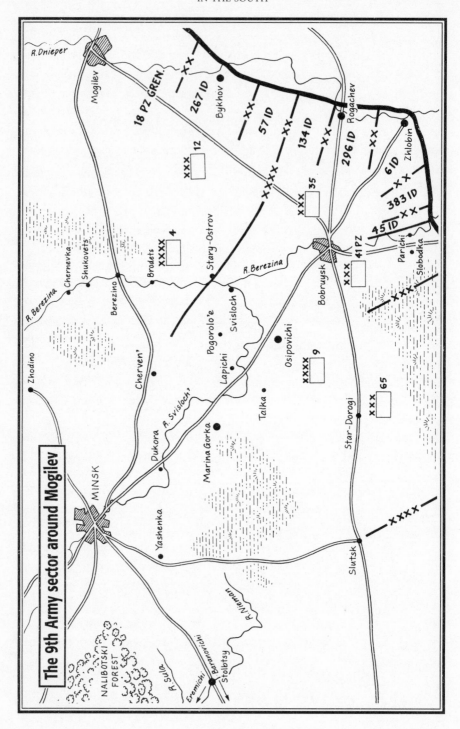

The 9th Army sector around Mogilev

progress in its advance north-westwards to cut off Bobruisk from the west. Although 20th Panzer destroyed some 60 Soviet tanks, its own tank strength had fallen to as low as 40, and it was unable to stem the Soviets' progress.

General Jordan and his Chief of Staff now realized that unless 20th Panzer Division could hold up the Soviet encircling forces, the formations of XXXV Corps to the east of Bobruisk would be in great danger. Field Marshal Busch turned down their request: 'I was expecting this request. But the communications centre of Zhlobin is to be held. I can't agree to it this evening, I must clear it with OKH. It's too late to do that now [*sic*].'[2] The operations log of Ninth Army for 25 June reads: 'Since Army Group has given us no reinforcements, Ninth Army too is in no position to contain the breakthrough as long as 20th Panzer Division has to remain committed to its attack. This attack faces a marsh and at least one tank corps; it no longer has any chance of success.'

By now General Jordan was completely disillusioned with the Field Marshal's conduct of the battle, as is revealed in the War Diary: 'HQ Ninth Army is fully aware of the disastrous consequences of all these orders. It can accept them only inasmuch as, after representing his opposing view upwards in a responsible manner, a commander in the field is obliged to carry out the orders of his superior, even if these go against his own convictions. It is a bitter pill to swallow, though, when one feels that, behind these Army Group instructions which so utterly ignore one's own pressing suggestions, and behind the answers given by the Field Marshal and his Chief of Staff, one can see no sign of a commander showing any purposeful will to do his utmost, but just the execution of orders whose basis has long since been overtaken by events.'[3] Clearly General Jordan had no doubts about the fate that was staring his Army in the face, but even he had not grasped the dimensions of the disaster looming on the horizon as the Soviets not only encircled Bobruisk but pressed on to Minsk and Slutsk.

On the morning of 26 June it became obvious that 20th Panzer could do nothing more to the south of Bobruisk and it was ordered to disengage and block the south-western approaches to the city. Enemy tank forces had demolished the bridge on the direct route and the Division had to make a wide detour across the road bridge over the Berezina in the suburb of Titovka. Half the Division managed to get across before Soviet tanks from 9th Tank Corps arriving from Mogilev to the north captured the bridge.

On the Soviet side the mobile forces of the left wing of First Belorussian Front were released with 1st Tank Corps advancing north-west to encircle

Bobruisk from the west and Lieutenant-General I. A. Pliev's cavalry/mechanized group of 1st Guards Cavalry Corps and 1st Mechanized Corps aiming directly westward for the vital communications centre of Baranovichi through which German reinforcements would be brought forward.

On 26 June Busch flew to the Obersalzberg to present the facts of the rapidly deteriorating position to Hitler and try to get some change in his 'Hold Firm' policy so that some of the formations of Army Group Centre could be salvaged before it was too late. The Field Marshal was accompanied by General Jordan who had been summoned by Hitler to explain his conduct of the battle, in particular his use of 20th Panzer Division. Although Army Group Centre had appreciated that the two major Soviet thrusts would join eventually in the area of Minsk, they still had not recognized that the Soviet plan was even more ambitious, and aiming farther west. Hitler agreed to Ninth Army's retiring into the Bobruisk position, not knowing that the move had been afoot since midday. During the morning, Soviet 9th Tank Corps blocked all road and river crossings north and east of Bobruisk, thus cutting off the greater part of Ninth Army.

The deployment of 20th Panzer Division to the north of the Army area was understandable but premature because now it was unable to move south in sufficient time to deal with the far more dangerous threat developing in the south. Just when it was most needed, when even its low strength would have had a limited effect on the Soviet advance, its tanks, artillery and infantry were entangled on bad roads crowded with refugees. Some authorities believe that the lesser of two evils would have been to split the Division into two groups which could have bought time by meeting the Soviet thrusts head on, but it is difficult to believe that this would not have meant the destruction of this fine Division. For his part in the deployment of the Division, although its movements were approved if not ordered by Army Group Centre, General Jordan was dismissed by Hitler, his command of Ninth Army having lasted for only a few weeks. He was replaced by General der Panzertruppen Nikolaus von Vormann. The next day Field Marshal Busch was dismissed and replaced by one of Hitler's favourite generals, Field Marshal Walter Model. This was recorded in Ninth Army's War Diary on 29 June: 'The news of Field Marshal Model's arrival is noted with satisfaction and confidence.'

NOTES

1. Buchner, p. 159.
2. Niepold, p. 109.
3. *Ibid.*, p. 110.
4. *Ibid.*, p. 159.

15
5TH PANZER DIVISION AND 5TH GUARDS TANK ARMY

On the morning of 24 June, Hitler decided to release 5th Panzer Division from Army Group North Ukraine for employment in Army Group Centre's area, despite the belief in OKH that the main blow of the Soviet summer offensive was yet to fall. The 5th Panzer Division was part of LVI Panzer Corps and had taken part in the spring fighting to raise the siege of Kovel, an important communications centre. The commander of LVI Corps was an unusual soldier. For almost four years, General of Infantry Friedrich Hossbach had been, as a major, Hitler's Wehrmacht Adjutant. This was a position of more influence than is implied by the English rendering of the word 'Adjutant'. In Germany it meant more a confidential military adviser. Hossbach had held his appointment during the formative years of the Wehrmacht. He is known particularly for the notes he took of the secret meeting held at the Chancellery on 5 November 1937 at which Hitler told his senior commanders that if necessary he would go to war to achieve his long-term aims. Hossbach expanded his notes into a memorandum, later known as the 'Hossbach Memorandum', which was used as evidence at the Nuremberg war crimes trials. Hossbach was dismissed by Hitler because of the part he had played at the time of the Blomberg/Fritsch affair; he had warned General Fritsch that he was to be prosecuted for homosexuality. After the war began, Hossbach commanded an infantry division on the Eastern Front until taking command of LVI Panzer Corps; in 1945 he was commanding Fourth Army in east Prussia and was dismissed by Hitler for attempting to break out with his troops without permission.

The 5th Panzer Division had been formed in November 1938, its personnel being from Silesia and the Sudetenland which had only recently been annexed by Germany. It had fought well in France in 1940 and in the Balkans. Its 2nd Panzer Regiment was used to form the famous 11th Panzer Division. It fought on the central sector of the Eastern Front from June 1941, playing a prominent part in the fighting for Moscow, and in the unsuccessful Kursk offensive. During the spring of 1944, the Division had fought in the area east of Bobruisk, where Soviet forces were trying to take Rogachev, and was then moved to re-establish communications with Kovel until May.

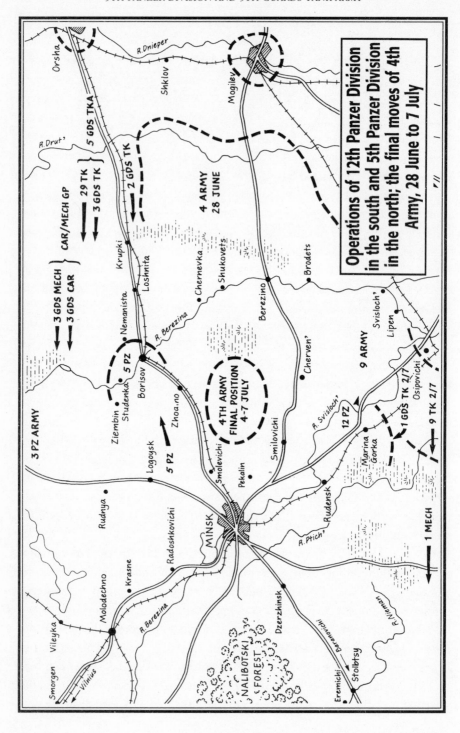

Operations of 12th Panzer Division in the south and 5th Panzer Division in the north; the final moves of 4th Army, 28 June to 7 July

After the heavy fighting endured by the Division, it was allowed 12 days' rest and recuperation. During this time 1st Battalion, 31st Panzer Regiment returned from a lengthy period in Germany where it had been re-equipping with Panzer V (Panther) tanks. The Division now had a tank strength of 70 Panzer V and 55 Panzer IV (Long Gun) tanks, but it was weak in infantry, the panzer grenadier companies having an average strength of 35 as against the establishment figure of about 150.[1]

The Commander of 5th Panzer Division was Major-General Karl Decker, a very experienced 'panzerman' who had served continuously on the Eastern Front from June 1941. Later, he commanded a panzer corps until the end of the war. Although not a general staff officer, he was an excellent commander and was deeply concerned about the welfare of his men, who regarded him as a superb fighting divisional commander.

The Division's First General Staff officer or '1a' ('Chief G3' in modern NATO terminology) was Lieutenant-Colonel Anton Detlev von Plato, a Hanoverian whose family had lived in the same village near the Elbe since the year 900. When he joined the cavalry in 1930, his father insisted that he enlist in Saxony rather in one of the nearby barracks in Hanover so that he would not have to wear the hated black-and-white Prussian cockade. A surprising survival of regional feeling! After four years he was transferred to General Guderian's experimental armoured unit and once the trials were completed he was posted to 3rd Panzer Division, one of the first panzer divisions to be established. He held various appointments in one of the panzer grenadier regiments and was a commander of a motor cycle company at the beginning of the war. After his general staff course he was sent to 1st Panzer Division as 2nd General Staff Officer under Colonel Wenck, one of the best-known staff officers, who in 1945 commanded Twelfth Army around Berlin – Hitler's last hope. Lieutenant Colonel von Plato was appointed to 5th Panzer Division in October 1943 and remained with it until he was appointed Chief of Staff of the reconstituted XXVII Corps. After the war he joined the Bundeswehr and rose to the rank of lieutenant-general; he commanded the Armour School at Münster, and was the first German Chief of Staff at the NATO Northern Army Group, finally commanding a corps. He also wrote the history of 5th Panzer Division.

On 22 June the Divisional staff heard on the General Staff radio bulletin reporting that the Russians had attacked Army Group Centre in the Vitebsk area. No details were given because the 'need to know' principle was being strictly adhered to. On the 25th at 0100 hours the Division was ordered to move to the Bobruisk area, entraining at Chelm. During the journey, their destination was altered to Borisov and Krupki, east of the Beresina. There were numerous delays caused by partisan demolitions and low-flying fighter-bomber attacks. The first trains arrived at Borisov on 27 June. The very experienced Pioneer Battalion 89 was first to arrive and supervised the unloading of the Division, aided by the divisional reconnaissance battalion which was next to arrive. The command staff of the Division had already arrived by road, having received orders from HQ Army Group Centre at Minsk. On the 28th, unloading had to be transferred there because the constant air attacks made it impossible to unload at Borisov. The Panthers of Panzer Regiment 31, had to fight Soviet tanks from the railway wagons before they could be unloaded from the last train to reach Borisov. The engineer battalion tried to set up delaying positions along the highway to the east near Krupki under command of SS Gruppenführer Joachim von Gottberg who had an *ad hoc* force of two police regiments and some hastily assembled battalions. The 5th Panzer Division established its headquarters at Nemanitsa, six kilometres north-east of Borisov.

On 28 June, new orders were given to both the Soviet and German forces. The four Fronts were given the task of liberating Minsk as soon as possible and pressing on to the west. The German orders promulgated in Hitler Order No. 8 (Appendix VIII) were aimed at creating a defensive position along the line of the Berezina, with three counter-stroke panzer groups available to restore the situation if necessary.

That evening the first fruits of the appointment of Field Marshal Model became manifest. He recommended that two divisions be transferred from Army Group North to Minsk with that formation pulling back its right flank to Polotsk. In addition, the 28th Light (Jäger) Division to move from the south to Slutsk and the assembly of 4th Panzer Division at Baranovichi to be accelerated.[2]

That same evening the Army Group order to close the widening gap between Third Panzer and Fourth Armies was issued. To shield Borisov from the north-east and attempt to regain ground lost already Lieutenant-General Dietrich von Saucken, using the staff of XXXIX Panzer Corps, was to take command of 5th Panzer Division with 505th Heavy Tank Battalion (Tiger) under command, and HQ von Gottburg with various SS units also under command. One of the most highly decorated panzer officers on the Eastern

Front, and later to command the élite Grossdeutschland Panzer Corps, von Saucken was an old friend, his 4th Panzer having fought alongside the Division during the recent winter and spring battles. As he had no headquarters, he was lent personnel with vehicles and radios.

So little was known about the enemy's progress that the reconnaissance battalion was ordered to gather information on the attacks north and north-east of Borisov. They reported that Soviet tanks were moving westwards in large numbers, and that there was a force crossing the Berezina, 50 kilometres to the north. The 13th Panzer Grenadier Regiment was ordered to hold a line north-east of Borisov during the night, and at first light they were attacked by tanks and infantry. Close-quarter fighting lasted all day and as neither the German tanks nor artillery could move forward because of enemy aircraft dogging their every move, the grenadiers had to fight with grenades, bazookas and mines. When the Panthers eventually arrived they destroyed six Soviet tanks and the grenadiers were able to consolidate and hold their position. A further attack by fifty tanks was beaten off later that evening. These would appear to have been from 29th Tank Corps, on the right of 5th Guards Tank Army.

Two of the best-known armoured formations on either side had now come up against each other. 5th Guards Tank Army had been formed in March 1943, as a consequence of the Soviet wish to restructure the Red Army, in particular to give it formations powerful enough to sustain deep operational movement and capable of acting as the forward mobile groups of individual Fronts. The 5th Guards distinguished itself at Kursk and later in the Belgorod counter-offensive. It was commanded by General P. A. Rotmistrov, who was shortly to be promoted Marshal of Armoured Forces in the Stavka. With two tank corps, 3rd Guards Tank and 29th Tank, the army had a powerful strike force of 524 tanks and assault guns.

On the morning of 29 June reports came in that the Soviet tanks that had crossed the Berezina in the north were advancing westwards. To counter them the Division moved elements of 14th Panzer Grenadier Regiment supported by tanks of 31st Panzer Regiment, recently unloaded at Minsk, to a blocking position at Logoysk in the direction of Rudnia. These Soviet tanks were from 3rd Guards Mechanized Corps of the cavalry/mechanized group commanded by General Oslikovski.

The 5th Guards Tank Army kept up its pressure on the bridgehead of Borisov and attempted crossings further north to outflank the main position.

During the morning an attempt was made to cross the river near Studenka, 12 kilometres to the north of Borisov. This was where Napoleon built two trestle bridges after the Borisov bridge was destroyed during his retreat in November 1812.

The fighting at Rudnia continued throughout the 29th, five Soviet tanks being destroyed. The reconnaissance battalion managed to hold out to the west at Ziembin, and the '1a', Lieutenant-Colonel von Plato, himself took a battle group of 31st Panzer Regiment to support them which indicates the importance placed upon the services of the unit as the 'Eyes of the Division'. For his action on this day, von Plato received the *Ritterkreuz*. General von Saucken arrived to take overall command of the situation and found that he was ordered to delay the Soviet advance to Minsk for as long as possible and to keep open the Berezina crossings so that the remnant of Fourth Army would not be cut off.

The remnant was in a bad state: 'This was no longer a retirement, nor an orderly withdrawal, rather a mass of men hysterically fighting their way back through an extended area of forests and swamps, criss-crossed by many rivers and streams whose crossings had already been destroyed, over mostly poor roads, in tremendous heat, without adequate provisions, and threatened from all sides. Soon assailed from the flanks and pursued from the rear, the decimated regiments and battle groups had to hold off well-armed partisan bands and regular troops of the Red Army, cover and protect the main column, and fight their way back through Soviet blocking positions ... Soviet close-support aircraft repeatedly strafed the defenceless foot and horse-drawn columns by day and bombed them by night. There were no German aircraft to be seen.'[3]

As they drew nearer to the bridge the scene became even more incredible. Another eye-witness gives his impression: 'There were many assault guns, Panthers, Tigers, light and heavy artillery, completely new weapons and equipment from the "Feldherrnhalle", out of fuel, blown up, bombed. Close to the bridge, where the crush was greatest, scenes like none I had ever seen before were played out. Vehicles pressed towards the bridge from all directions, each trying to be first across. This obstacle had to be passed as quickly as possible. How much longer would the bridge be standing? The next artillery salvo could bring it down for good. Drivers were told not to allow any strange vehicles into their columns, and they were told not to stop. About ten columns pressed towards the bridge side by side; however only one could cross at a time. The vehicles on the "highway" had every intention of being the first across. There was cursing and fighting. One horse-drawn vehicle drove into another. Wheels broke. More wrecks were added to the vehicles already destroyed. The military police were powerless. Finally everyone ran for his own life. The bridge had to be crossed!'[4]

There were a few other bridges over the Berezina where the same desperate scenes were played out. At Berezino the bridgehead was guarded by a task force drawn from 31st and 267th Infantry Divisions under command of General Vincenz Müller, Commander XII Corps. On the 29th the bridge received a direct hit. The engineers who bravely tried to repair it were under constant attack from the air, as were the columns of men piling up and waiting to cross. It was hit again during the day and another 15 metres of the structure was destroyed. The engineers said that they would still be able to meet their deadline of 1700 hours, but by dint of superhuman efforts, they managed to improve even on this and the bridge was ready by 1600 hours.

All attacks on the bridgehead at Borisov were repelled during the 29th, but other pressures were beginning to make themselves felt. Soviet tanks of the cavalry/mechanized group were striking towards Minsk and Molodechno from the north, and forces had to be found to deal with this threat. Permission was given to contract the bridgehead, and this was held against constant attack throughout the 30th by 13th Panzer Grenadier Regiment's battle group. Finally permission to blow the bridges was given during the evening and after the covering forces had withdrawn they were blown by 89th Engineer Battalion.

The day of 1 July was relatively quiet in the north with a few armoured thrusts which were easily repulsed by the tanks of 31st Panzer Regiment and the 'Tigers' of 505th Heavy Tank Battalion. The fiercest action took place along the axis west of Borisov where elements of the division retired behind a succession of small river lines.

The rivers posed problems for the Soviet mobile forces as well. On the southern flank of 5th Guards Tank Army, 2nd Guards Tank Corps, acting as the mobile group for 31st Army was ordered to cross the Berezina south of Borisov, and advance to the Moscow-Minsk railway line near Zhodino and then on to Minsk. The original intention was to 'bounce' a crossing on the march, but this failed. General Burdeiny then decided to mount an assault crossing in the area of Chernyavka, where the river was only 100-110 metres wide. However attempts to cross were hampered by a wide flood plain stretching for 600-800 metres in front of the river, which made it difficult for tanks to approach. He ordered the submachine-gun battalions of the Corps to make the crossing supported by the entire Corps artillery. Rafts were prepared to take the leading tanks and anti-tank guns across the river.

The leading engineers found that the Germans had set the existing bridge on fire. They managed to extinguish the flames, and then set about the construction of a makeshift bridge using the surviving piles and spans. They also laid a road across the flood plain using trees and brushwood from the banks of the river, with a ramp up to the remaining section of the bridge. The situation improved when the pontoon battalion arrived and set up a floating bridge. Once the crossing was under way, the Corps Commander and his staff went forward to meet the commander of the partisan group operating in the forests to the west of Chernyavka. He was able to give valuable information concerning routes along which the tanks could travel at a speed of up to 30km/hr despite the bad roads, and indicate the German positions and possible road-blocks.[5]

Lieutenant Degan of 2nd Guards Separate Tank Brigade describes an amusing incident when he crossed the Beresina as part of the follow-up forces: 'When we got to the banks of the Berezina, we looked for somewhere for our tanks to cross. We had 20 or 21 tanks, a battalion. There was no place to cross. Then we approached the bridge in Borisov, a railway bridge, but it was completely destroyed. Next to it a new pontoon bridge had been built. A colonel was commanding the crossing. He said: "I cannot allow tanks over. This bridge won't hold them." But my battalion commander had ordered me to find a crossing come what may. So I went up to this colonel and started to argue with him: "Comrade Colonel, I've got to get these tanks across." He just said: "Go away!" and there was no talking to him. At that very moment I happened to see a Marshal getting out of a jeep. For the first time in my life I was seeing a real live Marshal. I recognized him immediately as Marshal Vasilevsky. Vasilevsky caught sight of me. I was in overalls and he couldn't see my shoulder tabs. "Tank driver! Come here!" I went up to him. "What's the matter?" he asked. "Comrade Marshal of the Soviet Union," I said, and I told him how I had to get the tanks across, but there was no crossing. "How many tanks have you got?" he asked. "Twenty-one," I said. "Colonel!" he said, "Let these tanks cross." The colonel replied: "I cannot let these tanks cross, the bridge won't hold them." Then the Marshal tore a strip off the colonel, swearing at him. "Do you think we're fighting this war in motor cars? Let these tanks over first!"

And so this was how I managed, quite by chance, to carry out my orders successfully, all thanks to meeting a Marshal. Now there's a thing!"[6]

To return to 5th Panzer Division. The reports that Krasnoe and Molodechno had fallen proved false, as only reconnaissance patrols had been in the area. But the situation developed and a fierce battle for Krasnoe erupted on 2 July. In effect, the Division was fighting in three completely different directions. Combat Group 1 with 2nd Battalion, 14th Panzer Grenadier Regiment, the Field Replacement Battalion with elements of 31st Panzer Regiment and 89th Engineer Battalion were fighting for the Krasnoe–Molodechno position. Combat Group 2 with 13th Panzer Grenadier Regiment, the main body of 89th Engineer Regiment, and elements of 31st Panzer Regiment were struggling for Radoshkovichi against heavy tank and infantry attacks. Combat Group 3 with 1st Battalion, 14th Panzer Grenadier Regiment, Tiger Battalion 505, and some tanks from 31st Panzer Regiment were fighting for Logoysk. Effectively the Division was facing north-west, north and north-east at the same time and conducting three separate battles over a distance of more than 70 kilometres. Only radio communication was possible, and this stretched the limited command facilities to the utmost.

The Divisional Commander was supported by his principal staff officer, '1a' and three subordinate staff officers: the '1b' who looked after the administration of the Division, the '1c' who was responsible for intelligence, and the '1d' who assisted '1a'. At this stage in the war, the '1c' and sometimes the '1d' at division were not general staff officers. The specialist officers were normally the commanding officers of the supporting arms; for example, the commanding officer of the divisional artillery regiment was also the artillery adviser to the Divisional Commander. In this situation the Division established two command posts: the '1a'" with half the command post set up in the north-west near Molodechno, and General Decker, the Divisional Commander, used the other half to command Combat Groups 2 and 3.

Combat Group 1 succeeded in retaking Molodechno, despite almost continuous attacks from the air. The significance of this was that the railway line to Vilnius was re-opened and reinforcements could be brought forward. It was also the main line of retreat for the troops fighting to the north of the Borisov—Minsk highway, as the dense Nalibocki forest prevented any major movement to the west. Almost immediately after the recapture, reinforcements started to arrive. On 2 July, elements of 170th and 221st Divisions began to arrive together with an assault gun battalion.

The recapture of Minsk, the capital of Belorussia, would be of considerable propaganda value to the Soviet High Command. Its loss would be a bitter blow to the Germans. Not only was it a nodal point of road and rail links, of extra importance in this area of poor communications, but it had also been the Headquarters of Army Group Centre. Thus a considerable administrative infrastructure had grown up in and around the city with local government and Party officials, Army administrative units and supply dumps. Perhaps the greatest problem was the number of wounded who had been evacuated from the front to the network of hospitals around the city. As the Russian forces drew nearer to Minsk it became apparent that a degree of panic was breaking out among the rear area troops.

As late as 29 June, Army Group Centre still hoped to stabilize the situation around Minsk and earmarked two divisions from Army Group North to be sent there. These were 170th and 132nd Infantry Divisions. Next day, Fourth Army recognized that there was a grave danger of a further encirclement in the Minsk area. Early on the morning of the 30th, responsibility for 'Fester Plätz Minsk' had been transferred to Ninth Army which had been ordered to improve the state of the city's defences. All that the Commandant had at his disposal were 1,800 men mostly unfit or stragglers without their weapons. However the feeling was growing at Army Group and OKH that there just were not enough troops to hold Minsk, particularly as it was adjudged more important and practical to hold the line Baranovichi—Molodechno. The demolition of military and civilian installations was authorized to begin during the night of 1/2 July. There were still 53 trains in the city, and 15,000 men unfit for battle, without weapons or ammunition, some without proper clothing. On 1 and 2 July, some 8,000 wounded and 12,000 rear echelon personnel, including a large number of female auxiliaries, left on three hospital and 43 other trains. Army Group now accepted that it would not be possible to get the formations of Fourth and Ninth Armies back to the area of Minsk. The Field Marshal told Chief of Staff OKH that his main task was to keep open the corridors leading to the west so that reinforcements could be brought in to stabilize the situation. That night Hitler agreed to 'Fester Platz Minsk' being evacuated.

During the afternoon of 2 July, 2nd Guards Tank Corps continued its dash towards Minsk. After driving nearly 50 kilometres, they liberated Smolovichi, but after that they came up against a German delaying position and lost a number of tanks. The Corps Commander, General Burdeiny, was furious, and blamed commanders and staff alike for not having made adequate reconnaissance and for becoming careless. They paid for this in unnecessary losses. It was apparent that the colossal strain was beginning to show. The tank crews had been fighting day and night for eight days and were extremely tired. The 4th Guards Tank Brigade was in the lead at this stage. It was commanded by Colonel O. A. Losik, who became a Marshal of Armoured Troops after the war. He decided to make a night assault with submachine-gunners following closely behind the leading tanks. They mopped-up another delaying position, destroying four tanks, some guns and two companies of infantry.

The Brigade Commander reported his success to the Corps Commander and was ordered to continue his pursuit up to the eastern outskirts of the city, which he reached at 0200 hours. He was ordered to continue the assault at dawn, which would have been imminent at this time of the year. At this stage, the Soviet commanders were uncertain whether the city would be defended.

The Brigade Commander decided to send in a tank platoon to make a reconnaissance. Under Guards Junior Lieutenant Dimitry Frolikov, they entered the city from the north-east, crushing a German battery before it could get off a single round. There were no other obstacles and this was reported back. Colonel Losik put in two tank battalions in the north-east along the Logoysk road, and the third to the south of the Minsk highway. All three battalions carried submachine-gunners on the tanks. The tanks stormed into the eastern outskirts of the city supported from the flanks by two batteries of self-propelled guns. After overcoming enemy defences on the outskirts, the tanks advanced along parallel streets firing on the move. The submachine-gunners destroyed enemy rocket-launcher teams as they tried to engage the tanks at close quarters. When there was no resistance they travelled on the tanks, keeping a wary eye on the windows of the buildings they passed.

Frolikov's crew acted courageously. His tank was the first to move on to the Leninskiy Prospekt, having destroyed an assault gun, an anti-tank gun and about 30 infantrymen. The tank in which the Minsk citizen, Guards Sergeant Belkevich, was the driver-mechanic, was the first to penetrate the centre of Minsk. He drove among the ruins of his native city along the main street, and at an intersection, destroyed an anti-tank gun and rushed on to Freedom Square. The Brigade then consolidated its position and sent out reconnaissance patrols before resuming its advance to the west.[8] On 3 July, forward units of 1st Guards Tank Corps of First Belorussian Front arrived from the south-east. Minsk, capital city of the Belorussian Republic, had been liberated after three years of war. The Motherland honoured the bravery of 4th Guards Tank Brigade by awarding it the honorary title of 'Minsk' and bestowing the Order of the Red Banner. Colonel Losik was given the title of Hero of the Soviet Union, as was Guards Lieutenant Frolikov. The T-34 tank which today stands in the centre of Minsk is the one that was commanded by Frolikov in his dash on the morning of 3 July 1944.[9]

Once Hitler had agreed to give up Minsk without serious opposition, 5th Panzer Division concentrated on keeping open its withdrawal route to the north-west through Molodechno. The 13th Panzer Grenadier Regiment held a blocking position east of Radoshkovichi to allow the Division to reassemble behind it, in order to counter-attack, as ordered, to the south-west. But this attack was continually postponed and eventually cancelled through lack of fuel, held up because of the congestion on the roads. Heavy fighting swayed back and forth throughout the day.

Colonel von Plato recorded that during the first six days of combat, the Division and Tiger Battalion 505 destroyed some 295 tanks, but their own losses were correspondingly high. Lieutenant Degan tells how difficult it was to fight the German tanks: 'I must confess we knew the German tanks were very powerful. For example, they had tanks like the Tiger, the Panther, and the self-propelled gun, the Ferdinand. We thought that they were very fearsome because for a start they had much thicker armour: the frontal armour on a Tiger was 300mm and on the T34 it was 120mm. The German guns were much more powerful than our 85mm. Their guns had a much higher muzzle velocity and they could hit us quickly at a distance of 2 kilometres.

'I couldn't do anything with a German tank like a Tiger or a Panther if I met it head on. If I was going to win, I had to find its weak spot, and that meant approaching it from the side. So our usual tactics, when we were advancing and knew that there might be a tank ambush ahead, was to advance suddenly, stop and open fire as if we knew there was something there, and often turn round and take to our heels. We hoped they would open fire, and we would then be able to see where they were firing from and could then fight back.'[10]

During the night of 3 July, 5th Panzer Division was given orders for a further attack to the south on the flank of the Soviet thrust from Minsk towards the north-west. However the attacks of 3rd Guards Cavalry Corps and 3rd Guards Mech Corps of the cavalry/mechanized group under General Oslikovski aimed at cutting the road and rail link between Smorgon and Molodechno presented a greater danger, so the orders were altered. The Division would attack towards the Smorgon area to the north-west. It extricated itself with difficulty from the current battle around Radoshkovichi. The fighting of the next few days was very confusing with the Division attacking to the north to try to delay the Soviet forces heading for Vilnius.

For the Germans, the priority was to try to build a defensive line along the railway line north-west to Vilnius, and to close the gap between the remnant of Third Panzer Army in the north in the area around Polotsk and those elements of Fourth Army fighting for their lives outside the large pocket to the east of Minsk. The role of 5th Panzer Division in this plan was to delay the Soviet advance on Vilnius for as long as possible, despite their exhaustion. Against very heavy odds, they had been fighting an enemy who was able to introduce new formations at will, with a superiority in tanks of 20:1 and in artillery 35:1, and with constant air support.

However the Soviet troops were beginning to feel the strain of advancing so far in a relatively short period of time, surpassing anything that had been attempted before. It is not easy to learn details of the difficulties encountered by the Soviet armoured formations, because the memories of them were forgotten in the euphoria of their achievement. However Lieutenant Degan gives an indication of the state of his platoon in 2nd Guards Independent Tank Brigade: 'In Borisov, we got new tanks and new crews but we didn't manage to move out of the rear. The brigade had no fuel, no shells and no ammunition. My platoon was re-equipped and was given everything there was. We got our shells from other tanks and we got fuel from others and our spare fuel tanks were filled. Then we were ordered to proceed to Vilnius.'

The closing of the pocket around Minsk marked the end of the second of the planned stages of the Soviet offensive, and the Stavka and its representatives in the field now began to implement the third stage, designed to push the German forces farther to the west. This involved a considerable regrouping of forces and moving of Front boundaries in order to achieve their new objectives. Three operations took place simultaneously. In the north, First Baltic Front, its boundary moved southwards, began an operation designed to clear the German forces from northern Belorussia and advance into Lithuania. This was called the Dvina Operation by the Soviets and eventually included Second Baltic Front.

In the Vilnius operation, Third Belorussian Front was ordered to continue its advance towards that important city, and was allocated continued use of 5th Guards Tank Army. It became the spearhead of the operation, but by now it was beginning to lose its effectiveness. Soviet armour had advanced 200 to 250 kilometres which was close to its operational limits of sustaining forward momentum. Most of the Soviet armoured units had to be recalled for re-fitting and re-supply half way through the offensive.

The Bialystok/Brest operation in the south pushed back the remnant of Army Group Centre to the borders of eastern Poland. At the end of the second phase of the Soviet offensive, 5th Panzer Division had virtually fought itself to a standstill. The Division had started out with a formidable tank strength of 70 Panthers and 55 Panzer IV (Long) tanks supported by 20 Tigers of 505 Heavy Tank Battalion. By 9 July, tank strength was down to 12 Panthers and 6 Mk IV (Long) and an unknown number of Tigers. However, for the first time in the fighting they were close to their own workshops which were able to repair most tanks that were recovered. On 9 July, tank strength increased to 25 Panthers, 25 Pz IVs and 15 Tigers, all battleworthy. The Division reported that since 27 June it had destroyed 486 Soviet tanks, 11 assault guns, 119 anti-tank guns and 100 trucks.[11]

When the situation became quieter, the commander of 13th Panzer Grenadier Regiment, Major Friedrich, wrote: 'The fighting was the heaviest we had ever experienced. We fought by camouflaging ourselves, firing everything we had, withdrawing and then attacking again from a different direction. This meant that everyone from the Commander down to the youngest grenadier had to give of their utmost. Sleep was totally out of the question. These days of heroism, sacrifice and privation cannot be described in words. It would be wrong to mention individuals or units because all gave of their best.'

Perhaps the greatest compliment was heard on the Soviet radio net: 'If you meet 5th Panzer, try to go round them!'[12]

NOTES

1. This chapter was based on interviews with Generalleutenant von Plato, and upon his address to the 1985 Art of War symposium.
2. Niepold, p. 149.
3. Buchner, p. 162.
4. Hinze, Rolf, *Der Zusammenbruch der Heeresgruppe Mitte im Osten*, Stuttgart, Motorbuch Verlag, 1980, as quoted in Buchner, p. 164.
5. Storodumov, Major-General I., The 2nd Guards Tanks Corps in the Belorussian Opera-

tion, Moscow, Voyenno-Istoricheskiy Zhurnal, Translated AMC, p. 35.

6. Interview with Professor Degan at Tel Aviv.
7. Shorodumov, pp. 36-7.
8. Belousov, Colonel A., 'Tank Attack' in *Voyenny Vestnik*, No. 7, 1979, Translated AMC, p. 45.
9. *Ibid.*, p. 46.
10. Professor Degan.
11. Symposium, p. 409.
12. *Ibid.*, p. 405.

16
12TH PANZER DIVISION IN THE SOUTH

During the afternoon of 27 June, the train carrying the advance party of 12th Panzer Division arrived in the area of Marina Gorka–Osipovichi in the rear of Ninth Army. With reluctance Hitler had released this panzer division from Army Group North to stem the advance of the right wing of Rokossovsky's First Belorussian Front which was already threatening to cut off the whole of Ninth Army east of Bobruisk, a situation made yet more critical by the hasty commitment of 20th Panzer Division three days earlier.

The 12th Panzer Division had been formed in 1940 from 2nd Motorized Division and had fought continuously on the Eastern Front since June 1941. By 1944 the once almost 100 per cent Pomeranian content had been diluted and now it had men from all over Germany, even from Alsace. Of the latter there were some who had served in the French Foreign Legion. Divisional strength was 11,600 officers and men with some 681 Russian '*Hiwis*', auxiliaries mostly recruited from Russian prisoners of war, many of them of German ethnic origin. The Divisional Commander was Lieutenant-General Erpo Freiherr von Bodenhausen, a former cavalry officer; at the time of the offensive he was on leave in Germany, so the Division was commanded by Colonel Gerhard Müller who had lost an arm fighting with the Afrika Korps and had been highly decorated. However he had had little experience on the Eastern Front and so more than usual responsibility fell upon the '1a' or first general staff officer (Chief G3 in NATO terminology).

Lieutenant-Colonel Gerd Niepold had joined the German Army in 1932, attended the Berlin General Staff Course in 1941, and was appointed personal staff officer to General Paulus, who was then responsible for the planning of 'Barbarossa', and later, as a field marshal, surrendered Sixth Army at Stalingrad. By 1944, Niepold was a highly experienced staff officer who, somewhat unusually in the German Army, had served previously in 12th Panzer Division. He had recently returned to the Division from the staff of another panzer corps. After the war he was a lieutenant-general in the *Bundeswehr* and finally served as a corps commander.[1]

Although the Division was incomplete, it still required 53 trains to move it to its new position. Only 2nd Battalion, Panzer Regiment 29 was present with 35 Panzer IV Long and 9 Panzer III Long tanks, the 1st Battalion being in Germany at Putlos converting to Panzer V Panthers. There were four infantry or panzer grenadier battalions, one of which was carried in armoured personnel carriers (SPWs) and the other three in unarmoured trucks. Panzer Artillery Regiment 2 had 22 guns including 12 'Wespe' self-propelled howitzers mounted on Panzer II chassis. Only one company of the divisional anti-tank battalion was present, the remainder plus the reconnaissance battalion, the anti-aircraft battalion and part of the engineer battalion were refitting in Germany, or in Kurland. Their absence would be felt keenly in the weeks to come.

Having passed train-loads of administrative troops and civilians with their baggage, all travelling westwards, the Division's first train arrived in fine sunny weather in the Marina Gorka area, only to be halted by a railway official with the news that the line ahead had been demolished to prevent its use by the Soviets and that the unloading ramp was about to be blown up so speed of unloading was imperative. A company of tanks and two mechanized infantry companies were swiftly off-loaded and sent to secure high ground to the east.

The '1a' set out for Ninth Army's command post where he met the Chief of Staff of the Army, Major-General Helmut Staedke, who had been his Tactics Instructor at the General Staff Course in Berlin in 1941. He greeted him with: 'Good to see you! Ninth Army no longer exists!' He was told that the remnant was in parlous straits. The double prong of Marshal Rokossovsky's attack had succeeded in surrounding the greater part of the army in the Bobruisk area and he was just about to release his exploitation force to the east. This was General Pliyev's cavalry/mechanized group consisting of 4th Guards Cavalry Corps and 1st Mechanized Corps – an unusual grouping but one that the Soviets used extensively as best suited in difficult country such as they faced in the swamps and thick forests of Belorussia.

The position to the east of Bobruisk was chaotic with elements of two corps fighting on the east bank of the Berezina, and only a narrow railway bridge across the river linking them with the city. The 20th Panzer Division had lost most of their tanks in attempting to recapture the wooden road bridge. The Army had first received orders from Field Marshal Busch to plug the gap to the south of the city and later counter-orders to break out from the encircled city. Orders from Hitler later still, insisted that Bobruisk be held, but these were countermanded before the first order was received. Not surprisingly there was a lack of trust in the higher leadership! The final order read: 'New orders from Army Group Commander. XXXXL Panzer Corps and XXXV Corps are to fight their way through to the line Osipovichi – Stary Ostrov and establish a new defensive position there. General Hamann with 383rd Infantry Division is to hold Bobruisk as a "*Fester Platz*". Confirm intention to comply.' This order to break out of the encircled city was virtually the same as the first counter-order, but much irreplaceable time had been lost.

The first priority was to get as many men as possible back across the bridge into Bobruisk. Lieutenant-Colonel Niepold stated later: 'All semblance of order ceased. All over the place vehicles were being blown up and guns spiked. It was simply a confused column of men streaming over the railway bridge into Bobruisk. With the enemy pouring in shells and bombs, the chaos reached its climax.'

For two days elements of XXXV Corps tried to break out to the north but were destroyed in the attempt. The Corps Commander, Lieutenant-General Kurt-Jürgen Freiherr von Lützow, collapsed from the strain and was taken prisoner; he was not released until 1956.

After five 5 days of the offensive, Hitler and OKH in their far-distant headquarters at the Berghof near Berchtesgarden, maintained their view that Army Group North Ukraine had yet to face the main Soviet offensive in the near future. Hitler had lost confidence in Field Marshal Busch and decided to replace him with one of his most trusted generals, Field Marshal Model – this would also have the effect of making it easier to extract reinforcements from Army Group North Ukraine for the poor relation in the north. Himmler reflected the attitude prevalent at the Berghof when he wrote two days earlier: 'In my view the Army Group's command was too soft and war weary.'

Field Marshal Busch had never really been tested in battle as von Runstedt and von Manstein had been, and owed his promotion to his strong Nazi sentiments. General Niepold traces Busch's reluctance to stand up to OKH to Hitler's forceful rejection of the Army Group's proposal to shorten the front and his remark that he had only just realized that the Field Marshal was yet another of those generals who spent their whole time looking over their shoulder. The result was that any attempt by his army commanders to withdraw in front of the enemy to prevent encirclement and to create reserves were rejected out of hand. General Niepold comments: 'There is no disputing that the Army Group Commander felt himself unable to take any independent decision, even over small things. Nor could he brace himself to stand up really firmly to Hitler and argue with his decisions. By his attitude he crippled the ability of his armies to take the kind of action the situation called for.'

Hitler had come to trust Field Marshal Model's ability to stabilize and restore disastrous situations. Withdrawals suggested by other generals would be rejected without discussion, but were accepted if recommended by Model. Hitler called him '*Mein bester Feldmarschall*' and allowed him considerable latitude. An example that gives an idea of their relationship was when Ninth Army, then commanded by Model, faced encirclement during the Battle for Moscow and Model argued with Hitler about the deployment of a vital reinforcement. Finally Model glared at Hitler through his monocle and asked: 'Who commands the Ninth Army, my Führer, you or I?' Hitler uncharacteristically backed down and accepted that Model knew what was happening at the front and should make the tactical decisions. Fortunately for Model, events before Moscow turned out as he had forecast.[2]

In addition to his new command of Army Group Centre, Model retained command of Army Group North Ukraine, exercised through a deputy, Colonel-General Josef Harpe, it being thought that the flow of reinforcements between the army groups would be made easier. Although Model was hard on senior officers, he was popular with the troops who appreciated some of his idiosyncrasies. One such was that he would take a divisional commander up with him in his aircraft, land and then tell the unfortunate, 'Now get out and bring up your division', and then he would fly off again![3]

General of Panzer Troops Nikolaus von Vormann arrived to take over command of Ninth Army and found that the only formation capable of fighting, 12th Panzer Division, was still in the process of arriving.

The shambles in Bobruisk was becoming increasingly chaotic as more troops minus their heavy weapons and vehicles poured across the narrow railway bridge under constant artillery and air attack. Many of the buildings were burning furiously, covering the city with thick smoke. The Soviet forces were maintaining their pressure and were only beaten off at the expense of heavy losses. On 28 June the commander of XXXXI Panzer Corps asked for permission to break out of the encirclement, and this he received but was told to leave one division to defend the '*Fester Platz*'. This requirement was later rescinded, but it was too late for Lieutenant-General Walter Hamann who was captured and later executed by the Russians for alleged war crimes in Bobruisk.

During the afternoon, the staff prepared the plan for the breakout and the Corps Commander, Lieutenant-General Edmund Hoffmeister, issued his orders. The first wave would start at 2300 hours with the armoured group of 20th Panzer Division in the lead followed by the infantry divisions. Only tracked vehicles, 4x4 Volkswagen Field Cars and saddle horses could accompany the column, the remainder were to be destroyed. The rearguard would remain in position until 0200 hours next day.

General Hoffmeister had to make the heart-rending decision to leave behind the seriously wounded who numbered 3,500. They were left in the citadel with the very brave medical staff to care for them, but no one had any delusions about the fate that awaited them, and as many as possible staggered out to try to join the columns leaving the burning city. Many fell out and either shot themselves or were killed by partisans.

After dusk the troops formed up as best they could amidst the rubble and the burning vehicles and under constant Soviet artillery fire. Leaderless soldiers milled around, their numbers swollen by civilians anxious to get out to escape the vengeance of their own countrymen. At one time spontaneous singing broke out, thousands of soldiers singing the German equivalent of 'Why are we waiting?' followed by an emotional rendering of a patriotic song, '*Oh Deutschland hoch in Ehren*'.

The actual breakout was made by the panzer grenadiers of 20th Panzer Division supported by their few remaining tanks attacking to the north-west along the west bank of the Berezina. They broke through the Soviet positions with little difficulty, but after daylight they were attacked by T-34s and strafed from the air by cannon and machine-gun fire. Inevitably the column split up into smaller groups which continued to march in a north-westerly direction. One large group was surrounded within a few kilometres of the German relieving forces and General Hoffmeister and the commanders of 36th and 45th Divisions, Major-Generals Alexander Conrady and Joachim Engel, were captured. Only General Conrady was to survive.

The 20th Panzer Division led by General von Kessel was more fortunate. They captured some Soviet stores and were able to deploy a Josef Stalin self-propelled gun at the rear of their column. Other columns were intercepted by messengers in clean German uniforms who tried to mislead them into partisan ambushes or into the path of regular Soviet formations. Many were thought to be former German soldiers 'turned' in the Russian prisoner-of-war camps under the influence of the 'National Committee for a Free Germany'. This produced an hysteria similar to that produced by German soldiers dressed in US uniforms during the Ardennes offensive in December 1944. Those without adequate identification papers were summarily shot.

The second and third waves that set out during the course of the 29th fared less well and most were captured or killed, vanishing without trace. Only small groups reached the Svisloch, to the north-west. The history of 45th Infantry Division tells of the fate of one party fortunate enough not to be shot immediately on capture by partisans or regular Soviet troops: 'An unpleasant fate awaited the masses of captured troops. The many wounded were put aboard primitive panje wagons, in which they travelled for days. Many died before the survivors were assembled in overcrowded Russian field hospitals. There was much suffering there and little medicine, even though the Russian female doctors did what they could. Although completely exhausted from the terrible days of the past weeks, the remaining soldiers were forced to assemble in columns of several hundred men each and were marched to a large camp at Zhlobin, receiving nothing to eat for several days.'4

Others were less fortunate: 'We had to stay in a tent. Other prisoners arrived, amongst them wounded that had broken out of Bobruisk. Then a Russian Commissar ordered them to be taken outside. We understood immediately what they intended to do with them. They were all shot in the back of the neck. One of them shouted "*Fünf Malinki*" [five children]. Subsequently I asked the Commissar why he had done that. He said that it was too far to the transport for these wounded men. Later we saw our comrades dead and plundered lying in ditches beside the road.'5 The surviving prisoners were put on trains at Zhlobin, jammed 80 men to a cattle truck and sent to Moscow. Here they received their first warm meal and were deloused. They were then forced to take part in the Victory March through the streets of Moscow.

It is now necessary to look back at the efforts being made to help extricate the survivors of Ninth Army. On 28 June more trains carrying elements of 12th Panzer Division arrived throughout the day and were unloaded in the Marina Gorka area. A panzer grenadier battalion was sent forward to take up a screening position along the Svisloch between Talka and Pogoreloje. The assembly of the Division continued throughout the 29th and 30th, while Headquarters Ninth Army debated how best to use them to help the troops breaking out from Bobruisk.

In the evening of 29 June, there were Soviet attacks across the Svisloch into the large military camp at Lapichi. Major-General M. F. Panov, Commander of 1st Guards Tank Corps, reported that his 17th Guards Tank Brigade had seized a bridgehead across the river, but German reports stated that the bridgehead had been eliminated. We shall probably never know which report was correct. Next day there was heavy fighting as further Soviet attempts to cross the Svisloch were repelled.

At 1500 hours on the 30th, the Army Commander, General von Vormann, spoke on the telephone to the '1a' and asked him if he thought that the Division were capable of attacking towards Svisloch town to help the breakout. Niepold replied that the Division could not disengage from the present attempts to prevent the Russians from forming bridgeheads over the Svisloch. Some minutes later General von Vormann telephoned an order that the Division mount a relief attack from Pogoreloje towards the Svisloch as early as possible next day, but left it to the Division to use what forces it could spare to achieve its objective. All that could be spared from holding the river line was the mechanized panzer grenadier battalion and a company of tanks under the command of Major Blanchbois.

During the late afternoon they were disengaged from the fighting around Lapichi and replenished with fuel and ammunition. Setting off in darkness to cover 35 kilometres along narrow tracks through the forest, they encountered no resistance until they were approaching their objective, but before the head of the column reached the only bridge over the river in that sector, they received an unpleasant surprise. The Russians had dug-in and concealed an extensive defensive position featuring no less than fifteen heavy anti-tank guns on the far side of the bridge. As the leading vehicle began to cross the bridge, it received a direct hit on one of its tracks. For the remainder of the morning there was savage confused fighting as the Germans tried to clear the bridge and the Russians counter-attacked with tanks and artillery. This prevented the battalion from reaching the main group of XXXI Panzer Corps who were merely a few kilometres behind the anti-tank gun position. Only a few exhausted German soldiers were able to slip away, but General Hoffmeister and the other generals were forced to surrender as we have already seen.

A large group of 'Bobruiskers' managed to cross farther along the river; the rear elements of the battalion group saw in the shimmering midday heat a long column of exhausted men dragging themselves along the road to the rear of their positions. Major Blanchbois sent an officer to the crossroads to direct them to the German lines. He told them: 'Twelfth Panzer's mechanized battalion is here to get you out. It is 20 kilometres to the German lines. You have managed to get here and you can make the last stretch.' Major Blanchbois told the author that the men were in a terrible state and were at the end of their tether. They had been constantly harried on the ground by partisans and attacked from the air by fighters and fighter-bombers. They had struggled along without cohesion, hungry, exhausted and with only stagnant marsh water to quench their burning thirst. Many had discarded their boots to swim across the rivers and had wrapped their feet in rags and straw. The wounded were hobbling along with the help of sticks and crutches.

When told that the battalion was there to get them out, some men immediately demanded motor transport to take them on, and when this was refused tried to rush the panzer grenadiers' SPWs. They had to be restrained at gunpoint. Many units had been broken up and the men did not trust strange officers as there had been so many examples in the last few days of enemy agents in German uniforms giving false directions. The only person they would trust was Major Blanchbois and they crowded around him and accused others of being spies, demanding their immediate execution. In some instances they carried out executions themselves. Major Blanchbois had constantly to exhort them to continue marching to the north-west.

During the afternoon the Battalion was ordered to break off and retire as it was needed elsewhere. Despite dire threats Major Blanchbois refused to obey until the stream of 'Bobruiskers' had dried up. The Battalion withdrew shortly after 1800 hours, with the worst of the wounded on their vehicles; they arrived back in the German lines after midnight. Estimates vary as to how many men were saved, but it was probably in the order of 15,000–20,000. This was the only successful relief operation during the offensive. Some days later Major Blanchbois was awarded the *Ritterkreuz* of the Iron Cross.[6]

Lieutenant-Colonel Niepold watched the first columns struggling past the Divisional Command Post on their way to the railway yards at Marina Gorka. 'It was a pitiful sight to see these men, this defeated army, some with and some without their weapons, with many wounded hobbling along on sticks and crutches. A shattering sight.'[7] One of the last groups to arrive was that of 20th Panzer Division led by General von Kessel and some of his officers. He demanded a truck and returned eastwards looking for more survivors of his Division. Niepold doubted whether they would ever meet again.

The Soviet force that had opposed the 12th Panzer Division relief force had consisted of one of General Panov's 1st Guards Tank Corps' brigades – the other two were thrusting towards Marina Gorka through Talka south of Minsk. This meant that 12th Panzer would have to retire rapidly to avoid being caught in the encirclement of Minsk that was now obviously part of the Soviet plan. But Army Group Centre was even more concerned about the extensive threat that was developing to the south-west of Minsk, aimed at preventing the arrival of German reinforcements and gaining as much ground as possible to the west. General Pliyev's cavalry/mechanized group had been ordered to seize the communications centre of Baranovichi. To counter the emergence of this threat Field Marshal Model decided to move 12th Panzer Division to the west to try to protect the lines of communication running to Minsk.

General Rokossovsky saw that reinforcements were beginning to arrive in the Baranovichi area and changed the objective of the cavalry/mechanized group, directing them to seize the Niemen crossings at Stolbtsy. German air reconnaissance confirmed that Russian cavalry were heading for the Niemen bridges, and 12th Panzer were ordered to send an advanced detachment in an attempt to forestall them. It became known later that on 4 July the Stavka ordered First Belorussian Front to advance to Brest-Litovsk to establish a bridgehead on the western Bug. The battalion from Panzer Grenadier Regiment 5 could not be disengaged until the evening of 1 July. It moved via Dukora along minor roads crowded with civilian refugees and retreating administrative troops. After an exhausting night drive of 160 kilometres, the Battalion arrived half an hour too late: the tanks of 1st Guards Cavalry Corps had seized the river crossings. Despite their fatigue, the panzer grenadiers attacked immediately but were unable to prevent the Russians from blowing the vital road bridge; the railway bridge was also held by the Russians. Shortly after midday the Battalion received welcome support from some Stukas, but they were unable to dislodge the Russian cavalrymen.

The Headquarters of Ninth Army made its way westwards but in so doing lost most of their signal communications equipment and so were out of touch with their subordinate formations and with Army Group.

It was hoped that 28th Jäger Division from Army Group North Ukraine would be able to reach Stolbsty from the south, but they encountered heavy opposition so it was decided to send an officer from Ninth Army to order 12th Panzer to move westwards as soon as possible to clear up the enemy bridgehead at Stolbtsy from the north. But the withdrawal of the Division removed the southern pivot of Fourth Army which was struggling to get back to Minsk.

The Division first dispatched a panzer grenadier battalion with a company of tanks in support to act as a flank guard along the Minsk–Slutsk road in the area of Yashenka. There they found a battalion of 'Feldherrnhalle' Division already in contact with the Soviet mechanized forces and took them under command until the Niemen was crossed. This augmented battalion group of 12th Panzer suffered heavy losses in preventing the Soviet tanks of the cavalry/mechanized group from attacking the remainder of the Division while it moved from east to west.

The Division marched through the night and throughout the next day along very bad minor roads and sandy tracks, its progress hindered by troops from other formations breaking into the column and causing blockages. Where possible the trucks picked up soldiers on foot who were hastening to avoid being encircled in Minsk, 20 kilometres to the north. By 1300 hours Minsk, the capital of Belorussia, was back in Russian hands after an occupation lasting three years. Lieutenant-Colonel Niepold related: 'On the withdrawal from Minsk to Stolbtsy the roads were congested by units in flight from the east – partly panic, partly disorder and partly bad discipline. There was a small bridge and some units tried to enter our column. When a large artillery truck towing a 2.10cm howitzer tried to cross the bridge, I ordered an officer to draw his pistol and restore order. And I was there too. This truck would have destroyed the bridge. That was traffic control!'

The divisional columns were attacked by partisans and threatened from the south by tanks. On the southernmost sector of their route the Soviet tanks got so close that the staff destroyed their classified secret documents, presumably including the daily keys for their enciphering machines. The only blessing was that the Soviet air force was too occupied with the reduction of the encircled Fourth Army to the north to have time to bother the Division.

By the evening of 3 July the leading elements of the Division had reached Stolbtsy, the column stretching back some 25 kilometres. During the march the troops had been told that there was to be a concentric attack on Stolbtsy: from the south 28th Jäger Division would attack west of the road and railway corridor as soon as possible after its arrival, and 4th Panzer would attack from the south-west. The 12th Panzer would provide the eastern arm of this movement. Shortly after 2000 hours, the Division was ordered to take and hold the Stolbtsy crossings and to make contact with 4th Panzer to the south. Colonel Müller and Lieutenant-Colonel Niepold went forward to Panzer Grenadier Regiment 25's command post to plan the attack. The '1a' remembers that the commanders' faces looked strained and that they were tired and depressed, not having much hope of success for the forthcoming attack. It was decided to attack with three panzer grenadier battalions abreast from Stolbtsy to the south-west with the aim of seizing crossings over the Niemen. The attack was planned to begin at 0400 hours and was to be supported by the tank battalion and the divisional artillery. The '1a' also shared the doubts about the possibility of success in the morning, and ordered a reconnaissance of an escape route to the north-west as all other routes were barred by the advancing Soviet tanks.

The attack had some initial success as did that of 4th Panzer, but both attacks gradually ground to a halt because of the greater Soviet strength and the exhaustion of the German troops. However, although communications with Army, now known as 'Von Vormann Force', were extremely poor, a message was received at 0900 hours confirming that 4th Panzer's attack had been halted and ordering 12th Panzer to cross the Niemen by the pontoon bridge at Eremichi to the north of Stolbtsy. This bridge had been constructed by 'Von Vormann Force' after General von Kessel and the remnant of 20th Panzer had forced a passage through the partisan positions in the southern tip of the almost impenetrable Nalibocki forest. The staff of 12th Panzer were very glad to hear of the reappearance of General von Kessel who had been given up for lost when he disappeared eastwards to pick up stragglers from his Division.

The 12th Panzer Division moved off to the north-west, protected in the rear by a battalion east of Stolbtsy, and one battalion east of the Nalibocki forest. The Division met many groups of survivors from Fourth and Ninth Armies, among them a battalion of the fusilier regiment led by Major Lemm who had escaped from Mogilev. The route was difficult, the area infested with partisans and to crown everything when they arrived at the wooden bridge over the River Sula they found that the partisans had set it on fire. The Division waited on a narrow sandy track while the staff debated what to do next. The only consolation was that the weather was sunny and warm. Just as the pioneers were about to be called forward to construct a makeshift bridge, an officer appeared on a motor-cycle from the nearby woods. He said that he was from 20th Panzer and that General von Kessel had sent him to take them to the bridge at Eremichi and that he knew the way. Initially there was some doubt as to his identity; many supposedly German officers had been working for the Russians, misdirecting columns into ambushes. But his papers appeared to be in order, and although he could not point out the way on the map, the staff decided to follow him. The column did an about-turn, not easy with heavy tracked vehicles on a narrow track, and followed the officer to another bridge over the Sula. Although the track remained bad and the partisan attacks persisted, the leading elements of the Division had crossed the Niemen by 1700 hours. It was not until the following afternoon that the administrative units and the rearguard got across. On the other side they learned that they had already been committed to attack on the western bank south towards 28th Jäger. However, there was great relief that the Division had succeeded in breaking out from the threatened encirclement, albeit at a heavy cost in men and *matériel.*

NOTES

1. This chapter was based on interviews with General Niepold and on his book *Battle for White Russia.*
2. D'Este, in *Hitler's Generals*, London, Weidenfeld and Nicolson, 1989, p. 324.
3. Interview with General von der Gröben.
4. Buchner, p. 196.
5. Interview with Major Blanchbois.
6. Niepold, p. 178.
7. Interview with General Niepold.

17
THE FATE OF FOURTH ARMY

The Commandant of '*Fester Platz* Mogilev', General Bamler, who had taken over that afternoon from von Erdmannsdorf, reported on the evening of 27 June: 'Under attack since midday from north, south, and east. Fighting on routes out of the city. Enemy has crossed River Dnieper in the east.' At 2200 hours the last message to be received from him read: 'Can only hold city centre now.'[1]

Fourth Army's situation was dismal. In the north, VI Corps had been shattered, with only a few formations fighting bravely on. XXVII Corps, XXXIX Panzer Corps and XII Corps were withdrawing under heavy pressure. Soviet forces were pouring through the gaps on the left and right flanks of the Army, and had made several penetrations in its centre.

On 26 June the Field Marshal flew to the Obersalzberg to present his appreciation of the situation to Hitler and try to reach agreement on the far-reaching measures to be taken if a substantial part of his Army Group were to be saved. But his appreciation was narrow as he considered that the aim of the Soviet offensive was confined to the encirclement of Minsk. Unfortunately no OKH War Diary exists and the Army Group's War Diary for 25, 26 and 27 June has not survived. This version of events relies on the memory of the officer who kept the Army Group War Diary. It is not mentioned in the post-war account written for the US Army by General von der Groeben, the '1a' of the Operations Branch at Army Group Centre.

Apparently Hitler agreed that Fourth Army should conduct a phased withdrawal to the River Berezina. On the morning of 27 June, however, Army Group Centre gave orders for Fourth Army to hold the Dneiper position. Possibly the Field Marshal thought that this was one of the phase lines, but otherwise the order is inexplicable. The result was that Fourth Army lost another irreplaceable day, which contributed significantly to the ensuing disaster. As Soviet forces had already crossed the Dnieper in several places, the order could not be carried out. General von Tippelskirch, the commander of Fourth Army, disregarded it and ordered the Army to withdraw to a position between the Rivers Dnieper and Drut, to be held for a maximum of 24 hours.[2]

Fourth Army was now looking over its shoulder continually because 5th Guards Tank Army was operating far to the rear of its left flank, and approaching the vital crossing over the Berezina at Borisov. The cheering news was that 5th Panzer, a very strong division, was arriving in the area. During the morning of 28 June, Fourth Army was ordered to withdraw behind the River Drut, the withdrawal to be completed by that evening.

That day, the 28th, must be seen as the last on which Fourth Army was capable of operating as a formation; after that its actions were those of individual corps. The bad state of the roads, packed with retreating administrative troops, and the lack of adequate bridges over small streams caused problems for the fighting troops trying to get across the Drut. Throughout the day the columns were under constant air attack, and two corps commanders, Generals Martinek and Pfeiffer, were killed. To add to their difficulties, Army Headquarters withdrew to the Berezino area, which was unsuitable for good radio communications.

During the afternoon Field Marshal Busch was able to speak to General von Tippelskirch by telephone and ordered Fourth Army to withdraw behind the Berezina. The Army Commander noted: 'Now the order is on its way – too late!' When it arrived, the confirmatory order indicated the extent to which Army HQ had lost touch with the situation. The Army was ordered to cross at Beresino and move north and south to hold the flanks. The Army Commander issued a characteristically direct order: 'Get to the Berezina as soon as possible!' Shortly afterwards Busch came to the Headquarters to announce his supersession by Field Marshal Model. Reading between the lines, this was no self-congratulatory farewell visit. General von Tippelskirch took the opportunity of blaming the state of his Army on the Headquarters of the Army Group and by implication on Busch personally. The Field Marshal departed and was only re-employed for a few days in Schleswig-Holstein at the end of the war. He died a prisoner of war in England in 1945 and was buried in an unmarked grave near Aldershot.[3]

On 28 June, the Stavka reviewed progress so far and then set new objectives. Basically these were to the west of Minsk, and once achieved they were updated on 4 July to include the cities of Kaunus, Grodno, Bialystok and Brest-Litovsk. At this stage it was possible to detect the movements that would close around Fourth Army to the east of Minsk. The 5th Guards Tank Army was closing in on the vital Berezina crossing at Borisov, with 2nd Guards Tank Corps aiming to reach the river to the south of Borisov. The southern wing of the encircling forces consisted of 9th Tank Corps, the mobile group of 3rd Army on the right of Third Belorussian Front. Between these two encircling wings the four armies of Second Belorussian Front were squeezing Fourth Army which was beginning its agonizing retreat to the Berezina.

The area through which the divisions were making their painful way was literally 'bandit' country; bad roads through thick forest criss-crossed by small rivers and large areas of swamp, where partisans had always operated at will. Held up time and again by demolished bridges, mines, and rows of trees cut down across the roads, the columns backed-up for miles. Short of fuel and ammunition, they were perfect targets for the partisans, and the marauding Soviet aircraft which patrolled ceaselessly overhead looking for opportunity tasks.

The picture of 4th Army on 29 June is of the four corps trying to get back across the Berezina as soon as possible, although some divisions were only just beginning to cross the River Drut, many miles to the east. It was difficult for the Army headquarters to keep in touch with progress as not only were the columns having to fight their way forward but they were moving through an area where radio communications were extremely poor.

In the south XII Corps were making slow progress through the Brodets area towards the Berezina where a bridge was being built. The work was being protected by a hastily assembled force consisting of a regiment from Ninth Army's 707th Security Division and 200 stragglers and administrative troops. Mention was also made of Russian auxiliaries, or 'Hiwis', who were reported to be panicky, which is not surprising because they knew what would happen to them if they were captured. Most German units had hundreds of *Hiwis* on their strength; some remained with their units throughout the war, and in 1945 were taken back to Germany under assumed names. To this day some even attend Old Comrades' reunions.

During the course of the day Fourth Army HQ continually urged on those corps that could be contacted. The others it was assumed were making their way back as best they could. The VI Corps seemed to have merged with XXXIX Panzer Corps under its commander, General Otto Schünemann until he was killed later in the day. It reported that it could only hold the Drut position until midnight and was told that it could withdraw to the Berezina. But this was easier said than done because traffic on the road to Berezino had ground to a halt. It was now recognized that the danger from the south was increasing as 9th Tank Corps moved to close the encirclement from the south. The 12th Panzer Division was now fighting against units of 65th Army's 18th Corps which had moved to the north-west after the reduction of Bobruisk. There were now only 50 kilometres between the two wings of the pincers closing in on Fourth Army, whose formations were still trailing back many kilometres to the east. The successful outcome of this battle would in the last resort depend on how long the two panzer divisions, 5th in the north and 12th in the south, could keep open the withdrawal routes to the west.[4]

The new commander of Army Group Centre, Field Marshal Model, met Colonel-General Zeitzler, Chief of Staff OKH, to discuss the situation. As the cavalry/mechanized group of Third Belorussian Front was rapidly advancing to the west and posed the greatest threat to German attempts to bring up reserves to stabilize the position, OKH agreed to send two infantry divisions to Minsk and a panzer division and a jäger division to hold Baranovichi. But there were insufficient forces to protect the vital river crossing at Borisov, and it was very doubtful whether such forces as could be mustered could get there before the fast-moving Soviet forces arrived.

Next day, the 30th, the Soviets maintained pressure to close the jaws of the trap set for Fourth Army. Attempts were made to hold bridgeheads over the Berezina through which the Army could withdraw when its units reached the river. As they struggled back they were buoyed up by the hope that they would find a strong position on the Berezina where they could reorganize and recuperate, but their hopes were dashed when they saw the conditions prevailing along the river line. Von Saucken Group held one of the main bridgeheads at Borisov on the Smolensk–Minsk highway. Flörke Group, based on 14th Panzer Grenadier Division commanded by Lieutenant-General Hermann Flörke, held a position on the western bank opposite Chernyavka where the bridge had been destroyed. The next crossing was a bridge constructed by VI Corps at Shukovets. The important bridge at Berezino was still open, but was being threatened by enemy probes across the road to the west towards Cherven.

In order to simplify the command structure to fight what had become virtually two separate battles, the commander of Fourth Army placed all troops south of Chernyevka under General Vincenz Müller, commander of XII Corps. He was ordered to extricate HQ XXXIX Panzer Corps and send it to Borisov where it was needed by General von Saucken who had been operating with makeshift facilities lent to him by 5th Panzer Division.[5]

The difficulty of communications is shown by the fact that the Army Group's orders issued on the 29th were not received until the 30th: 'The main task of Fourth Army remains to get its divisions back behind the Berezina in as good condition to resume fighting as possible; contact must be made with Ninth Army and maintained in the Cherven area; as the Army understands 12th Panzer is to bring to a halt any enemy advance on Minsk from the south-east; an aggressive attitude is called for by the flank guard to prevent the encirclement of Borisov.' The shortage of troops was now beginning to tell; there were insufficient fresh troops to hold some of these critical points. Field Marshal Model was already looking at the 'bigger' picture. His appreciation was that he did not have enough troops to defend Minsk, and he was becoming apprehensive of the Soviet thrusts towards the west, to Baranovichi and Molodechno. The loss of these rail centres would greatly inhibit the assembly of reserves from other fronts and from Germany itself.

During the day, Soviet forces advanced on a broad front from Polotsk down to Borisov where the German bridgehead collapsed and 5th Panzer Division was withdrawn to the west bank. The Soviet concept of operations in this sector was to cut communications between Minsk and Vilnius to the north-west, in addition to completing the encirclement of Fourth Army.

On 1 July Fourth Army was gradually being surrounded although at this stage there were plenty of gaps. The 5th Panzer Division withdrew to Smolovichi and Flörke Group to the south to join the remainder of VI Corps near Shukovets, where two bridges had been built. Formations were now calling for air resupply because they had little remaining fuel or ammunition. Müller Group vas still holding a sizeable bridgehead to the east of Beresino, and hoped to be able to get many men over the river by the night of 2/3 July. The Army's remaining divisions were still well to the east of the Berezina, and running short of ammunition and fuel. In vain, Army HQ passed back map references of dropping zones, and the troops waited against hope, straining to hear the sound of transport aircraft overhead. None appeared.

The 5th Panzer Division was now Fourth Army's only formation able to operate effectively. Delaying the Soviet advance on Minsk now took second priority to covering the off-loading of reinforcements in the Molodechno area. If the Molodechno—Baranovichi line were breached, there would be no other opportunity to halt a Soviet advance to the line Vilnius—Bialystok—Brest. During the afternoon of 2 July, therefore, 5th Panzer was ordered to break off its action near Smolovichi and move to the Molodechno area to fulfil its primary task. It must have been an agonizing decision for the Army Commander who realized only too well that he was virtually signing the death warrant for so many of his men.[6]

The three Corps were still crossing the Berezina, harassed by over-whelming Soviet forces. In the evening of 2 July, Fourth Army HQ sent a message to its three corps telling them that Minsk was threatened by tank columns from the north-east, and that they should try to retire through Smolovichi, where they would be re-supplied. After that they were to with-draw westwards to the south of Minsk. The situation was now exacerbated because 12th Panzer Division was being dispatched westwards to deal with the threat to Stolbtsy, which it was vital to hold for the reinforcement pro-gramme.

The withdrawal of the various formations now began, all trying to get through to the main German lines which were moving day by day farther west. Morale was much lower now that they had crossed the Berezina and dis-covered that the expected strong positions along the river bank were a delu-sion. Fear of falling into Soviet hands, particularly those of the partisans, was fuelled by the constant sight of savagely mutilated bodies of German soldiers and Russian civilians along the way. This fear was exacerbated when they con-templated the fate of their own wounded that had to be left behind.

A large pocket had formed near Pekalin, south of Smolovichi to the east of Minsk, and this held three complete divisions, 57th, 267th and 31st, and remnants of 260th, 25th Panzer Grenadier and 78th Sturm Divisions – in fact most of the original formations of XII Corps. The six divisional com-manders were all present, together with the corps commander Lieutenant-General Vincenz Müller and the commander of XXVII Corps, General of Infantry Paul Völckers. There were also elements of XXVII Corps in the pocket. Some of these divisions were still strongly armed: 25th Panzer Grenadier Division had brought a staggering total of no less than 32 assault and 20 self-propelled guns. But although there had been an air resupply of fuel, ammunition was very short – not more than 5–10 rounds per gun.

On 5 July the two corps commanders held a General Officers' confer-ence to assess the situation and to decide upon future action. The overriding fact was that the nearest German lines were more than 100 kilometres to the west, and this seemed an impossible distance for their weary troops to cover without strong Luftwaffe support. Without fuel or ammunition they could not use their heavy weapons so the idea of a breakout seemed hopeless, but the thought of falling into Russian hands made any risk seem worthwhile. Major-General Adolf Trowitz, who had escaped from the Cherkassy pocket with his 57th Infantry Division during the previous winter, agreed to this, as did Major-General Günther Klammt of 260th Division. Lieutenant-General Hans Traut was undecided because of the wounded, probably numbering as many as 5,000, who would have to be abandoned. The decision was made to break out in two corps groups, XXVII Corps to the west and XII Corps to the north-west. The remaining formations of XXXIX Panzer Corps were allocated to the other two Corps. The decision was taken during the evening, despite General Völcker's strong recommendation to stand and fight.[7]

The breakout began at 2359 hours with 25th Panzer Grenadier Division striking out to the west towards Dzerzhinsk, south-west of Minsk. The wounded were left in charge of a doctor with a letter appealing to the Soviet commander to treat the wounded in accordance with the Rules of War. It is not known whether this had any effect. Having fired their last rounds, the gunners destroyed their weapons. The three groups charged with the bayonet shouting 'Hurrah!' Despite very heavy fire, Lieutenant-General Paul Schürmann got out with his group after overpowering a Soviet battery, but with only 100 men left out of his original 1,000. The Soviets now counter-attacked and the groups were split up into smaller groups, all trying to make their way to the west. Apparently some succeeded because Schürmann was not captured and the division was reformed in Germany later in the year.

General Trowitz's 57th Infantry Division broke out the same evening but was almost immediately hit by heavy fire. The columns retained their cohesion and joined up with the remnant of 'Feldherrnhalle' Division at dawn on the 6th. The two divisional commanders decided to act together to cross the Cherven—Minsk road which was held by Soviet forces. The two divisions waited until nightfall before moving. 'Feldherrnhalle' was scattered and most of its men were captured. Once across the road 57th Division, which still numbered 12—15,000 men, split up into smaller groups. The divisional commander's group, the last to cross the road, had two VW Schwimmwagen to carry the wounded. At daylight the group found itself in the midst of a network of Soviet positions and decided to wait for nightfall before moving again. They took cover in a field of rye and the exhausted men fell asleep until early evening when they were woken by rifle and mortar fire. One by one the small groups were taken prisoner. General Trowitz and the remaining groups were rounded up during the next two days.

General Traut's 78th Sturm Division had a similar fate. A survivor gave the following account: 'The troops formed up for the assault at 2300. Individual units began to sing the '*Deutschlandlied*' [the German national anthem]. The survivors will never forget that night. Burning villages, howitzer and rifle fire, dull explosions mixing with the thunderous shouts and singing of the attacking units. Enemy forces which tried to resist were overrun and surrounded again. The breakout succeeded ...

'By dawn of 6 July the enemy encircling positions had been left behind. However, the scattered Russian units quickly regrouped. Enemy motorized forces arrived. The larger breakout groups were soon caught and surrounded again. The only chance was to break up into very small groups.' Most of 78th Sturm including their divisional commander General Traut were captured.[8]

This story was repeated with different emphasis by all the divisions that tried to break out from the pocket. The order issued by Lieutenant-General Otto Drescher to his 267th Infantry Division read: 'Soldiers of my victorious 267th Infantry Division. While enemy penetrations in the sector of Army Group Centre made a withdrawal inevitable, the enemy brought forward strong forces on 3rd and 4th July against XII Corps. Our division acted as the rearguard of the Corps and successfully repelled all attacks, allowing the other divisions to withdraw safely. You, the soldiers of my division, have proved your valour and heroism in your commitment to the soldiers in the other Divisions.

'During this battle the enemy succeeded in encircling our troops. This encirclement must be broken and we must fight our way to freedom and to our homeland. If we are to see our homeland and families again, we must fight. I want no one to doubt that the way will be difficult and great sacrifice will be required. Whoever prefers the dishonourable fate of captivity will be subjected to the habitual cruelty of the Bolshevik murderers. I have no doubt that the choice will not be difficult. On comrades! On to the decisive attack, back to freedom and our homeland! Drescher.'[9]

Among the measures ordered by General Drescher were careful evaluation of reconnaissance reports; preparation of copies of a good scale map with wide distribution; silent destruction of vehicles, guns and even the battalion cooking equipment; and the formation of a cavalry squadron from artillery horses. All troops, where ever they came from, were taken into the combat groups, and weapons were distributed equally.

The 267th Infantry Division broke out in three columns, their first objective being to cross the Orsha—Minsk railway, and then the main road, which was protected by infantry posts. The left-hand column crossed both the railway and the highway, but Soviet armour arrived and fired at random into the dense mass of troops. Resistance was pointless and this column surrendered. Some of them later managed to escape to the west. The rout of the right-hand column led through dense forest infested with partisans, and the column split into smaller groups. Those that were captured were marched by the partisans along the highway to Borisov.

The remaining groups struggled on to the north-west. Some were attacked by two Soviet infantry companies supported by mortars. The Germans, who had only their rifles with not more than ten rounds per man, fought valiantly but to no end; all were either killed, or captured and sent to Borisov.

A Soviet senior lieutenant who was captured by the Germans made this statement: 'East of Minsk, I saw two columns of German prisoners of war, about 400 to 600 men, marching in the direction of Moscow. The majority of the prisoners were barefoot. In spite of the heat, they were allowed no water from the local streams during the march, therefore they drank muddy water. Whoever staggered was beaten, if a prisoner collapsed, he was shot. Once I saw a row of executed German prisoners lying in a roadside ditch. When they passed through a town, they would beg for bread, but the civilians did not dare give them any. I saw a German senior lieutenant sitting on the edge of a trench. He wore a uniform shirt with shoulder insignia and bravery awards, but he had no trousers and was barefoot. The guards removed the better clothes from the prisoners, in order to trade them for liquor with the civilian population.'[10]

The central column under personal command of General Drescher fared rather better. They crossed the railway as well as the highway and on the first day made considerable progress to the north-west in the direction of Molodechno. As food was now in very short supply and everyone would have to exist on what could be found in the forest, General Drescher decided to split the columns to make foraging easier. He then laid down the direction to be followed by each group and ensured that each had a commander with some experience of orienteering. Even the divisional chaplain was given a group of 100 men to lead. During the march many groups were split up even more, either of their own volition or because of swamps or partisan activity.

Most of them were killed or captured, but as comparatively few captives returned the details of their fate will never be known.

One of the most successful columns was that of 25th Panzer Grenadier Division led by General Schürmann, the first to leave after the commanders' conference. As we have seen, the main group split up during the actual break-out, but his group went on to cross the Bobruisk—Minsk railway line which was already covered by the Soviets. He then attempted to cross more outpost lines without success and decided to turn eastwards and bypass Minsk to the north. This was successful and he managed to lead his ever dwindling detachment, which now numbered only 30 men, to the German lines north of Molodechno and south of Vilnius. His was the largest group to reach the German lines. The remnant of the Division was withdrawn to the training area in Bavaria. It was then employed in the west until the Ardennes offensive failed when it was sent to help defend Berlin. General Schürmann remained with the Division until February 1945.

It is interesting to look at the breakout phase from the Soviet point of view. The following is an extract from the Soviet *Military History Journal* published in 1984, which describes the outline of the reduction of the German encirclements and breakout groups: 'The actions to eliminate the surrounded enemy in the area to the east of Minsk can be conditionally divided into three stages which are characterized by the use of different methods. Thus, in the first stage [from 4 to 7 July] the enemy endeavoured to break out to the west in an organized manner, with the chain of command still intact and receiving some air supply. During this period our troops made concentrated attacks to split the enemy groups into smaller parties, and forced them to abandon heavy military equipment and weapons. In the second stage [to 9 July] individual Nazi detachments were still endeavouring to put up organized resistance, advancing along forest roads and paths and attempting to escape from encirclement. The Soviet troops destroyed these isolated groups by intercepting them on advantageous lines and destroying them with fire and attack by the main forces of divisions and regiments. In the third stage [9 to 11 July], the scattered small enemy groups, now chaotic and without organized resistance, endeavoured to break out of the snare to the west. The Soviet forces 'combed' the forests and fields and captured small enemy groups, using small composite detachments (a rifle company or battalion reinforced by a tank platoon, a battery of anti-tank guns and a mortar company) mounted on motor vehicles.'

In the various accounts the impression is given that some of the German generals were lukewarm about continuing the unequal struggle. This appears to be the line they took at the commanders' conference on 5 July. The foremost among these appears to have been General Vincenz Müller, the commander of XII Corps and acting commander of Fourth Army. One day, during the breakout, a German officer carrying a white flag appeared in the Soviet lines saying that an important German general wished to meet a Soviet general of equal seniority, to discuss the surrender of his troops.

This was General Müller who gave 'the impression of a sullen, depressed man in untidy uniform with only one shoulder-strap and his boots were dirty. General Smirnov, the commander of the Soviet 121st Infantry Corps, asked him if he wanted to tidy himself up. He answered "Yes, thank you." The general was taken to a separate house. After he had tidied himself, he came out accompanied by his orderly.' It was then suggested to General Müller that he write an order instructing his soldiers to lay down their arms. This would then be scattered over the area by Soviet aircraft. Müller agreed with this and added that he did not want the blood of his soldiers to be spilt.[11]

NOTES
1. Niepold, p. 130.
2. *Ibid.*, pp. 135-6.
3. *Ibid.*, p. 142.
4. *Ibid.*, p. 149.
5. *Ibid.*, p. 166.
6. Symposium, p. 402.
7. Hinze, p. 236; Buchner, p. 176.
8. Buchner, p. 185.
9. Hinze, p. 241.
10. Hinze, p. 250.
11. Smirnov, *In the Mogilev direction*, p. 19.

18
AFTERWARDS

Once the German soldier had surrendered or been captured his initial survival depended upon the whim of his captor. Often when the Russian soldier or partisan had an old score to settle there was just a tightening of the trigger finger and all was over. Most prisoners were treated fairly although harshly. They were sent under guard to a collecting point where there were limited facilities for feeding and primary medical care, and their survival was very much a matter of chance. The problem for the Soviet side was made much worse by the large numbers of prisoners taken. It is impossible to state with any certainty whether any provision was made for such an influx during the planning of the offensive.

A very large number of prisoners were taken shortly after capture to a transit camp at Zhlobin. The exhausted men received nothing to eat for three days while they were shuffling along in the slow-moving columns. Men who were unable to keep up because of wounds or exhaustion were shot. At Zhlobin they were given a bowl of thin watery soup once a day, their only sustenance. It is recorded that some men ate grass and seeds to try to assuage their hunger. After being kept in the camp for several days, they were packed into cattle trucks and sent to Moscow. Here some 57,600 prisoners were packed into the Hippodrome, in preparation for a Victory March through the streets of Moscow.

Stalin's biographer, Volkogonov, attributes this idea to Stalin who thought that it would raise the morale of the people and incite the troops to finish off the 'Fascists' more quickly. Within a week 26 trains had been organized to bring the prisoners from behind the front line to the Hippodrome, the horse-racing centre of Moscow, first built in 1883, some miles to the north-west of the centre of the city. The 55,000 or so prisoners led by eighteen generals and 1,200 officers would be guarded by Russian soldiers on foot and by Cossacks on ponies, and would march towards Red Square. The streets of Moscow were lined with people watching this spectacle, some jeering and spitting; others watched silently, no doubt remembering sons and husbands, fathers and brothers. After the parade the columns were broken up and directed towards the railway stations where trains were waiting to take them to camps in distant areas of the Soviet Union. Years of captivity awaited them, and many thousands of them would never return.[1]

There have been few English translations of accounts of the prisoner-of-war camps in the Soviet Union, though there are many in German. Details of some of them are given in the bibliography. All the accounts describe the attempts made by the Russians to 'turn' and use the prisoners in various ways. The pressure was greatest when the prisoner was newly arrived and had not had sufficient time to orientate himself or to be assimilated into a group of fellow prisoners.

On arrival at a camp, groups were split up, the other ranks separated from their officers and NCOs, and discussion groups were formed, aimed at promoting one or other of the two main pro-Soviet 'activist' organizations set up after Stalingrad. The most promising from the Soviet point of view was the 'Nationalkomitee Freies Deutschland' set up at Krasnogorsk near Moscow in the buildings which now house the National Film Archives. The president was Erich Weinert, a well-known German Communist, and in the upper echelons there were a number of these who had fled Germany to escape the concentration camp. The membership was a mix of officers and other ranks from all political parties and religions. This was a much more active group than many that flourished for a while and then collapsed. NKFD sported the old imperial colours on its newspaper which was widely distributed and dropped from the air on German formations fighting on the Eastern Front. The paper urged German soldiers to desert, promising fair treatment and repatriation after the war. It is doubtful whether many were hood-winked by this offer.

The other main movement was the *Bund Deutscher Offiziere* (BDO) which some German generals joined after Stalingrad. They took a different standpoint from the NKFD, for example, refusing to have a hand in inciting German soldiers to desert. But after discussions in which the Soviet government promised that if there were an Army-led rising against Hitler, Germany would be allowed to retain her 1938 frontiers, and with NKFD agreement to stop trying to persuade German soldiers to desert, the two organizations amalgamated in September 1943.[2]

Although most front-line German soldiers were unaffected by the propaganda of these subversive organizations, they were certainly subjected to the attentions of German-speaking Russians or, in some cases, German soldiers who had gone over to the Russians. There are countless reports of men dressed as German officers or NCOs offering guidance to safety and then leading their victims into partisan ambushes. These incidents unleashed such a phobia among the German troops that a stranger without plausible documentation was liable to be shot out of hand. The panic caused was very similar to that which occurred during the Ardennes offensive when German troops dressed as GIs infiltrated the US formations.

Many of the officers commanding corps and divisions caught in the various encirclements were either killed or committed suicide. A number of the captured officers became members of the NKVD though some, including Field Marshal Paulus, could not be persuaded to join until after the 20 July bomb plot. After their release, some of these generals started a new life in East Germany, many of them in government service. Most of the German officers who co-operated with the Soviets were looked upon with contempt by the remainder of the officer corps.

The majority of the German prisoners were not interested in political activity, being concerned only with survival and getting back to their families. Those who collaborated, known as 'activists', were employed by the Russians to run the prison camps in return for more rations and a few meagre privileges. They ran compulsory indoctrination lectures on Communism. Although most of the prisoners could sympathize with a moderate activist who probably only collaborated because his family lived in the Russian occupation zone of Germany and saw no other option other than to co-operate, the majority of them were held in contempt. General Bamler was one of these universally hated collaborators. One prisoner described him in the following words: 'He became one of the most active, cunning, unscrupulous, and dangerous leaders and organizers in the service of the NKVD. He signed everything the NKVD asked him to sign ... He collaborated with the Russians in gathering or fabricating evidence used to convict many of the people who were later sentenced to long prison terms. If he is still alive, he has the fate of many men on his conscience.'

Most of the prisoners had to endure captivity for more than ten long years until Chancellor Adenauer negotiated their release in 1955.

19
THE LONG MARCH HOME

Those groups of German soldiers who managed to evade capture by the Soviet regular troops and partisans in the first few hours and days after breaking out of the encirclement, and decided to try to make their way westwards to the German lines, faced almost overwhelming odds. The weather was extremely hot, rations were non-existent, they had no maps and little ammunition and above all they were harried on the ground and from the air. Many men did make it back, but in general they were the younger and fitter men; most senior officers rarely had the stamina to go on.

The columns travelled by night or in misty weather, lying up by day. They avoided centres of population and main roads and railway tracks as all these were likely to have Soviet troops moving along them. Guard posts had been set up and patrols were sent out to search for the German columns. Frequently larger groups split up into smaller groups in the hope that it might be easier to forage for food. Surprisingly many of the Russian or Polish peasants supplied them with food and water for a variety of reasons. Some could not believe that the Germans would not be back, and asked for receipts to show that they had helped German troops in their time of need. Some feared the partisans even more and dreaded the day when they would be back under the Soviet yoke.

In some areas farms were rare and difficult to find. In one instance a German column was being given food as another group was about to assault the buildings. In another some German soldiers were hiding in a corn stack and to their horror Soviet troops arrived to collect the corn from the local women who were probably Lithuanians. As the Soviets were removing the corn, one of the Germans put his finger across his lips. The woman nodded and managed to divert the attention of the Russians. The woman knew that she faced immediate death if the Germans had been discovered.

During the withdrawal of Fourth Army east of the Berezina, a man dressed as a German lieutenant appeared and gave orders for the bridge, over which the withdrawing troops were about to cross, to be demolished. The pioneer corporal refused to carry out the order because it seemed suspicious as there was still a long column waiting to cross. The bogus lieutenant was shot out of hand. The bridge was demolished after the column had crossed.

The Soviets appear to have put a great deal of effort into trying to mislead columns about to cross major rivers, particularly the Berezina. A wounded battery Commander in Fourth Army area reported that he met two unknown officers wearing staff rank badges two kilometres from the Berezina bridge. They directed vehicles into a swamp and offered to lead the soldiers to where they could cross the river in safety away from the bridge which they said had fallen into enemy hands. As the wounded officer could not hear any firing and thought that there was no chance of being able to find a way through the swamp, he decided to make a reconnaissance in an amphibious jeep. The two 'staff officers' tried to hinder this, but the battery commander reached the bridge and crossed it with his men.

Another column crossed the Dnieper and shortly afterwards a Lieutenant riding pillion on a motor cycle appeared and said : 'I come from the Division and have orders to lead you back. If you take this route', pointing to a new direction, 'you will find 150 German tanks which will take you to safety.' After about fifteen kilometres, this column was fired on by enemy artillery and mortars and finally were attacked by Soviet tanks and infantry.

Some attempts at subterfuge were not so successful. A member of 267th Infantry Division reported that near the Berezina, a major riding a horse appeared and ordered that the vehicles be destroyed. The men should swim across the river with the remaining horses as the bridge was not yet ready and the Russians were already on the west bank. The leader of the supply column found that this was untrue and crossed the bridge with his vehicles. The 'major' was summarily shot. He was found to be wearing a peculiar combination of uniform: flying trousers, riding boots, a Soviet-style tent cloth blouse topped by a flying helmet. Another bogus officer gave himself away when he tore his field-grey uniform and was seen to be wearing a Soviet commissar's uniform underneath.

Those Germans who fell into the hands of the partisans had very little hope of surviving. The more fortunate were shot immediately, but many were tortured before they died. The retreating columns passed many mutilated bodies of their compatriots along the way. One report describes over a hundred dead German soldiers who had been left behind as they were wounded. All had been shot in the back of the neck. One group of five men had been marched along the road, but then had been shot from behind. One of these men was not killed and was able to report the incident. On another occasion a group of prisoners was forced to undress and were beaten and mutilated until their remains were scarcely recognizable. How many similar tragedies took place is unknown as few soldiers who fell into enemy hands survived to tell their story.

The most difficult and hazardous part of their journey was the final few miles when they had to pass through the Soviet lines and then enter the German positions without being shot by their own side. They realised that they were approaching the danger zone as the signs of the front line increased – heavy artillery fire, lights and flares at night, heavy traffic, greater intensity of administrative units. The Soviets took stringent precautions to stop German soldiers crossing the lines with constant patrols and check points, all looking out for the ragged survivors awaiting their chance.

A captain and an NCO ran into a Soviet artillery position by night. They crept under a pile of sunflower stalks. While they lay there Red Army soldiers began removing the dried stalks. With great presence of mind the Germans grabbed a large bundle of the stalks and followed the Russians through the minefields. When the rearmost Red soldier asked them a question the German NCO swore at him in Russian. He remained silent from then on. The two crossed the Soviet trenches and were able to hide out in no man's land.[3]

Another account gives the flavour of those terrible days: 'Through the quiet of the late summer day, the thunder of the guns rumbled in the distance. At last we were close to the front. The most difficult part of our journey was about to begin. Carefully we slipped through the enemy rear in the darkness and approached the main line of Soviet resistance. The sky was filled with bright flashes, the night roared with thunderous crashes. Three nights and three days we lay just behind the Soviet front. On the first day we crawled into a wheat field. The shells from the German artillery were bursting uncomfortably close. We heard Russian soldiers talking, saw their shadows, and often they were so close that we thought they must see us.' The following night they tried again but had to retreat, being fired on twice. The third night they were determined to get through come what may. The tracer from machine-guns criss-crossed the sky and there was continual rifle fire as they crawled past sentries doing their rounds. A flare went up and there was a fierce exchange of fire. They dashed forward to take cover in a shell-hole, and there was a blinding flash as one of them stepped on a German mine. His companion then went forward to summon help and returned with stretcher-bearers. Their incredible journey of more than ten weeks was over. It is estimated that 10,000 to 15,000 men escaped from the encirclement of Fourth Army on the Berezina, and that not more than 900 made their way back to the German front lines. Most of the dead have no known grave, nor is it known how they died. The most senior survivor was a major wearing the Knight's Cross who made his way back alone, and barefoot. Once their identity was confirmed, the returnees were sent to a collecting centre at Schlossberg in East Prussia. In a very few cases there were enough survivors from a particular formation to justify reforming it, otherwise they were sent to new units. Their memories of the long bitter march must have remained imprinted on them for life.

NOTES

1. Volkogonov, pp. 476-7.
2. Knappe, Siegfried, *Soldat*, London, Airlife, 1992, p. 337.
3. The experiences of German soldiers trying to return to their own lines are taken from Hinze, Rolf, *Rückkämpfer, 1944*, published privately in Germany in 1988.

20
TO THE WEST

By early July, only the wings of Army Group Centre remained. Both Second Army in the Pripyat Marshes and the rump of Third Panzer Army in the north were still in fighting shape because the main thrusts of the Soviet attacks had bypassed them. Having achieved their main aim of destroying Army Group Centre, the Soviets' intention was to gain as much ground as possible to the west. 'Bagration' continued in the Army Group Centre sector at a much slower pace; not only were the mechanized forces beginning to outrun their logistical support but the Germans were assembling reserves to stabilize the position. The Soviet plan was to continue to move westwards in compliance with new instructions issued by Stavka. First Baltic Front was to advance towards Dvinsk; Third Belorussian Front towards Molodechno and then through Vilnius and Lida to the Niemen; Second Belorussian Front would complete the reduction of the forces around Minsk; the right wing of First Belorussian Front would pass through Baranovichi to Brest-Litovsk.[1]

The almost impenetrable Nalibocki forest separated the two narrow corridors leading to Baranovichi and Molodechno. The German attempts to hold these two centres were to dominate the fighting for the next few days. The Soviet forces were frustrated in their attempts to take Baranovichi in the southern corridor by a *coup de main* and had to mount an attack with a tank corps and a mechanized corps. The town fell on 8 July despite German attempts to reinforce the garrison. The focus then changed to the north, to the area of Molodechno and Vilnius.

The Soviet 5th Guards Tank Army bypassed 5th Panzer Division in its attempt to reach Vilnius, a '*Fester Platz*' with a very weak garrison. There was a real danger that Vilnius would follow the fate of Vitebsk, particularly as Hitler refused to alter the status of the city, going so far as to declare on 7 July: 'In view of its operational importance, under no circumstances must *Fester Platz* Vilnius fall into enemy hands.' Hitler was hoping to assemble four panzer divisions to attack towards Vilnius to restore contact with Army Group North, although it was pointed out to him that the divisions could not be assembled before 23 July at the earliest. It was in this atmosphere that the request to evacuate Vilnius was received at OKH. Hitler responded immediately by ordering that the city be held and stating that it would be resupplied by air if necessary.

Field Marshal Model met Hitler on the morning of the 9th with the commander of Army Group North, Colonel-General Johannes Friessner also being present. Both commanders wanted to withdraw Army Group North to the line Riga—Dvinsk—River Dvina, but Hitler said that this was out of the question because Gross-Admiral Dönitz wished to retain as much as possible of the Baltic to train his U-boat crews. Vilnius fell on 13 July, after heavy fighting which was particularly costly for 5th Guards Tank Army. By mid-July the impetus was going out of the offensive against Army Group Centre, and the Stavka now began to put pressure on the flanks, as part of their strategic plan for the summer of 1944, timed to take place while the German Army was fighting hard in the west and OKW needed every division it could get hold of. On 14 July, Marshal Konev's First Ukrainian Front opened their offensive upon Army Group North Ukraine, an offensive known to the Soviets as the Lvov—Sandomierz operation. The Army Group had lost three panzer and two infantry divisions to Army Group Centre and had to give ground rapidly. An entire German corps of 40,000 men was encircled at Brody and although some men managed to escape, about 25,000 Germans were killed and 17,000 captured.

The third phase of the summer strategic offensive, known as the Lublin—Brest operation, was launched by the left wing of Marshal Rokossovsky's First Belorussian Front on 18 July with the aim of thrusting towards Lublin and the River Vistula. By the end of the month, Soviet forces were making good progress and had effected several crossings. The most successful of these in Konev's sector was brought to a halt by a powerful counter-attack by Model who had managed to assemble three panzer divisions for the purpose. Meanwhile by September Rokossovsky halted on the east bank of the Rivers Vistula and Narew, and remained immobile while the Poles suffered the agony of the Warsaw Rising. Soviet forces maintained these positions until they launched the Vistula—Oder offensive in the following January.

The Red Army kept up the pressure on the north flank towards the Baltic and in the south towards the Balkans. In the north, the opening offensive of the summer had hastened Finland's departure from the war in August when she asked the Soviets for peace terms. On the immediate northern flank of Army Group Centre a wide gap had developed between it and Army

Group North, which in mid-July Soviet forces tried to exploit. Hitler accepted that the most effective way of dealing with the threat was to withdraw all troops to the River Dvina, but was not prepared to lose Latvian oil, Swedish iron ore and Finnish nickel. Therefore Army Group North was ordered to hold its positions. This was the final straw for the Chief of the General Staff, General Zeitzler, who, to Hitler's annoyance, reported himself sick. Whether this was a diplomatic illness in view of the imminent 20 July bomb plot will probably never be known. In the event, Army Group North was unable to maintain its positions and was preparing to retire behind the River Dvina, while Third Panzer Amy was standing on the eastern border of East Prussia. Other than a 30-kilometre-wide corridor, Army Group North was cut off, but Hitler still refused to agree to its evacuation.

The final act in the Soviet offensive operations of 1944 took place in the south, after German reserves had been drawn off to help stabilize the situation on the main Soviet strategic direction. During the summer, Army Group South Ukraine had given up six panzer divisions, two infantry divisions and two assault gun brigades, but the opposing Soviet forces had also given up five out of six tank armies to the main offensives in the north. Despite wide-ranging *maskirovka* operations, German intelligence had a good idea of the size and scope of the blow that was about to fall upon them. The offensive opened on 20 August with the aim of destroying German forces in Roumania which, in addition to depriving Germany of the irreplaceable output of the oilfields, would have a dramatic effect upon the political situation in the Balkans.

Second Ukrainian Front, commanded by General R. Ya. Malinovsky, had six rifle armies, a tank army, and some independent mechanized tank and cavalry corps supported by an air army, and was to attack southwards towards Yassy. General Tolbukhin's Third Ukrainian Front with four rifle armies, two independent mechanized corps and an air army was to attack eastwards from the Soviet positions to the west of the River Dniester. The main German force, Sixth Army, reconstituted after Stalingrad, faced north and north-east, with Roumanian formations on the flanks. As at Stalingrad, Soviet forces fell upon the Roumanians who were considerably less well-equipped than the Germans, and gave way almost at once. Within four days Sixth Army was completely encircled and making vain attempts to break out across the River Prut. The greater part of the Army was destroyed as was Roumanian Fourth Army; Roumanian Third Army surrendered. The 1st Roumanian Panzer

Division 'Greater Roumania' did not fire a single shot at the Russians, but fired in the air or at passing vehicles.

The remnant of 20th Panzer Division, which had been involved at Bobruisk and had managed to escape, was part of German Eighth Army; only one of their tanks, a commander's tank, had a radio. A staff officer stopped a train carrying tanks destined for other units and manned them with tank crews from 20th Panzer. They were able to block Soviet assaults and allow the left wing of Eighth Army to withdraw behind the Carpathians.

By 29 August, when the remaining German pockets had been eliminated, the Soviets were claiming 150,000 German troops dead and 106,000 captured. It is reported that 70,000 of these returned from captivity after the war.

A number of men managed to avoid surrender and escaped to safety in either Hungary or the Carpathians. Some authorities put the figure of these *Rückkämpfer* as high as 18,000 to 20,000 men, but the only confirmed figure is that 350 men of Sixth Army and 1,200 of Eighth Army returned. Some rear echelon troops managed to withdraw in time, as did three German divisions on the left wing of Eighth Army. It was a defeat of major importance which would have a considerable effect on the political and military aspects of the remaining months of the war.

NOTE
1. This chapter was based upon Glantz, *1985 Art of War Symposium*, and 'Notes on Army Group Centre' (unpublished).

21
50 YEARS ON

The year 1944 was disastrous for the German Army, particularly on the Eastern Front. Soviet fighting strength was at a peak and it had developed its command structure to take maximum advantage of this ascendancy. The events of the 1944 Soviet summer offensive have to be viewed as a whole in which strategic operations destroyed three German army groups in the centre and south of the Eastern Front. The first and most dramatic of these operations has been the main subject of this book, Operation 'Bagration', the destruction of Army Group Centre, which was accompanied by the liberation of Belorussia. This was so successful that formations, particularly the critical panzer divisions and assault gun brigades, had to be extracted from the flanking army groups in order to stabilize the situation. So when Army Groups North and South Ukraine had, in their turn, to face Soviet offensives in overwhelming strength their reserves had been dissipated thus contributing to their own downfall.

Apart from their great superiority in tanks, guns and aircraft, the Soviet success was the result of their use of *maskirovka* and their ability and flexibility in concentrating their forces to achieve a crushing superiority in critical sectors. Because of their relative weakness, the Germans could not react to these Soviet concentrations of strength until it was too late. However, on the German side even these disadvantages could have been partially ameliorated had it not been for Hitler's stultifying affect on operations at every level. German generals were denied the opportunity to use the mobility of their still powerful armoured divisions to bring the thrusts of the Soviet tank formations to a halt. Soviet production for tanks had risen to 29,000 tanks in 1944. In comparison, Britain produced only 5,000 as against 17,500 in America. Germany's production had increased dramatically after the rationalization and mass production measures introduced by Albert Speer after his appointment as Minister of War Production in September 1943. In 1944, the figure rose to 19,000 tanks and assault guns, despite the Allied bomber offensive.[1] However, unlike the Soviet Union which had only one major front to furnish with armoured vehicles, Germany had the ongoing ulcer of Italy, in addition to the new danger of the Allied invasion of north-west Europe. Germany's historical fear of having to fight a major war on two fronts was now a reality. Hitler saw at a very early stage that the real danger lay in the west where he had little scope for manoeuvre; even limited success would bring the Allies to the heartland of Germany.

Although the Germans were not constrained by the inability of their factories to produce new tanks and assault guns, this was only a short-term situation, there being an increasing lack of key raw materials. At the end of January 1945, Albert Speer told Hitler that the prospect for the future was not good, and that production would inevitably fall in the first months of 1945. The major shortage which affected every branch of the armed forces was that of oil. Not only was this required for actual operations but it was needed for training pilots and tank crews, and for general transportation. Oil was the Achilles' heel of the Third Reich and immense efforts were made to perfect the production of synthetic substitutes. This was brought to a halt temporarily by Allied bombing, but shows what could have been achieved if the bombers had concentrated on economic targets. The Roumanian and Hungarian oil fields were therefore of great importance.[2]

On the other hand, the Red army was well served by its munitions factories, and had no significant shortage of raw materials. The Allies provided considerable material assistance, principally the USA although the United Kingdom and Canada also made a significant contribution. However the Soviet Union maintained then and after the war that Lease-Lend was of little consequence to their war effort. In their view, American and British tanks were inferior in performance to the latest German and Russian models. That may be so, but evidence to the contrary lies in documentary newsreel film which show these tanks, particularly Shermans, in use until the end of the war. Perhaps of greatest importance were US motor vehicles, which by 1945 constituted more than 50 per cent of the total used by the Red Army. Although the Jeep was of considerable importance and was widely used in default of an adequate Russian equivalent, the most significant vehicle was the Studebaker. This most versatile truck with an amazing cross-country performance was used, as we have seen earlier, for artillery ammunition supply. It is doubtful whether the Soviet mechanized formations could have been sustained over the remarkable distances they covered in Operation 'Bagration' without these remarkable load carriers.

The overwhelming numbers of Soviet tanks and assault guns that produced such superiority when they were concentrated at critical points was one of the factors that brought about the success of 'Bagration'. Not only were there sufficient tanks to support the infantry during the savage fighting as the leading Soviet formations broke through the German defences, and made the first encirclements, but there were fresh formations available to exploit the collapse of the German defensive positions. In the north, the cavalry/mechanized group assigned to Third Belorussian Front and the Stavka reserve, 5th Guards Tank Army, and in the south assigned to the right wing of Marshal Rokossovsky's First Belorussian Front were able to strike deep into the German rear. It was these thrusts that caused the Germans so much difficulty when they tried to stabilize the situation by bringing forward reserves.

One problem for the military historian of the Second World War is to assess the relative superiority of German tanks. As early as the second year of the war, German tank commanders could only deal with some Russian tanks when they could fire at them from behind. The importance of this manoeuvring for position was just as important in 1944 as it had been earlier in the war, because neither side had an overwhelming superiority in their new and improved tank designs. One Soviet deficiency that had contributed so much to German success in tank-to-tank contests had been remedied. Every Soviet tank now had its own radio so that the commander knew what was going on, as opposed to having to react to flag signals, with little idea of what was happening outside, worse still if closed down.

In the German accounts of 'Bagration' one of the most consistent complaints is that few German aircraft were available either to provide tactical air support or to deter the Soviet ground attack aircraft which harried mercilessly the columns withdrawing across Belorussia. To some extent this illustrates the effect of Hitler's insistence on giving priority to the west, where Allied air power was having a devastating effect upon German movement in Normandy. The same aircraft were also needed to counter Bomber Command's raids on German cities. Göring's much-vaunted Luftwaffe was on its last legs.

After the numerical superiority of the Soviets in tanks and aircraft, the most decisive factor of the Soviet planning for the offensive was their use of *maskirovka*, coupled with their flexibility in assembling their forces to achieve force ratios to achieve their operational objectives. While it is certainly true to state that the Germans were expecting a Soviet summer offensive which would bring into play their great superiority in tanks, they had no idea where the first blow would fall, and how deep they were planning to strike. The Soviet success depended upon the secret deployment of three armies, 6th

Guards and 28th on the north and south flanks, and 5th Guards Tank as the Stavka reserve. The concentration of these forces achieved an overwhelming superiority which enabled them to crush the German defences and strike deep into their rear areas until the Germans were able to summon their reserves.

The defeat of Army Group Centre resulted in the destruction of about 30 divisions. It is difficult to be more precise because some divisions were only partly involved and others were introduced as reinforcements during the course of the fighting. It is impossible to find accurate figures of the losses suffered by Army Group Centre because some divisions disappeared almost without trace, and their survivors were killed after the fighting or died in captivity. The OKW's figure gives their version of the losses and quoted them as 300,000. Ziemke gives a breakdown based on 25 divisions, and says that Fourth Army lost 130,000 of its original 165,000-man strength, Third Panzer Army lost 10 divisions, and that 10-000 to 15,000 men of Ninth Army escaped through the intervention of 12th Panzer Division.[3] Buchner puts the losses as high as 350,000, including 150,000 captured by the Russians. He also states that losses including those killed on their way to assembly camps, deaths due to overcrowding and starvation on their way to prisoner-of-war camps and during their sojourn in those camps are estimated at 75,000, giving a total of 275,000 dead German soldiers. The exact total will never be known.[4]

This success was not cheap; Soviet losses were very high. Until recently it has been almost impossible to obtain any official figures of Soviet losses, but these are now available. Appendix V gives the recently declassified official figures, showing a total of more than 178,000 dead and missing, which was about 8 per cent of the forces involved. The German figure represents nearly 44 per cent of those engaged.

The destruction of Army Group Centre was the greatest military defeat suffered by Germany during the Second World War, surpassing even that of Stalingrad. The two senior staff officers of the panzer divisions that fought so hard to prevent the disaster, recognized its significance. General Niepold states: 'The loss of the entire Army Group Centre greatly accelerated the collapse of the German State. The war would have lasted much longer and the defence of the east could have continued if the divisions of Army Group Centre had not been smashed.' General von Plato agrees: 'The collapse in the east had already been foreshadowed by the defeat at Stalingrad, and this was the second indication, at the very moment that there had been a collapse in the west, that we could no longer win the war.' General von Kielmansegg gives the view as seen from OKH: 'It was the beginning of the end. The end on the Eastern Front, and in conjunction with the recent invasion of France, the beginning of the end of the War.'

Professor Erickson summarizes the importance of the loss suffered by the German Army: 'When Soviet armies shattered Army Group Centre, they achieved their greatest single military success on the Eastern Front. For the German army in the east it was a catastrophe of unbelievable proportions, greater than that of Stalingrad, obliterating between twenty-five and twenty-eight divisions, 350,000 men in all.'

NOTES

1. Seaton, *The Russo-German War 1941-45*, London, Albert Barker, 1971, p. 4O2.
2. *Ibid.*, pp. 403, 467, 554.
3. Ziemke, p. 325
4. Interview with Albert Speer, Seaton, p. 442; Ziemke, p. 32
5, Buchner, p. 2l2; Erickson, p. 228.

APPENDIXES

APPENDIX I – GERMAN ORDER OF BATTLE 23 JUNE 1944

ARMY GROUP CENTRE

Generalfeldmarschall E. Busch
Generalfeldmarschall W. Model (from 28 June 1944)
Chief of Staff   Generalleutnant H. Krebs
Army Group Reserve
14th Panzer Grenadier Division   Generalleutnant H. Flörke
707th Security Division   Generalmajor G. Gihr – captured
Panzer Grenadier Division   Generalmajor F.-C. von Steinkeller – captured
   'Feldherrnhalle'
20th Panzer Division   Generalleutnant M. von Kessel

THIRD PANZER ARMY

Generaloberst G. H. Reinhardt
Chief of Staff   Generalmajor O. Heidkämper
95th Infantry Division   Generalmajor H. Michaelis – captured
VI Corps
General der Artillerie G. Pfeiffer – killed
197th Infantry Division   Generalmajor H. Hahne – missing
256th Infantry Division   Generalleutnant A. Wüstenhagen – killed
299th Infantry Division   Generalleutnant L. R. Graf von Oriola
IX Corps
General der Artillerie R. Wuthmann – captured
252nd Infantry Division   Generalleutnant W. Melzer
Korps Abteilung D [Corps Det]   Generalmajor B. Pamberg
LIII Corps
General der Infanterie A. Gollwitzer – captured
206th Infantry Division   Generalleutnant A. Hitter – captured
246th Infantry Division   Generalmajor C. A. Müller-Bülow --captured
4th Luftwaffe Field Division   Generalleutnant Pistorius – killed
6th Luftwaffe Field Division   Generalleutnant R. Peschl – killed

FOURTH ARMY

General der Infanterie K. von Tippelskirch
Chief of Staff   Oberst E. Dethleffsen
XII Corps
Generalleutnant Müller (Vincenz) – captured
18th Panzer Grenadier Division   Generalleutnant K. Zutavern – killed
57th Infantry Division   Generalleutnant A. Trowitz – captured
267th Infantry Division   Generalleutnant O. Drescher – killed

XXVII Corps
General der Infanterie Völckers – captured
25th Panzer Grenadier Division	Generalmajor P. Schürmann
78th Sturm Division	Generalleutnant H. Traut – captured
260th Infantry Division	Generalmajor G. L. Klammt – captured

XXXIX Panzer Corps
General der Artillerie R. Martinek – killed
12th Infantry Division	Generalleutnant R. Bamler – captured
31st Infantry Division	Generalleutnant H. Ochsner – captured
110th Infantry Division	Generalleutnant E. von Kurowski – captured
337th Infantry Division	Generalleutnant O. Schünemann – killed

NINTH ARMY

General der Infanterie H. Jordan
General der Panzertruppen von Vormann (27 June 1944)
Chief of Staff Oberst Gundelach

XXXV Corps
Generalleutnant K. J. Freiherr von Lützow – captured
6th Infantry Division	Generalleutnant W. Heyne – captured
45th Infantry Division	Generalmajor J. Engel – captured
134th Infantry Division	Generalleutnant E. Philips – killed
296th Infantry Division	Generalleutnant A. Kullmer – captured
383rd Infantry Division	Generalleutnant E. Hoffmeister – captured

XXXXI Panzer Corps
General der Artillerie H. Weidling
Chief of Staff	Oberst Berger
35th Infantry Division	Generalleutnant Richert – captured
36th Infantry Division	Generalmajor A. Conrady – captured
129th Infantry Division	Generalmajor R. H. von Larisch

LV Corps
General der Infanterie F. Herrlein
Chief of Staff	Oberst Hölz
102nd Infantry Division	Generalleutnant W. von Bercken – captured
292nd Infantry Division	Generalleutnant R. John

SECOND ARMY

Generaloberst W. Weiss
Chief of Staff	Generalmajor H. von Tresckow

VIII Corps
Generalder Infanterie G. Hoehne
XX Corps
General der Artillerie R. Freiherr von Roman
XXIII Corps
General der Pioniere O. Tiemann
Security and Training Divisions - Rear Areas
201st Security Division	Generalleutnant A. Jacobi
221st Security Division	Generalleutnant H. Lendle

286th Security Division	Generalleutnant H. Oschmann
391st Security Division	Generalleutnant A. Baron Digeon von Montenon
390th Field Training Division	Generalleutnant H. Bergen

Belorussian Military District
General der Kavallerie E. von Rothkirch and Trach
Commandants of *Feste Plätze*

Bobruisk	Generalmajor A. Hamann – captured
Mogilev	Generalmajor G. von Erdmannsdorf (Bammler)

Orscha and Vitebsk were commanded by Generals Traut and Gollwitzer

APPENDIX II – COMPARATIVE RANKS

German	*British*
Generalfeldmarschall	Field Marshal
Generaloberst	General
General der Panzer Truppen, etc	Lieutenant-General
Generalleutnant	Major-General
Generalmajor	Brigadier
Oberst	Colonel
Oberstleutnant	Lieutenant-Colonel
Major	Major
Hauptmann	Captain
Oberleutnant	Lieutenant
Leutnant	Second Lieutenant

APPENDIX III – SOVIET ORDER OF BATTLE

NORTH

Stavka representative Marshal A. M. Vasilevsky

FIRST BALTIC FRONT

Army General I. Kh. Bagramayan
Chief of Staff Colonel-General V. V. Kurasov (as of 28 June 1944)

4th Shock Army	Lieutenant-General P. F. Malyshev
6th Guards Army	Colonel-General I. M. Chistyakov (as of 28 June 1944)
43rd Army	Lieutenant-General A. P. Beloborodov
1st Tank Corps	Lieutenant-General V. V. Butkov
3rd Air Army	Colonel-General N. P. Panivin (as of 19 August 1944)

THIRD BELORUSSIAN FRONT

Army General I. D. Chernyakhovsky (as of 26 June 1944)
Chief of Staff Colonel-General A. P. Pokrovsky (as of 23 August 1944)

39th Army	Lieutenant-General I. I. Lyudnikov
5th Army	Colonel-General N. I. Krilov (as of 15 July 1944)

11th Guards Army	Colonel-General K. N.. Galitsky (as of 28 June 1944)
2nd Guards Tank Corps	Major-General A. S. Burdeyny
31st Army	Colonel-General V. V. Glagolev (as of 15 July 1944)
Cavalry/Mechanized Group	Lieutenant-General N. S. Oslikovsky
3rd Guards Cavalry Corps	Lieutenant-General N. S. Oslikovsky
3rd Guards Mechanized Corps	Lieutenant-General Obukhov
5th Guards Tank Army	Marshal P. A. Rotmistrov (from 8 August 1944 Lieutenant-General M. D. Solomatin and from 18 August 1944 Lieutenant-General V. T. Vol'sky)
3rd Guards Tank Corps	General I. A. Vovchenko
29th Tank Corps	General E. I. Fominykh
1st Air Army	Colonel-General G. G. Khryukin

SOUTH

Stavka Representative Marshal G. K. Zhukov

SECOND BELORUSSIAN FRONT

Army General G. F. Zakharov (as of 28 July 1944)
Chief of Staff Lieutenant-General A. N. Bogolyubov

33rd Army	Lieutenant-General Kryuchenkin (from 9 July 1944 Lieutenant-general S. I. Morozov)
49th Army	Lieutenant-General I. T. Grishin
50th Army	Lieutenant-General I. V. Boldin
4th Air Army	Colonel-General K. A. Vershinin

FIRST BELORUSSIAN FRONT

Marshal K. K. Rokossovsky (as of 29 June 1944)
Chief of Staff Colonel-General M. S. Malinin

3rd Army	Colonel-General A. V. Gorbatov (as from 29 June 1944)
9th Tank Corps	Major-General B. S. Bakharov
48th Army	Lieutenant-General P. L. Romanenko
65th Army	Colonel-General P. I. Batov
1st Guards Tank Corps	Major-General M. F. Panov
28th Army	Lieutenant-General A. A. Luchinsky
61st Army	Colonel-General P. A. Belov (as of 26 June 1944)
70th Army	Colonel-General V. S. Popov
Cavalry/Mechanized Group	Lieutenant-General I. A. Pliyev
4th Guards Cavalry Corps	Lieutenant-General A. I. Pliyev
1st Mechanized Corps	Lieutenant-General S. M. Krivoshein
16th Air Army	Colonel-General S. I. Rudenko
Dnieper Flotilla	Captain 1st Rank V. V. Grigoriyev

(This Orbat is based on information provided by Colonel Glantz.)

APPENDIX IV – SOVIET CASUALTIES IN THE BELORUSSIAN OPERATION

Front	Strength	Killed and Missing	Wounded	Total
First Baltic	359,500	41,248	125,053	166,301
Third Belorussian	579,300	45,117	155,165	200,282
Second Belorussian	319,500	26,315	91,421	117,736
First Belorussian	1,071,100	65,779	215,615	281,394
Dneiper Flotilla	2,300	48	54	102
TOTALS	2,331,700	178,507	587,308	765,815

Source: G. F. Krivosheyev, ed.: [Secret classification removed; the losses of the Armed Forces of the USSR in wars, combat actions, and military conflicts]. Moscow, Voenizdat, 1993, p. 203. (Reproduced by kind permission of Colonel D. Glantz.)

APPENDIX V STAVKA DIRECTIVE: *MASKIROVKA*

(From a Directive of the Headquarters of the Supreme High Command to Front Commanders)

To ensure concealment of activities going forward on all Fronts, I order:

1. All movements of troops and equipment are to be done only at night, strictly observing all night march discipline. Movement during the day is to be authorized only in weather when flying is absolutely impossible, and only for individual groups that cannot be observed by the enemy on the ground. At daytime halting places and new assembly regions, troops and equipment are to be dispersed and carefully camou-flaged. Personnel must not communicate with the local population and movement of groups and sub-units along open roads and terrain sectors must be minimized. Direct special attention to concealment when replacing first-line troops.

2. During the entire period of regrouping and preparation for action keep up the existing fire situation. Establish a procedure for ranging artillery and mortar weapons that guarantee concealment of the artillery grouping in the primary axis.

3. Prohibit newly arrived formations from conducting ground reconnaissance.

4. Do not conduct commanders' reconnaissances in large groups simultaneously. To conceal the true sectors of action organize the work of commanders' reconnaissance groups on a broad front, including the passive sectors.

In necessary cases, command personnel on commanders' reconnaissances are autho-rized to wear the uniforms and equipment of privates. Tank soldiers are categorically forbidden to appear on commanders' reconnaissance in their special uniforms ...

13. Organize careful daily checks on execution of all orders relating to concealment. Make daily checks from the air of the concealment of headquarters and troop posi-

tions, for which purpose special officers from the front and army staffs must be appointed ...

Report on orders issued by 1st June 1944.   Zhukov
1900, 29 May 1944.   Antonov

(Source: TSAMO SSSR [Central Archives of the USSR Ministry of Defence] fund 48-80, inventory 1795, file 3. sheets 3-5. original.)

This and the following Appendix are reproduced by kind permission of Colonel D. Glantz from his *Soviet Military Deception in the Second World War*, p. 616.

APPENDIX VI – FRONT DIRECTIVE: *MASKIROVKA*

From the 30th May 1944 Directive of the Military Council of the 1st Baltic Front to ensure concealment during preparations and to achieve surprise in conduct of the operation.

I Order:

A. Concerning Concealment of Troops and Maintenance of Troops of Military Secrecy.
1. All movements of troops and rear services are to be done only at night between 2200 and 0400 with an exactly determined travel distance. Do not try to travel long distances. End marches in forested, sheltered regions. Do not permit columns to stretch out or lagging sub-units to move during daytime.
No matter where troops and their rear services may be when light comes, all roads must be perfectly still; all movement must stop.
2. Motor vehicles can travel only at night with headlights out. Set up white signs that are plainly visible at night on the roads. Paint the front part of the hood and rear sides of vehicles white. Travelling at high speed or passing vehicles on the march is categorically forbidden. The movement of troops, transports, motor vehicles, and combat equipment must follow strictly routes that are planned and scouted in advance, with no diversion to parallel roads and trails ...
5. When single enemy planes or small groups appear anti-aircraft weapons and troop units on the march and at unit lines must not open fire. It is permitted to fire at enemy aircraft operating in large groups and threatening troops on the march and at unit lines ...
8. During the entire period of regrouping and preparation for action maintain the existing fire conditions. Establish a procedure for ranging artillery and mortar weapons that ensures concealment of the artillery grouping in the main axis.
9. When enemy aircraft appear during tactical exercises sub-units and units must take cover immediately and, according to predetermined signals, quickly deploy and simulate defensive construction on natural lines.
10. Establish rigorous control at communications centres and do not permit discussion, especially open discussion of activities on wire communications.

11. Make defensive subjects paramount in the Red Army press, and categorically forbid running any articles and notices that in any way treat questions of preparation for upcoming actions.

12. No activity (troop movement, hauling supplies, commanders' reconnaissance, and so on) can be permitted or carried out before steps have been taken to conceal this activity.

For this purpose:

— Select one assistant chief of staff at all unit and formation headquarters to be assigned to work out instructions for camouflaging troops in all types of combat activity and to see that specially designated officers monitor this closely;

— Army and Corps Commanders must establish an order for commanders' reconnaissance which precludes clustering of such groups. Commanders' reconnaissance groups may only travel on roads and trails where defensive forces ordinarily travel;

— In zones scheduled for vigorous actions, step up defensive works, paying special attention to the quality (convincingness) of construction on dummy minefields and the like.

B. Concerning Discipline on the March and at Unit Lines.

1. Raise standards demanded of subordinate commanders and troops, and continuously explain to them the rules of troop behaviour on the march, at unit positions, and on the job.

2. Persistently explain to troops and demand that they increase vigilance, especially on the march, and maintain military secrecy.

3. Establish constant checks by officers on the behaviour on the march and at unit lines.

4. Prohibit familiarization flights over territory occupied by the enemy for the personnel of new units joining the air army. Only the leaders can be authorized to make such flights a day or two days before the start of the action. In this case establish an overflight zone whose depth guarantees that the plane if damaged by enemy fire can land in our territory ...

C. Concerning the Provost Service

1. The entire Front region should be broken into the following zones for purposes of more precise organization of the provost service:

a. The Front zone, from the line of Front bases (city of Nevel) to the line of army bases (Zheleznitsa, Bychikha). The organization of provost work in this zone is assigned to the chief of staff of the Front.

b. Army zone, from the line of army bases (Zheleznitsa, Bychikha) to the line of division exchange points.

c. Troop zones, from the line of division exchange points to the forward edge of defence.

Organization of provost service in the army and troops zone and in the unit areas should be assigned to the military councils of the armies and commanders of the corps...

3. Provost and security service must be organized and carried out strictly on all front, army and troop roads beginning at 1800 of 2 June 1944 ...

Each provost must be given a group of officers from the army and front reserve and entire rifle sub-units and units to perform provost duty on the roads and in troop areas. Determination of the composition of the groups of officers and sub-units for provost service must be based on the following considerations:

a. One provost officer post with two officers for each 3-5 kilometres of road and one two-man post operated by soldiers and sergeants for every 1-2 kilometres of road.

b. Two officers and 3-5 two-man posts for each battalion in the troop unit area ...

5. Front and army signal chiefs must ensure constant wire communication and telephones on all routes, at every officer front provost post and every provost office. Provost officers in charge of roads and regions must be given necessary mobile equipment for this purpose ...

7. To ensure concealed movement of troops, trains, vehicle transport, combat equipment, and individual groups of soldiers and officers and to camouflage engineer work to prepare the springboard for the offensive, immediately determine the ground enemy's fields of vision in the forward zone (troop zone) and organize the strictest provost and security service. Take steps to establish vertical screens. Prohibit daytime travel by all motor vehicles (including cars) through fields of visibility and set markers at the boundaries of fields of visibility with especially rigorous provost officer posts.

8. Determine the limit for truck traffic in a day figuring 100 trucks for each army and front unit. The front chief of rear services should make up and issue special passes to armies and front units for daytime vehicle traffic within the established limit.

9. Categorically forbid written communications relating to activities being carried on. Only the restricted circle of scheduled persons should be permitted to see the content of essential documents, and documents must not go beyond the headquarters that prepared them.

10. Prohibit direct submission of requests from directorates, staffs, and chiefs of the arms of troops to the corresponding directorates of the fronts, sending them only through the army and front staffs.

11. In reports to front headquarters at 2100 each day report the results of the concealment inspection.

Do not put this Directive in written or printed form, disseminate it to the commanders of regiments and detached battalions by personal communication and instruction of subordinate commanders.

Guards Army Gen I. Bagramayan, commander of the 1st Baltic Front

Lt Gen Leonov, member Military Council 1st Baltic Front

Lt Gen Kurasov, chief of staff of the 1st Baltic Front

30 May 1944.

(TSAMO SSSR, fund 235, inventory 2074, file 75, sheets 2-10). Source: A. Izosomiv, 'On the 35th Anniversary of the Belorussian Operation', VIZH, No. 6 (June 1979), pp. 49-52. Translated by JPRS [Joint Publications Research Service].)

APPENDIX VII – HITLER'S *FESTER PLATZ* ORDER

The Führer	Führer Headquarters,
High Command of the Army	8th March, 1944.
Führer Order No. 11	

(Commandants of Fortified Areas and Battle Commandants) In view of various incidents, I issue the following orders:

1. A distinction will be made between 'Fortified Areas' [*Feste Plätze*], each under a 'Fortified Area Commandant', and 'Local Strongpoints' [*Ortsstützpunkte*], each under a 'Battle Commandant'. The 'Fortified Areas' will fulfil the functions of fortresses in former historical times. They will ensure that the enemy does not occupy these areas of decisive operational importance. They will allow themselves to be surrounded, thereby holding down the largest possible number of enemy forces, and establishing conditions for successful counter-attacks. Local strongpoints deep in the battle area, which will be tenaciously defended in the event of enemy penetration. By being included in the main line of battle they will act as a reserve of defence and, should the enemy break through, as hinges and corner stones for the front, forming positions from which counter-attacks can be launched.

2. Each 'Fortified Area Commandant' should be a specifically selected, hardened soldier, preferably of General's rank. He will be appointed by the Army Group concerned. Fortified Area Commandants will be personally responsible to the Commander-in-Chief of the Army Group. Fortified Area Commandants will pledge their honour as soldiers to carry out their duties to the last. Only the Commander-in-Chief of an Army Group in person may, with my approval, relieve the Fortified Area Commandant of his duties, and perhaps order the surrender of the fortified area. Fortified Area Commandants are subordinate to the Commander of the Army Group, or Army, in whose sector the fortified area is situated. Further delegation of command to General officers commanding formations will not take place. Apart from the garrison and its security forces, all persons within a fortified area, or who have been collected there, are under the orders of the Commandant, irrespective of whether they are soldiers or civilians, and without regard to their rank or appointment. The Fortified Area Commandant has the military rights and disciplinary powers of a Commanding General. In the performance of his duties he will have at his disposal mobile courts-martial and civilian courts. The staff of Fortified Area Commandants will be appointed by the Army Group concerned. The Chiefs of Staff will be appointed by High Command of the Army, in accordance with suggestions made by the Army Group.

3. The garrison of a fortified area comprises: the security garrison, and the general garrison. The security garrison must be inside the fortified area at all times. Its strength will be laid down by Commander-in-Chief Army Group, and will be determined by the size of the area and the tasks to be fulfilled (preparation and completion of defences, holding the fortified area against raids or local attacks by the enemy). The general garrison must be made available to the Commandant of the fortified area in sufficient time for the men to have taken up defensive positions and be installed when a full-scale enemy attack threatens. Its strength will be laid down by Commander-in-Chief Army Group, in accordance with the size of the fortified area and the

task which is to be performed (total defence of the fortified area) ...

signed: ADOLF HITLER.

(Reproduced from Trevor-Roper: *Hitler's War Directives*, Pan Books, 1978.)

APPENDIX VIII – HITLER'S OPERATION ORDER No. 8

issued by Army Group Centre
TOP SECRET
Distribution – List 3 5 copies.
This message passes on to Army Commanders
the Führer's orders to Army Group Centre.

To ensure security, their tactical content is to be passed to corps and divisional commanders orally and only to the extent that it concerns them. The Führer's other
requirements are to be passed on in an appropriate manner to all ranks. The orders
are to be destroyed once read and understood. The orders for the 'firm positions'of
Bobruisk and Mogilev under Führer Order No. 11 are not affected by these orders.

(signed) Busch
HQ Army Group Centre

Operation Order No. 8
Instructions for the further conduct of operations by Army Group Centre.
The enemy advance on Army Group Centre's sector must now be halted once and for
all. To this end I have ordered reinforcement with panzer and infantry divisions and
assault gun brigades from other Army Groups and from Germany, this on a scale and
at a pace only to be achieved at the cost of weakening other fronts. I have also reinforced 6th Air Force to an extent which makes it by far the strongest of the air forces
on the Eastern Front. What I now expect of the Army Group is, however, that no
yard of ground shall be given up without fighting for it, and that every commander
and man in the Army Group shall have instilled in him the iron will to hold firm.
The furthermost line at which the Russian offensive must be halted, cost what it may,
is as follows: Lake Chervonoye—Lyuban—Star Dorogi—Osipovichi—River Svisloch—River Beresina to Beresino—Lake Lukomlskoye—present position of 3rd
Panzer Army. To the extent that the enemy has already passed this line, he is to be
thrown back forthwith by the ruthless employment of all available troops. To the
extent that this line may be forced further back, it is to be restored gradually by whatever means are possible in short, rigidly controlled bounds. Our troops must make it
a point of honour to take all their equipment with them. Ground ceded to the enemy
is to be scorched as far as possible; any weapons and stores that our troops are forced
to leave behind must be completely destroyed. The task of the Panzer formations, following the principles whose success is so well proven, is to destroy enemy groups that
have forced their way forward by a series of swift, sharp punches. I forbid the use of
panzer formations in containing positions.
My detailed orders are these:

1. Three counterstroke groups [lit. 'intervention groups'] are to be formed:

a. In Ninth Army area, 12th and 20th Pz Divs under HQ XXXXI Pz Corps.

b. In Fourth Army area, 5th Pz Div and 505 HY Tk Bn (Tiger), under command of Lt-Gen von Saucken; to this end HQ XXXIX Pz Corps is to be placed at his disposal for the time being.

C. In Third Pz Army's area, 212 Inf Div and 227 and 232 Assault Gun Brigades.

d. A decision on the employment of 4th Pz Div will be taken at the appropriate time.

2. Ninth Army is to restore a continuous front on its sector by pulling back its centre and left and making offensive use of its mobile formations. During these operations, it must not lose contact with Fourth Army's right. The critical factor here is Fourth Army's rate of movement.

3. Fourth Army is to fall back by short bounds with a continuous front on to the line River Beresina—Lake Lukomlskoye. In doing this, it must use mobile formations to support its left flank. Mogilev and Orsha are to be held for at least a matter of days, so as to tie down enemy forces and thus facilitate the build-up of the final defensive front further to the rear. Every man in these garrisons must be made aware of the decisive importance of his task.

4. Third Pz Army is to continue holding its present positions or, as needs be, to fight itself clear. Under no circumstances must it let itself be forced further back.

I am confident that the Army Group will do everything in its power to accomplish the task set it. I expect my confidence be justified.

signed ADOLF HITLER
Authenticated , Lieut.

(Reproduced by kind permission of General Niepold from *Mittlere Ostfront Juni '44*, as translated by the late Brigadier Simkin.)

APPENDIX IX – VETERANS INTERVIEWED

German

Gen Graf von Kielmannsegg	la Ops Sec OKH
Maj Gen von der Groeben	la Ops Sec AG Centre
Lt Gen Lemm	Bn Comd 12 Inf Div
Col Fricke	Adjt Pz Gren Regt 20 Pz Div
Lt Gen Niepold	la 12 Pz Div
Lt Gen von Plato	la 5 Pz Div
Col Blanchbois	Comd Pz Gren Bn 12 Pz Div
Lt Schulze	Sqn Ldr Fighter Bombers

Russian

Lt Degen	OC Tk Coy 3 BE FRONT
Sgt Fukson	Arty Bde 3 SHOCK 2 BALT FRONT
Lt Col Herbert	Tech Offr Tk Bde 3 BE FRONT
Maj Morderer	DCOS 69A 1BE FRONT
Col Vilensky	CO Rifle Regt ? 1 BALT FRONT

Note. German ranks are those gained during post-war service in the Bundeswehr. Russian ranks are wartime.

ANNOTATED BIBLIOGRAPHY

Art of War Symposium. Proceedings of symposia held in 1984, 1985 and 1986 at the US Army War College, Carlisle, Penn., and in 1987 at Garmisch-Partenkirchen, to investigate the methods by which the Soviet Army conducted offensive operations. Colonel Glantz chaired the proceedings and went through the various operations with the aid of detailed maps which he prepared for each day of the successive operations. The proceedings are an invaluable source for the Eastern Front and cover many different facets of Soviet and German conduct of operations.

Barnett, Corelli (ed.). *Hitler's Generals*, London: Weidenfeld and Nicolson, 1989. An excellent series of short biographies of the most prominent German generals.

Buchner, Alex. *The German defensive battles on the Russian Front 1944*, Schiffer Military History, West Chester, Penn. A translation of a German work on the battles of 1944 on the Eastern Front, it gives a lively account of the Belorussian offensive and includes a number of personal accounts of the breakout.

Bullock, Alan. *Hitler and Stalin, Parallel Lives*, London: Harper Collins.

Carell, Paul. *Scorched Earth: Hitler's War on Russia*, vol. 2, London: George Harrap Ltd, 1970. An excellent account of the events of 1943 and 1944, mostly from the German point of view, and includes interesting details about Soviet agents at German Headquarters.

Cooper, Matthew. *The German Army, 1933-1945; The German Air Force, 1933-1945; The Phantom War*, London: Macdonald and Jane's, 1978-81. The first two books are very interesting with regard to development of the services. The third book was written from material assembled for the first two. I found it particularly helpful on German anti-partisan operations.

Deist, Wilhelm. *The Wehrmacht and German Rearmament*, London: Macmillan 1981. This gives an account of the expansion of the *Wehrmacht* after Hitler's accession to power.

Edmonds, Robin. *The Big Three: Churchill, Roosevelt and Stalin*, London: Hamish Hamilton, 1991. A very useful account of the relationship between the Allied leaders and in particular the development of the plans for the Second Front which the offensive in Belorussia was timed to support.

Erickson, John. *The Road to Stalingrad; The Road to Berlin*, London: Weidenfeld and Nicolson. Professor Erickson was the first non-Soviet scholar to be allowed access to Soviet archives and was able to interview many of the Soviet war leaders. His extensive knowledge of the Soviet war effort is unequalled in the West.

Glantz, David. Cass Series on Soviet military theory and practice: 1. *Soviet Military Deception in the Second World War*, 2. *Soviet Military Operational Art*, 3. *Soviet Military Deception in War*, 4. *Soviet Military Operational Art.– The Military Strategy of the Soviet Union*, London: Frank Cass. Colonel Glantz's works are based on meticulous research into Soviet sources from which he has been able to assemble a highly detailed account of Red Army operations. His study of *maskirovka* covers previously unknown ground. In the immediate post-war period much of what was known about the Eastern Front was based on German accounts, and it is particularly valuable to be able to set these against the detailed accounts in Colonel Glantz's works. With the advent of glasnost, a vast amount of previously classified material continues to become available, and we are fortunate to have a scholar of his ability to assimilate this material.

Hinze, Rolf. *Der Zusammenbruch der Heeresgruppe Mitte im osten 1944*, Stuttgart: Motorbuch Verlag, 1980. Dr Hinze, who served throughout the Belorussian offensive as an artillery officer in the 267th Division, was one of those '*Rückkämpfer*' who managed to return to the German lines, having suffered incredible hardships. He has written and published privately a number of very valuable and informative books on this period of the war, quoting many personal accounts which are not available elsewhere.

Keilig, Wolf. *Die Generale des Heeres*, Friedberg: Podzun-Pallas, 1983. A useful alphabetical list of German Second World War generals.

Knappe, Siegfried. *Soldat. Reflections of a German Soldier, 1936-1949*, London: Airlife Publishing, 1992. The interesting personal experiences of an artillery officer on the Eastern Front, particularly important for account of life in Soviet prisoner-of-war camps and the attitude and behaviour of General Bamler.

Mitcham, Samuel W. *Hitler's Legions*, London: Leo Cooper, 1985. This book gives the details of the German order of battle, division by division, including their composition, commanders and an outline of their services.

Niepold, Gerd. *Mittlere Ostfront Juni 1944*, Herford: Mittler & Sohn, 1985; translated as *Battle for White Russia: the Destruction of Army Group Centre, June 1944*, London: Brassey, 1987. General Niepold was the senior general staff officer of 12th Panzer Division and attended the 1985 Art of War Symposium to share his experiences of the Belorussian offensive. His book gives a day-by-day account of the course of the offensive as seen through German eyes. When read with Colonel Glantz's account from the Soviet side it presents a very full picture of the disaster which befell Army Group Centre, in particular the weaknesses and miscalculations of the German High Command.

O'Neill, Robert. *The German Army and the Nazi Party*, London: Cassell, 1966. A masterly study of the relationship between the German army and Hitler in the years after he came to power.

Rokossovsky, Marshal K. *A Soldier's Duty*, Moscow: Progress Publishers, 1970. The autobiography of the commander of First Belorussian Front, it gives interesting details of the period of preparation, but is not particularly good on the progress of the offensive.

Seaton, Albert. *The Russo-German War, 1941-45*, London: Albert Barker, 1971. The outstanding general history of the war on the Eastern Front. The judgements made are confirmed by more recently released documents. A *tour de force*. – *The German Army, 1933-45*, London: Weidenfeld and Nicolson, 1982. An excellent description of the development of the German Army, particularly its organization.

Shtemenko, S. M. *The Soviet General Staff at War 1942-1945*, Moscow: Progress Publishers, 1985. The fullest account of Stalin and the higher direction of the war. General Shtemenko served as Head of the Operations Staff of the Stavka, and was involved in the planning of the Belorussian offensive.

Shukman, Harold. *Stalin's Generals*, London: Weidenfeld and Nicolson, 1993. Short biographies of the most distinguished Russian wartime generals, many of whom are relatively unknown in the West.

Trevor-Roper, H. R. *Hitler's War Directives, 1939-1945*, London: Pan Books, 1978. A very useful source book giving the texts.

Volkogonov, Dmitri. *Stalin, Triumph and Tragedy*, London: Weidenfeld and Nicolson, 1991. General Volkogonov is an eminent historian as well as an important political figure in his own right. A most valuable revisionist history based upon hitherto classified documents.

Warlimont, Walter. *Inside Hitler's Headquarters, 1939-1945*, London: Weidenfeld and Nicolson, 1964 republished by Presidio Press. The only full account of how OKW functioned under Hitler, with its Byzantine rivalries and the struggle for power of the various factions within the Services and the Party.

Zhukov, Marshal G. K. *The Memoirs of Marshal Zhukov*, London: Macdonald, 1969 (originally published in Moscow). The autobiography of Stalin's Deputy who participated in all the important decisions of the war. More interesting on the planning and preparations than on the course of the offensive.

Ziemke, Earl F. *Moscow to Stalingrad: Decision in the East; Stalingrad to Berlin: The German Defeat in the East*, US Army Historical Series, Office of the Chief of Military History, Washington, DC, 1968, 1987. These are the two basic works on the Eastern Front and are invaluable for giving a wide-ranging picture from both sides.

INDEX